MACHINE LEARNING & DEEP LEARNING WITH PYTHON

USE PYTHON JUPYTER TO IMPLEMENT MATHEMATICAL CONCEPTS, MACHINE LEARNING ALGORITHMS AND DEEP LEARNING NEURAL NETWORKS

JAMES CHEN

Published by James Chen, 2023

ISBN: 978-1-7389084-0-0 (Paperback)

ISBN: 978-1-7389084-1-7 (Hardcover)

Table of Contents

1. Introduction

W hile more and more people are talking about *artificial intelligence, machine learning* and *deep learning* not only in the technology domain but also in the commercial, business and other domains in recent years; more and more companies and business owners are leveraging these innovations to build intelligent applications to resolve their complicated business problems; more and more technology companies, data scientists and researchers are promoting new initiatives to take advantage of these emerging technologies, there are still some misconceptions about what these terms exactly mean. Although sometimes the three terms are used interchangeably, each has distinct and different meanings within its domain.

1.1 Artificial Intelligence, Machine Learning and Deep Learning

As a very high-level overview of the three terms, to simply put, deep learning (DL) is part of machine learning (ML), and machine learning is part of artificial intelligence (AI), as shown in Figure 1.1.

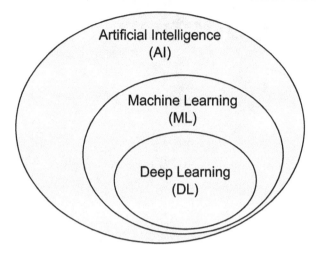

Figure 1.1 Artificial Intelligence, Machine Learning and Deep Learning

Artificial Intelligence (AI)

Artificial intelligence is to develop the machines and applications that can imitate human perceptions and behaviors, it can mimic human cognitive functions such as learning, thinking, planning and problem solving. The AI machines and applications learn from the data collected from a variety of sources to improve the way they mimic humans.

As some examples of artificial intelligence, autonomous driving vehicles like Waymo self-driving cars; machine translation like Google Translate; chatbot like ChatGPT by OpenAI, and so on. It's widely used in the areas such as image recognition and classification, facial recognition, natural language processing, speech recognition, computer vision, etc.

Machine Learning (ML)

Machine learning, an approach to achieve artificial intelligence, is the computer programs that use mathematical algorithms and data analytics to build computational models and make predictions in order to resolve business problems.

Different from traditional computer programs where the routines are predefined with specific instructions for specific tasks, machine learning is using mathematical algorithms to analyze and parse large amounts of data and learn the patterns from the data and make predictions and determinations from the data.

Deep Learning (DL)

Deep learning, as a subset of machine learning, uses neural networks to learn things in the same, or similar, way as human. The neural networks, for example artificial neural network, consist of many neurons which imitate the functions of neurons of a biological brain.

Deep learning is more complicated and advanced than machine learning, the latter might use mathematical algorithms as simple as linear regression to build the models and might learn from relatively small sets of data. On the other hand, deep learning will organize many neurons in multiple layers, each neuron takes input from other neurons, performs the calculation, and outputs the data to the next neurons. Deep learning requires relatively big sets of data.

In recent years the hardware is developed with more and more enhanced computational powers, especially the graphics processing units (GPUs) which were originally for accelerating graphics processing, and they can significantly speed up the computational processes for deep learning, they are now an essential part of the deep learning, and new types of GPUs are developed exclusively for deep learning purpose.

In this book, the word "machine learning" includes both machine learning and deep learning.

1.2 Whom This Book Is For

This book is written for people with different computer programming levels, from those with limited programming skills to experienced ones. If you are a beginner in computer programming, don't worry, the book begins with very basic and straightforward Python statements in the codes, and they are easy to understand. Although it's helpful if you read together with some Python tutorials, it's totally fine to read this book alone to understand all the contents and will become familiar with Python very soon. This book is not intended to introduce the tricks of Python programming, instead it will focus on how to implement the algorithms and mathematical concepts using the packages and libraries, therefore no need to worry about programming skills.

If you are experienced in Python or other similar languages like R, Java, Java scripts or VB scripts, and so on, you might find no difficulties to understand the Python codes, and you will focus more on how the mathematical algorithms are implemented by Python codes, and you will understand what Python packages and libraries provide supports to the different algorithms.

No matter a beginner or an experienced programmer, as long as you want to learn machine learning with Python, you will benefit from this book.

Sometimes people might think that machine learning especially deep learning requires extensive and in-depth mathematical background, it's not the case with this book, a high school level of math knowledge is enough to start. Chapter 3 introduces the math fundamentals from very basic concepts and covers everything used in this book. If you have lots of math background and knowledge, feel free to skip the chapter and re-visit it when necessary.

1.3   How This Book Is Organized

In order for beginners to get started, this book begins with some basics such as installations and environments setup, if you have experiences and/or already known how to do it, please feel free to skip the sections.

Python with Jupyter Notebook is used as the programming language throughout this book. Chapter 2 is to recommend some programming environments for practice when reading this book, from the cloud environments where no need to manage and configure the hardware and software to locally hosted environments with more flexibility. It's recommended to use the cloud environments as much as possible, and shift to a local environment when doing deep learning topics where extensive and long-time computational resources are required and might not be provided by the cloud vendors. The prerequisite is the local machine should be equipped with powerful hardware which can provide enough computational capabilities.

Chapter 3 is to cover the mathematical fundamentals used by this book, a high-school math level can get started from there. It introduces vectors, matrices and related operations and attributions, then calculus, functions and derivatives, differential and gradient descent which are used in most of machine learning algorithms behind the scenes. This chapter also introduces the most often used functions like sigmoid, tanh, relu, softmax etc. This chapter does not explain the tedious and boring stuffs like a normal textbook, instead it comes with Python codes to implement those math concepts and use Python to generate plots and diagrams to visualize those math concepts.

If you believe you are familiar with those math concepts, feel free to skip the chapter and revisit it when necessary.

Chapter 4 is to explain machine learning in 12 topics, it covers linear and logistic regressions, k-means clustering, principal component analysis, support vector machine, k-nearest neighbors, and anomaly detection as machine learning; and then artificial and convolutional neural networks, recommendation systems, and generative adversarial networks as deep learning. Each topic comes with explanation and Python implementations. Most of the topics introduce not only the Python packages and libraries but also the implementation from scratch, meaning not leveraging any advanced Python packages but using the very basic stuffs, the purpose is to explain what's happening behind the scenes.

All right, enjoy the wonderful world of Machine Learning!

2. Environments

This chapter will prepare the environments for running the machine learning codes in this book. A good environment helps to provide services and tools for data querying, data processing, model training and tuning, testing, code versioning, packages and libraries managing and so on. An environment consists of hardware and software components, the hardware includes the CPUs, GPUs, memories, storage etc., when a machine learning model, especially a deep learning model is in the training process, extensive computational resources are required, in most cases CPUs plus memories are not enough and the GPUs are helpful to provide the added computational capabilities. Therefore, the hardware equipped with GPUs would be an ideal environment for this purpose.

The software also plays important roles in machine learning and deep learning projects. Python and Jupyter Notebook are used as primary software tools in the book. There are many packages are required when running Python codes, the necessary packages have to be downloaded from the public repository and installed in the environment. Section 2.5 depicts the required packages used in this book.

The software is also important to leverage the computational power of GPUs, even though the hardware is equipped with GPUs, without a software package to support them, they will not be used by the machine/deep learning projects. Therefore, it's important to choose the right packages to install into the environment.

The environment can be a virtual one that is available from the cloud providers, it can also be installed, configured and hosted in a local machine if it's equipped with powerful hardware.

Section 2.2 introduces two cloud environments that widely used for machine/deep learning and data science purpose, they are pre-installed, pre-configured and ready to use, and it's convenient to install any additional packages as needed, and no need to worry about hardware. They can also be configured to use GPUs as easy as selecting a menu item.

The cloud providers have free and paid plans, the free plans usually have limitations, for example, the usage of GPUs and continuous execution time. In some cases, especially for deep learning, it could take many hours, sometimes overnight or even more to train the model, the free plan might not work in this case. If not want to upgrade to paid plans to overcome these limitations, section 2.3 and 2.4 explains the installation on local machines.

The environments hosted by local machines are more flexible and have no limitations on running time, the deep learning training can be done overnight or even more time. If the powerful GPUs are equipped with the local machines, they will also be helping the computation. Section 2.3 explains how to install them on the docker containers, where the GPUs could be leveraged. And section 2.4 explains how to install them on the local machine, on Windows as well as Linux.

It's recommended to use one of the cloud environments to start, and when move to the deep learning sections later in this book, where the extensive computation resources are required, then move to the docker hosted local environments as described in section 2.3. If for some reasons docker does not work, then move to the installation of local machine as section 2.4.

2.1 Source Codes for This Book

The source codes for this book are located at Github:

https://github.com/jchen8000/MLDLwithPython.git

All the codes are tested and working with the latest version of the packages at the time of this writing.

It's recommended to clone the source codes to the local machine, by the following command:

```
git clone https://github.com/jchen8000/MLDLwithPython.git
```

If `git` is not installed, install it follow the instructions, https://git-scm.com/book/en/v2/Getting-Started-Installing-Git

2.2 Cloud Environments

There are several cloud providers can be used for executing Python codes. Here introduce two of them -- Google Colab and Saturn Cloud.

Google Colab

Google Colab is used basically throughout this book except the deep learning sections in the later chapters. Then what is Google Colab?

> Colab, or "Colaboratory", allows you to write and execute Python in your browser, with
> - Zero configuration required
> - Access to GPUs free of charge
> - Easy sharing
>
> Whether you're a student, a data scientist or an AI researcher, Colab can make your work easier. Watch Introduction to Colab to learn more, or just get started below!
>
> From https://colab.research.google.com/notebooks/intro.ipynb

Google Colab, hosted by Google, provides Python & Jupyter environment, so you don't use any local computer resources to run the Python codes. The machine/deep learning projects normally require lots of computational resources, such as GPU and memory. If run them on a local machine without powerful hardware the greatest bottleneck could be the lack of computational resources, Google Colab provides these resources, and you have the freedom to use them at your disposal with free or paid plans, although the free one has limitations. Currently Google Colab provides GPU (Graphics Processing Units) and TPU (Tensor Processing Units) supports, the latter is developed by Google for machine learning purpose. It also provides memory and disk spaces. However, these resources are not persistent, meaning they are available only when you connect to Google Colab, and you lose everything when you disconnect.

Jupyter is an open-source and web-based coding environment that allows the users to create and share live interactive codes together with rich text elements for descriptions and documentations, it's convenience and widely used for data science and machine/deep learning. It supports many programming languages including Python.

Google Colab can be accessed at https://colab.research.google.com/

You might think to go through the Getting Started guide if not familiar. A Google account is needed to access the Google Colab, the codes will be stored either in Google Drive or Github. It's recommended to store all codes in Github and use Google Colab to access them, it can access the private Github repositories as well.

There are some tutorials on the web that can help to get started with Google Colab, such as:

https://colab.research.google.com/github/cs231n/cs231n.github.io/blob/master/python-colab.ipynb
https://www.tutorialspoint.com/google_colab/index.htm
https://towardsdatascience.com/getting-started-with-google-colab-f2fff97f594c

Saturn Cloud

Saturn Cloud, at https://saturncloud.io/, provides a workspace for the purpose of data science and machine/deep learning, it gives you a virtual machine of your choice, hardware specs, memories, CPUs, GPUs, and so on. It supports many languages for data science and machine learning, like Python, R, Jupyter notebook, etc.

You can choose the specs of the virtual machine from the given templates and run the Jupyter environment easily, and it connects to Github to retrieve the code files. There are also free and paid plans, at the time of this writing, the free plan does not require credit card and has 30 hours of running time per month, with 64GB RAM or a GPU, but GPU running time is limited to one hour.

There would be more choices if upgrade to paid plans.

Pros and Cons

The cloud environments save the time of setup and configuration, they are ready to use. However, they are less flexibility, and there are limitations, like Google Colab will make the GPUs unavailable without notice during the running. Of cause the limitations can be eliminated by upgrading to the paid services.

2.3   Docker Hosted on Local Machine

An effective way of running Python and Jupyter on local machine is a *docker* which is widely used today for software development, and of cause for data sciences and machine/deep learning.

Docker uses containers to create virtual environments that isolated from the OS and other applications on the local machine, meaning applications within docker will not impact any other applications running on the same machine. It's suggested using docker to build the Python and Jupyter environment, all the executions are within the docker container. It leverages all hardware resources of the host machine, like memories, GPUs, CPUs, storages and so on.

If not familiar with docker, you might want to get started by reading some tutorials, for example, https://docs.docker.com/get-started/

And then install the docker on the local machine if it's not installed:

- On Windows machine: https://docs.docker.com/desktop/windows/wsl/
- On Linux machine: https://docs.docker.com/engine/install/ubuntu/

Leverage GPU

If the local machine comes with GPUs, it's a good idea to leverage them because they help to speed up the computation, depends on the specs of the GPUs, it could significantly make the training faster, especially useful for the deep learning projects introduced in the later sections of this book.

Usually, the GPU drivers need to be updated to the latest version, go to the GPU makers' website to update driver. The below instructions are specifically for Nvidia GPU devices.

Install Nvidia CUDA drivers at https://www.nvidia.com/Download/index.aspx

Open a terminal in Linux or cmd in Windows, and type:

```
docker run -it --gpus=all --rm nvidia/cuda:11.3.0-
base-ubuntu20.04 nvidia-smi
```

If the results are something like below, meaning the GPU is ready for the docker container:

```
+-----------------------------------------------------------------+
| NVIDIA-SMI 527.92.01 Driver Version: 528.02 CUDA Version: 12.0  |
|-------------------------------+----------------------+----------------------+
| GPU Name Persist... | Bus-Id Disp.A          | Volatile Uncorr. ECC |
| Fan Temp Perf ...   | Memory-Usage| GPU-U... | GPU-Util Compute M.  |
|===============================+======================+======================|
| 0 Quadro K620 On  | 00000000:01:00.0 On  | N/A                    |
| 34% 45C P8 1W/30W | 223MiB / 2048MiB     | 1% Default             |
 . . .
```

If you don't see the above results, unfortunately the GPUs are not available for some reasons. Only the CPUs are available in this case.

Pull the Image from dockerhub.com

I have built a docker image and made it available at dockerhub.com, it's ready to use for running the codes in this book, type the following command in terminal or cmd window:

```
docker pull jchen8000/tf_gpu_jupyterlab:latest
```

Alternatively, Build a Docker Image

There are many prebuilt docker images for this purpose, we will choose one that meets our needs, and build our own from there.

In the terminal in Linux or cmd in Windows, create a directory with any name you like, for example, `mydocker`, then go to the directory:

```
mkdir mydocker
cd mydocker
```

Create a file named `Dockerfile` in the directory, the contents of the file:

```
1    FROM tensorflow/tensorflow:latest-gpu-jupyter
2    RUN apt-get update && apt-get upgrade -y
3    RUN apt-get install graphviz -y --fix-missing
4    RUN python3 -m pip install --upgrade pip
5    RUN pip install matplotlib
6    RUN pip install jupyterlab
7    RUN pip install sympy
8    RUN pip install pandas
9    RUN pip install scipy
10   RUN pip install pydot
11   RUN pip install scikit-learn
12   RUN pip install seaborn
13   CMD ["/bin/bash"]
```

Line 1 is to leverage a prebuilt docker image that provided by tensorflow at https://hub.docker.com/r/tensorflow/tensorflow/, it comes with Python, tensorflow which is deep learning related libraries, Jupyter and it is leveraging GPUs. The size of this image is about 6GB. The keyword FROM means to build a new image based on this one. And line 2 is to update and upgrade it.

The base image does not include some packages which are needed for this book, they should be installed. Line 3 to 12 are to install them, if you want to install more libraries, feel free to do it by adding new lines before line 13.

Line 13 gives a bash shell after the docker is running.

Then from the terminal or cmd window, build the image with a name of your choice, for example `tf_gpu_jupyterlab`:

```
sudo docker build -t tf_gpu_jupyterlab .
```

Since the base image is big and lots of packages will be installed, it could take a while to complete. The results are something like:

```
Successfully built 0b74513e1286
Successfully tagged tf_gpu_jupyterlab:latest
```

The final docker image size is about 8GB.

Run the Docker Image

In the terminal or cmd window, type:

```
docker run --gpus all -p 8888:8888 -v [your
folder]:/tf/[target folder] -it --rm
jchen8000/tf_gpu_jupyterlab:latest bash
```

Or if you build it by yourself:

```
docker run --gpus all -p 8888:8888 -v [your
folder]:/tf/[target folder] -it --rm
tf_gpu_jupyterlab:latest bash
```

The parameter   gpus all means using all available GPUs, however if the GPUs are not available, remove this parameter.

-p 8888:8888 will map the port to 8888.

-v [local folder]:/tf/[target folder] will map the local folder to the docker folder. For example, if want to map C:/MachineLearning to the docker, it should be:

-v C:/MachineLearning:/tf/MachineLearning

Everything under C:/MachineLearning will be available within the docker under /tf/MachineLearning folder. The github repository can be cloned into the local folder and they are available within the docker.

After the docker is run, the Linux shell appears, optionally examinate the installed packages by typing the following command:

```
pip list
```

A full list of installed packages is displayed. From there launch the JupyterLab:

```
jupyter-lab --notebook-dir=/tf --ip 0.0.0.0 --no-
browser --allow-root --port=8888 --
NotebookApp.port_retries=0
```

The JupyterLab will be started, there are lots of message displayed, look for the message like below:

```
http://127.0.0.1:8888/lab?token=72a3ca4d424eaba99b...
```

Copy and paste it in a new browser window, JupyterLab is available there.

JupyterLab is an enhanced version of Jupyter Notebook, it's better to organize project files and looks like an IDE environment.

Lightweight Docker Image to Run Machine Learning Only

The above docker image is about 8GB in size, if you want to do machine learning codes only (before section 4.9), a lightweight docker image is good to go:

```
docker run -p 8888:8888 -it --rm -v [your_folder]
:/home/jovyan/work/[target_folder] jupyter/scipy-
notebook
```

This will pull and run a ready-to-use docker image, about 3GB in size, but it will not run the deep learning codes (after section 4.9), and it will not use the GPUs.

2.4 Install on Local Machines

As an alternative, the environment can be installed and hosted on local machine, this section introduces the methods to install Jupyter on Windows and Linux machines.

2.4.1 Install Jupyter on Windows

It's suggested that non-experienced users go with installing Anaconda, it will install the latest version of Python and Jupyter, as well as other useful tools for data science and machine/deep learning.

This web page describes the steps of the installation on Windows,

https://test-jupyter.readthedocs.io/en/latest/install.html

It's straightforward to go through the installation process, download Anaconda package from its website at https://www.anaconda.com/products/distribution, install it following the instructions, and run it.

2.4.2 Install Jupyter on Ubuntu

Update Python and install PIP tool

Ubuntu 20.04 comes with preinstalled Python 3. PIP (Package Installer for Python) is a package management tool for Python and is used to install and manage packages and libraries, it connects to an online repository of public packages. As the first step, Python 3 and PIP will be updated and installed.

Execute the following command in a Terminal window,

```
sudo apt update
sudo apt install python3-pip python3-dev
```

Install Python Virtual Environment

A Python virtual environment is a self-contained directory tree in the local machine that has a Python installation for a particular version together with a number of required packages. After a virtual environment is created all the packages installed are only available to this environment, it does not affect other virtual environments.

Run the following commands to upgrade pip and install virtual environment.

```
sudo -H pip3 install --upgrade pip
sudo -H pip3 install virtualenv
```

Create a Project Folder

A project folder is the place to hold all project relate files, the virtual environment is also built on the project folder. The following command create a folder called machine_learning_python from the home, you can create it in whatever name and location you like.

```
mkdir ~/machine_learning_python
```

Create a Virtual Environment

Go to the project folder and create virtual environment,

```
cd ~/ machine_learning_python
virtualenv venv
```

And then activate the virtual environment,

```
source venv/bin/activate
```

At this point the virtual environment is completed and ready to install Jupyter.

Install Jupyter and Run it

Now install Jupyter,

```
pip install jupyter
```

Then run it,

```
jupyter notebook
```

2.5 Install Required Packages

The following Python packages are needed to be installed to the virtual environments to execute the codes in this book, use the following commands to install them.

```
apt-get install graphviz
pip install numpy
pip install pandas
pip install scipy
pip install seaborn
pip install matplotlib
pip install opencv-python
pip install sympy
pip install scikit-learn
pip install tensorflow
```

```
pip install keras
pip install pydot
```

The GPUs are only needed when working together with `tensorflow` and `keras`, if the environment is installed on local machines without the docker as section 2.4, the latest version of `tensorflow` package will automatically run on a single GPU.

If installed with docker on a local machine, section 2.3 explained how to make GPUs available for the environment.

Congratulations, we are ready to go!

3. Math Fundamentals

T his chapter will introduce the math fundamentals that are widely used for machine and deep learning and also used throughout this book, although this book is not a math textbook and does not intend to be one. The basic concepts, brief descriptions and examples are explained in this chapter, the most important thing is how to implement the mathematical concepts and methods in Python, the examples and code snippets are included in this chapter, and this is the main focus of this book.

If you would like to understand more about related mathematical topics, there are many reference materials listed in References section at the end of the book, they would be very helpful for a better understanding of the mathematical related details.

Section 3.1 explains the linear algebra, vectors, matrices, the concepts, operations and attributes of them, and most important, how to implement and calculate them with Python libraries.

Section 3.2 explains calculus, functions, univariate and multivariate, derivatives and differential, as well as gradient descent – a widely used algorithm in machine learning and data sciences. It sounds like very difficult when touching these topics, I try to explain them as easily as possible and try to avoid those difficult stuffs, and whenever possible introduce Python-provided libraries and functions to help with these difficult things. And trust me eventually you will find it's quite easy, with the help of Python, to understand them and to resolve the problems.

Section 3.3 will introduce some advanced functions that widely used for machine and deep learning, such as Sigmoid or Logistic function, Identity or Linear function, Tanh function, Relu and Leaky Relu function, Gaussian function and Normal Distribution.

All the code snippets in this book can be found in the Github repository, they are tested and working.

Enjoy the Math Fundamentals!

3.1 Linear Algebra

3.1.1 Vectors

Vector is a very important concept not only for machine learning and data science, but also for many other areas. A vector has two attributes, *magnitude* (or size) and *direction*. For example, consider a vector is when a car moves from location A to B, the *magnitude* is the distance from A to B; if draw an arrow on the map from A to B, that is the *direction* of the vector.

There are two ways to describe a vector -- geometrically and algebraically. Here is an example of Vectors that described algebraically, it doesn't matter if the numbers are arranged in horizontal or in vertical order:

$$\vec{v} = \begin{bmatrix} 2 \\ 3 \end{bmatrix}, \text{ or } [2 \quad 3]$$

There are two numbers in this vector, the first is 2, the second is 3. This is called 2-dimensional, or 2-D, vector.

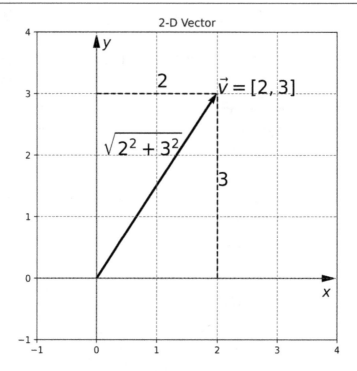

Figure 3.1 A Vector and its Magnitude

Generated by source code at Vectors.ipynb

The *magnitude* of the 2-D vector is calculated by the following formula:

$$|\vec{v}| = \sqrt{(x^2 + y^2)} = \sqrt{(2^2 + 3^2)} = \sqrt{13}$$

The vector can also be depicted geometrically, as Figure 3.1. The value in the *x*-axis is 2, and the value in *y*-axis is 3, the *magnitude* is the size, or length, of the vector.

Below are some more examples of 2-D vectors, in algebraical and geometrical representations.

$$\vec{v} = \begin{bmatrix} 2 \\ 3 \end{bmatrix}, \quad \vec{u} = [-1 \quad 2], \quad \vec{w} = [3 \quad -2]$$

Figure 3.2 is their geometrical representations.

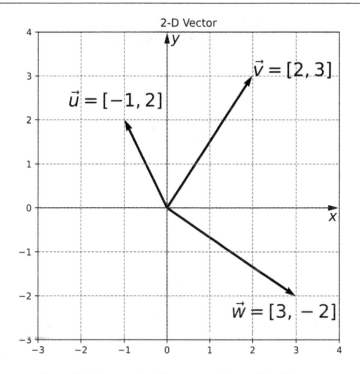

Figure 3.2 Geometrical Representations of the Vectors
Generated by source code at Vectors.ipynb

Below are the code snippets to define the Vectors in Python:

```
1   import numpy as np
2   v = np.array([2,3])
3   u = np.array([-1,2])
4   w = np.array([3,-2])
5   print("v =", v)
6   print("u =", u)
7   print("w =", w)
```

The results are shown below:

```
v = [2 3]
u = [-1  2]
w = [ 3 -2]
```

And they are plotted in the Figure 3.2 above.

This is the way that Python handles Vectors. The number of elements in a vector is called *dimension* of the vector. All the above examples have two numbers, which means they are 2-dimensional vectors. The 2-dimensional vectors can be geometrically represented on a 2-dimensional plane (or space).

Below are some examples of 3-dimensional vectors:

$$\vec{v} = [3 \quad 2 \quad 2], \quad \vec{u} = \begin{bmatrix} 1 \\ -3 \\ -1 \end{bmatrix}, \quad \vec{w} = [-3 \quad 1 \quad 2]$$

These 3-D vectors can be represented in a 3-dimensional space, as Figure 3.3.

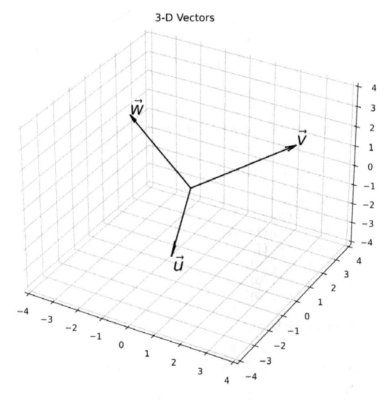

Figure 3.3 3-Dimensional Vectors
Generated by source code at Vectors.ipynb

The vectors more than 3-D can not be drawn geometrically, normally they are represented in algebraical way. Here is an example of a higher dimensional vector:

$$\vec{v} = [2 \quad 5 \quad 3 \quad -1 \quad 3 \quad 7 \quad 5]$$

In general, a n-dimensional vector is written as:

$$\vec{v} = [v_1 \quad v_2 \quad \cdots \quad v_n]$$

The magnitude is denoted and calculated by:

$$\|\vec{v}\| = \sqrt{(v_1^2 + v_2^2 + \cdots + v_n^2)}$$

In Python the vector is defined as below Line 1, and its magnitude is calculated as Line 2.

```
1   v = np.array([2,5,3,-1,3,7,5])
2   v_mag = np.linalg.norm(v)
```

```
v = [ 2  5  3 -1  3  7  5]
|v| = 11.045361017187261
```

3.1.2 Vector Addition and Subtraction

A vector can be added to another vector, say there are two vectors:

$$\vec{v} = \begin{bmatrix} 2 \\ 3 \end{bmatrix}, \quad \vec{u} = \begin{bmatrix} -1 \\ 2 \end{bmatrix}$$

The addition of the two vectors:

$$\begin{aligned} \vec{w} &= \vec{v} + \vec{u} \\ &= \begin{bmatrix} 2 \\ 3 \end{bmatrix} + \begin{bmatrix} -1 \\ 2 \end{bmatrix} \\ &= \begin{bmatrix} 2 + (-1) \\ 3 + 2 \end{bmatrix} \\ &= \begin{bmatrix} 1 \\ 5 \end{bmatrix} \end{aligned}$$

The geometrical representation of vector addition is shown as Figure 3.4,

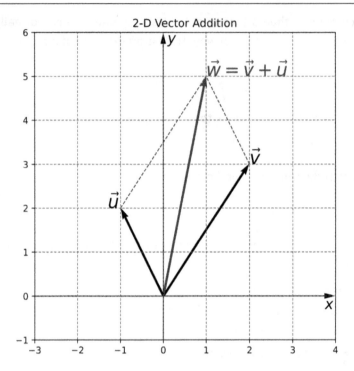

Figure 3.4 Vector Addition
Generated by source code at Vectors.ipynb

Similarly, a vector can be subtracted from another, the subtraction of the two vectors:

$$
\begin{aligned}
\vec{w} &= \vec{v} - \vec{u} \\
&= \begin{bmatrix} 2 \\ 3 \end{bmatrix} - \begin{bmatrix} -1 \\ 2 \end{bmatrix} \\
&= \begin{bmatrix} 2 - (-1) \\ 3 - 2 \end{bmatrix} \\
&= \begin{bmatrix} 3 \\ 1 \end{bmatrix}
\end{aligned}
$$

Its geometrical representation is as Figure 3.5:

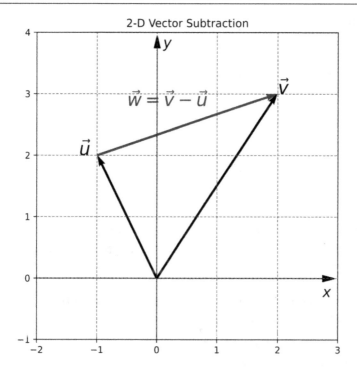

Figure 3.5 Vector Subtraction
Generated by source code at Vectors.ipynb

It's quite simple for Python to do the vector addition and subtraction,

```
1    v = np.array([2,3])
2    u = np.array([-1,2])
3    w1 = v + u
4    w2 = v - u
```

Line 1 and 2 define the two vectors, and Line 3 is vector addition, Line 4 is subtraction.

3.1.3 Vector Norm and Distance

The distance of vector from the origin is called *vector norm*. See Figure 3.1 for a 2-D vector $\vec{v}$, the norm is also referred as magnitude or length of the vector. The norm is denoted as:

$$\|\vec{v}\| = \sqrt{(x_2 - x_1)^2 + (y_2 - y_1)^2}$$

where the origin is $(x_1, y_1) = (0, 0)$, and (x_2, y_2) is the coordinate of the vector.

In general, a n-dimensional vector:

$$\vec{v} = \begin{bmatrix} v_1 & v_2 & \cdots & v_n \end{bmatrix}$$

The norm is defined as:

$$\|\vec{v}\| = \sqrt{(v_1^2 + v_2^2 + \cdots + v_n^2)}$$

Please note the norm is same as magnitude or length, just different terms.

This formula is called *Euclidean distance*, it's defined as a distance between two points, the distance is also the length of line segment between the two points.

It can be calculated using `numpy.linalg.norm()` function in Python, it's same as calculating the magnitude in previous section.

```
1   v = np.array([2,5,3,-1,3,7,5])
2   norm = np.linalg.norm(v)
```

Or it can be calculated as:

```
1   norm = np.sqrt(np.sum(v**2))
```

The results are same.

The vector distance is the distance between two vectors, as Figure 3.5, the vector subtraction will result a new vector $\vec{w}$, the norm of $\vec{w}$ is the distance between $\vec{v}$ and $\vec{u}$.

Therefore, it's denoted as:

$$\|\vec{v} - \vec{u}\|$$

Similarly in Python it can be calculated as:

```
1   v = np.array([2,5,3,-1,3,7,5])
2   u = np.array([1,4,2,-4,-1,2,3])
3   distance = np.linalg.norm(v-u)
4   print(distance)
```

```
7.54983443527075
```

Or,

```
1   distance = np.sqrt(np.sum((v-u)**2))
2   print(distance)
```

7.54983443527075

The results are same.

3.1.4 Vector Scalar Multiplication

A scalar is a number, the vector scalar multiplication is to multiply a vector by a scalar, means to multiply each item of the vector by the scalar. The scalar multiplication will change the magnitude (or the size) of the vector, but not the direction.

This is an example of scalar multiplication:

$$\vec{v} = \begin{bmatrix} 2 & 3 \end{bmatrix}$$
$$\vec{w} = 2\vec{v}$$
$$= 2 \cdot \begin{bmatrix} 2 & 3 \end{bmatrix}$$
$$= \begin{bmatrix} 2 \times 2 & 2 \times 3 \end{bmatrix}$$
$$= \begin{bmatrix} 4 & 6 \end{bmatrix}$$

Figure 3.6 is its geometrical representation, the scalar multiplication changes the magnitude to 2 times of the original vector, but the direction does not change.

The Python code is simply as below,

```
1   v = np.array([2,3])
2   u = 2*v
```

This is the generic formula of Scalar Multiplication for a n-dimensional vector:

$$\vec{w} = \lambda\vec{v}$$
$$= \lambda\begin{bmatrix} v_1 & v_2 & \cdots & v_n \end{bmatrix}$$
$$= \begin{bmatrix} \lambda v_1 & \lambda v_2 & \cdots & \lambda v_n \end{bmatrix}$$

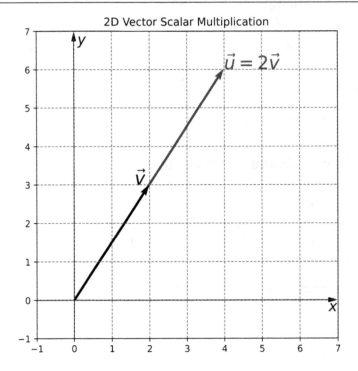

Figure 3.6 Vector Scalar Multiplication
Generated by source code at Vectors.ipynb

3.1.5 Vector Dot Product

The dot product is also called scalar product, it returns a scalar value. For example, there are two vectors,

$$\vec{v} = \begin{bmatrix} 2 \\ 3 \end{bmatrix}, \quad \vec{u} = \begin{bmatrix} -1 \\ 2 \end{bmatrix}$$

The dot product of the two vectors is calculated as,

$$\begin{aligned} \vec{v} \cdot \vec{u} &= \begin{bmatrix} 2 \\ 3 \end{bmatrix} \cdot \begin{bmatrix} -1 \\ 2 \end{bmatrix} \\ &= 2 \times (-1) + 3 \times 2 \\ &= 4 \end{aligned}$$

The geometric representation of dot product of two vectors is:

$$\vec{v} \cdot \vec{u} \;=\; \|\vec{v}\| \cdot \|\vec{u}\| \cdot \cos(\theta)$$

θ is the angle between the two vectors, the $||$ symbol is the magnitude of the vector.

Figure 3.7 is the geometric representation of the dot product of two vectors.

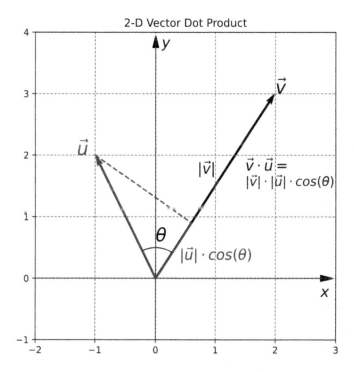

Figure 3.7 Vector Dot Product
Generated by source code at Vectors.ipynb

In general, the formula of dot product is as below, there are two vectors,

$$\vec{v} = \begin{bmatrix} v_1 & v_2 & \cdots & v_n \end{bmatrix}$$

$$\vec{u} = \begin{bmatrix} u_1 \\ u_2 \\ \cdots \\ u_n \end{bmatrix}$$

The dot product is defined as:

$$\vec{v} \cdot \vec{u} = \begin{bmatrix} v_1 & v_2 & \cdots & v_n \end{bmatrix} \cdot \begin{bmatrix} u_1 \\ u_2 \\ \cdots \\ u_n \end{bmatrix}$$

$$= v_1 u_1 + v_2 u_2 + \cdots + v_n u_n$$

$$= \sum_{i=1}^{n} v_i u_i$$

The result of dot product is a scalar, meaning it's a number not a vector.

The sum of square can be expressed by a vector dot product itself:

$$\vec{v} \cdot \vec{v} = \begin{bmatrix} v_1 & v_2 & \cdots & v_n \end{bmatrix} \cdot \begin{bmatrix} v_1 \\ v_2 \\ \cdots \\ v_n \end{bmatrix}$$

$$= v_1^2 + v_2^2 + \cdots + v_n^2$$

$$= \sum_{i=1}^{n} v_i^2$$

The dot product in Python is as below, np.dot() will calculate the dot product of vectors.

```
1   v = np.array([2,3])
2   u = np.array([-1,2])
3   w = np.dot(v, u)
4   print("Dot product of v and u =", w)
```

```
Dot product of v and u = 4
```

3.1.6 Vector Cross Product

Unlike dot product which results a scalar, the cross product of two vectors is a vector, meaning the result has a magnitude and a direction.

The direction of the result vector is perpendicular to both vectors, it follows right hands rule, as shown in Figure 3.8, with your right hand, point index finger aligns with the first vector and the middle finger with the second vector, then the direction of the cross product will align with thumb finger.

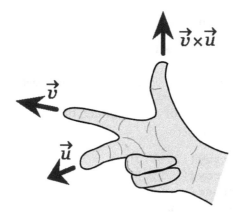

Figure 3.8 Right Hands Rule
Acdx, CC BY-SA 3.0 <http://creativecommons.org/licenses/by-sa/3.0/>
via Wikimedia Commons and modified by author.

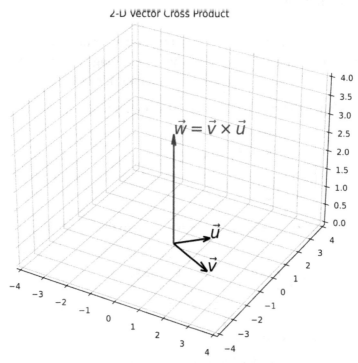

Figure 3.9 Vector Cross Product
Generated by source code at Vectors.ipynb

The magnitude of the cross product is equal to the area of the parallelogram shaped by both vectors.

The cross product is denoted as,

$$\vec{v} \times \vec{u} = \|\vec{v}\| \cdot \|\vec{u}\| \cdot \sin(\theta)$$

The geometric representation of cross product is shown as Figure 3.9,

Here are the Python codes for cross product, the function `np.cross()` calculates the cross product.

```
1   v = np.array([2,-1,0])
2   u = np.array([1,1,0])
3   w = np.cross(v,u)
4   print("w = v x u = ", w)
```

```
w = v x u = [0 0 3]
```

3.1.7 Matrices

A matrix, or matrices in plural, is a rectangular, or square array of numbers, expressions, or symbols, which are arranged in rows and columns. If a matrix has m rows and n columns, it's called a $m{\times}n$ matrix.

As an example, the matrix A below has 3 rows and 4 columns, it's called a $3{\times}4$ matrix.

$$A = \begin{bmatrix} 3 & 8 & 5 & 12 \\ -5 & 28 & 3 & 10 \\ -6 & 2 & 15 & 3 \end{bmatrix}$$

In Python, `numpy.array()` function is used to define a matrix, for example:

```
1   A = np.array([[3, 8, 5, 12],
2                 [-5, 28, 3, 10],
3                 [-6, 2, 15, 3]
4                 ])
5   print("A =", A)
```

As the result of running above code snippets:

```
A = [[ 3   8   5  12]
     [-5  28   3  10]
     [-6   2  15   3]]
```

In general, a $m \times n$ matrix is denoted as:

$$A = \begin{bmatrix} a_{11} & a_{12} & \cdots & a_{1n} \\ a_{21} & a_{22} & \cdots & a_{2n} \\ \cdots & \cdots & \cdots & \cdots \\ a_{m1} & a_{m2} & \cdots & a_{mn} \end{bmatrix}$$

Equality of Matrices

How to decide the equality of matrices, the two matrices A and B are equal if: 1) the rows and columns of matrix A are same as that of matrix B, and 2) the elements of the matrix A are equal to the corresponding elements of B.

Python provides some functions to check the equality of two matrices numpy.array_equal() function returns True if two matrices are equal, and False if not.

```
1    A = np.array([[3, 8, 5, 12],
2                  [-5, 28, 3, 10],
3                  [-6, 2, 15, 3]
4                  ])
5    B = np.array([[3, 8, 5, 12],
6                  [-5, 28, 3, 10],
7                  [-6, 2, 15, 3]
8                  ])
9    print("A = B?", np.array_equal(A,B))
10   C = np.array([[2, 8, 5, 12],
11                 [-5, 28, 3, 10],
12                 [-6, 2, 15, 3]
13                 ])
14   print("A = C?", np.array_equal(A,C))
```

The results are:

```
A = B? True
A = C? False
```

Another Python function to check equality is `numpy.equal()`, it checks element by element and gives the result of True or False for each element.

```
1    print("A = B?\n", np.equal(A,B))
2    print("\nA = C?\n", np.equal(A,C))
```

The results are:

```
 A = B?
  [[ True   True   True   True]
   [ True   True   True   True]
   [ True   True   True   True]]
 A = C?
  [[False   True   True   True]
   [ True   True   True   True]
   [ True   True   True   True]]
```

In machine learning the matrices contain the calculated numbers, in most of cases it's difficult to get exact same matrices, instead, the two matrices are considered equal if they are close enough. `numpy.isclose()` function uses a tolerance limit to decide if two matrices are equal, if the differences between the elements less than the tolerance limit value, they are considered close enough and said to be equal.

Below example uses tolerance = $1e\text{-}2$ to compare two matrices, $1e\text{-}2$ simply means $10^{-2} = 0.01$. The results are True for all elements. You can adjust the tolerance value to change the threshold to define how you consider they are equal.

```
1    A = np.array([[3.005, 8.492, 4.996, 12.001],
2                  [-5.002, 27.993, 3.002, 10.0045],
3                  [-6.0034, 2.00012, 15.003, 2.9995]
4                  ])
5    B = np.array([[2.998, 8.5, 5.001, 11.997],
6                  [-4.992, 28.0004, 3.0015, 9.9994],
7                  [-6.0023, 2.00045, 14.9996, 3.0001]
8                  ])
9    print(np.isclose(A,B,atol=1e-2))
```

```
 The result is,
  [[ True   True   True   True]
```

```
[ True    True    True    True]
[ True    True    True    True]]
```

3.1.8 Addition and Subtraction of Matrices

Here is the formula to calculate addition or subtraction of two matrices:

$$A \pm B = \begin{bmatrix} a_{11} & a_{12} & \cdots & a_{1n} \\ a_{21} & a_{22} & \cdots & a_{2n} \\ \cdots & \cdots & \cdots & \cdots \\ a_{m1} & a_{m2} & \cdots & a_{mn} \end{bmatrix} \pm \begin{bmatrix} b_{11} & b_{12} & \cdots & b_{1n} \\ b_{21} & b_{22} & \cdots & b_{2n} \\ \cdots & \cdots & \cdots & \cdots \\ b_{m1} & b_{m2} & \cdots & b_{mn} \end{bmatrix}$$

$$= \begin{bmatrix} a_{11} \pm b_{11} & a_{12} \pm b_{12} & \cdots & a_{1n} \pm b_{1n} \\ a_{21} \pm b_{21} & a_{22} \pm b_{22} & \cdots & a_{2n} \pm b_{2n} \\ \cdots & \cdots & \cdots & \cdots \\ a_{m1} \pm b_{m1} & a_{m2} \pm b_{m2} & \cdots & a_{mn} \pm b_{mn} \end{bmatrix}$$

Matrices A and B must be in the same size to perform addition and subtraction operations, there will be errors otherwise.

Properties of Addition and Subtraction:

1. Commutative Law: $A + B = B + A$
2. Associative Law: $(A + B) + C = A + (B + C)$
3. Identity of the Matrix: $A + O = O + A = A$, where O is zero matrix
4. Additive Inverse: $A + (-A) = (-A) + A = O$
5. $A - B = A + (-B)$

In Python, the `numpy.add()` function is used for matrix addition and *numpy.subtract()* for subtraction. For example:

```
1  A = np.array([[3, -1, 2], [-16, 2, -3]])
2  B = np.array([[8, 2, -8], [2, 1, 10]])
3  print ("A =\n", A)
4  print ("\nB =\n", B)
5  C = np.add(A, B)
6  print ("\nC = A + B =\n", C)
7  D = np.subtract(A, B)
8  print ("\nD = A - B =\n", D)
```

The results are:

```
A =    [[   3   -1    2]
        [-16    2   -3]]
B =    [[ 8   2 -8]
        [ 2   1 10]]
C = A + B =
        [[ 11    1   -6]
        [-14    3    7]]
D = A - B =
        [[ -5   -3   10]
        [-18    1 -13]]
```

There will be errors if two matrices with different size perform addition or subtraction operation. Here is an example that shows the error, when a 2×2 matrix add to a 2×3 matrix:

```
1   A = np.array([[3, -1], [-16, 2]])
2   B = np.array([[8, 2, -8], [2, 1, 10]])
3   C = np.add(A, B)
4   print ("\nC = A + B =\n", C)
```

The errors are shown as below:

```
ValueError      Traceback (most recent call last)
<ipython-input-3-eb3cd430eceb> in <module>()
      1 A = np.array([[3, -1], [-16, 2]])
      2 B = np.array([[8, 2, -8], [2, 1, 10]])
----> 3 C = np.add(A, B)
      4 print ("\nC = A + B =\n", C)
ValueError: operands could not be broadcast together
with shapes (2,2) (2,3)
```

Scalar Addition and Subtraction

The addition and subtraction can be performed between a matrix and a scalar (or a number), the result is the matrix with each item added to or subtracted by the scaler.

$$C = k \pm A$$

$$= k \pm \begin{bmatrix} a_{11} & a_{12} & \cdots & a_{1n} \\ a_{21} & a_{22} & \cdots & a_{2n} \\ \cdots & \cdots & \cdots & \cdots \\ a_{m1} & a_{m2} & \cdots & a_{mn} \end{bmatrix}$$

$$= \begin{bmatrix} k \pm a_{11} & k \pm a_{12} & \cdots & k \pm a_{1n} \\ k \pm a_{21} & k \pm a_{22} & \cdots & k \pm a_{2n} \\ \cdots & \cdots & \cdots & \cdots \\ k \pm a_{m1} & k \pm a_{m2} & \cdots & k \pm a_{mn} \end{bmatrix}$$

For example in Python,

```
1  A = np.array([[3, -1], [-16, 2]])
2  k = 5
3  print ("A =\n", A)
4  print ("\nk =", k)
5  C = np.add(A, k)
6  print ("\nC = A + k =\n", C)
7  D = np.subtract(A, k)
8  print ("\nD = A - k =\n", D)
```

The results:

```
A =
[[  3  -1]
 [-16   2]]
k = 5
C = A + k =
[[  8   4]
 [-11   7]]
D = A - k =
[[ -2  -6]
 [-21  -3]]
```

3.1.9 Multiplication of Matrices

Two matrices can be multiplied only when the number of columns in the first matrix equals to the number of rows in the second. I.e., the first matrix is $m{\times}n$, and the second is $n{\times}k$. The result of the multiplication has the number of rows the same as the first matrix and the number of columns the same as the second matrix. I.e.

$$(m{\times}n)(n{\times}k) = (m{\times}k)$$

In Python, the `numpy.matmul()` function is used for matrix multiplication. For example,

$$\begin{bmatrix} 3 & -1 & 2 \\ -16 & 2 & -1 \end{bmatrix} \cdot \begin{bmatrix} 8 & 2 \\ 2 & 1 \\ 3 & 2 \end{bmatrix} = \begin{bmatrix} 28 & 9 \\ -133 & -36 \end{bmatrix}$$

The matrices multiplication involves dot products between rows of first matrix and columns of the second matrix. See vector dot product in Section 3.1.5.

As shown in Figure 3.10, the first step is the dot product between the first row of the first matrix and the first column of the second matrix. The result of this dot product is the element of resulting matrix at the first row and first column.

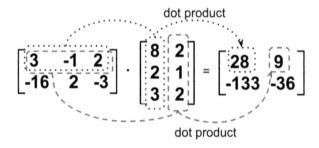

Figure 3.10 Matrices Multiplication

$$[3 \quad -1 \quad 2] \cdot \begin{bmatrix} 8 \\ 2 \\ 3 \end{bmatrix} = 3 \times 8 + (-1) \times 2 + 2 \times 3 = 28$$

Then the dot product between the same row of first matrix and the second column of the second matrix, and the result is positioned at first row and second column.

$$[3 \quad -1 \quad 2] \cdot \begin{bmatrix} 2 \\ 1 \\ 2 \end{bmatrix} = 3 \times 2 + (-1) \times 1 + 2 \times 2 = 9$$

And the same steps for the second row in first matrix doing dot product against columns of second matrix, as below:

$$[-16 \quad 2 \quad -3] \cdot \begin{bmatrix} 8 \\ 2 \\ 3 \end{bmatrix} = (-16) \times 8 + 2 \times 2 + (-3) \times 3 = -133$$

$$[-16 \quad 2 \quad -3] \cdot \begin{bmatrix} 2 \\ 1 \\ 2 \end{bmatrix} = (-16) \times 2 + 2 \times 1 + (-3) \times 2 = -36$$

In Python `numpy.matnul()` function is used for multiplication of matrices, here is the code example:

```
1   A = np.array([[3, -1, 2], [-16, 2, -3]])
2   B = np.array([[8, 2], [2, 1], [3, 2]])
3   print ("A(2x3) =\n", A)
4   print ("\nB(3x2) =\n", B)
5   C = np.matmul(A, B)
6   print ("\nC(2x2) = A x B =\n", C)
```

```
The result:
A(2x3) = [[   3   -1    2]
          [-16    2   -3]]
B(3x2) = [[8 2]
          [2 1]
          [3 2]]
C(2x2) = A x B = [[   28     9]
                  [-133   -36]]
```

In general, the matrix multiplication is denoted as:

$$C_{(m \times k)} = A_{(m \times n)} \cdot B_{(n \times k)}$$

$$= \begin{bmatrix} a_{11} & a_{12} & \cdots & a_{1n} \\ a_{21} & a_{22} & \cdots & a_{2n} \\ \cdots & \cdots & \cdots & \cdots \\ a_{m1} & a_{m2} & \cdots & a_{mn} \end{bmatrix} \cdot \begin{bmatrix} b_{11} & b_{12} & \cdots & b_{1k} \\ b_{21} & b_{22} & \cdots & b_{2k} \\ \cdots & \cdots & \cdots & \cdots \\ b_{n1} & b_{n2} & \cdots & b_{nk} \end{bmatrix}$$

$$= \begin{bmatrix} c_{11} & c_{12} & \cdots & c_{1k} \\ c_{21} & c_{22} & \cdots & c_{2k} \\ \cdots & \cdots & \cdots & \cdots \\ c_{m1} & c_{m2} & \cdots & c_{mk} \end{bmatrix}$$

Where, $c_{ij} = a_{i1} b_{1j} + a_{i2} b_{2j} + \ldots + a_{in} b_{nj}$

The sum of square can be calculated by dot product or multiplication for a vector by itself, this is widely used formula in machine learning and often used later in this book. For example there is a vector $A = [\ a_1 \ a_2 \ \ldots \ a_n\ ]$,

$$\sum_{i=1}^{n} a_i^2 = a_1^2 + a_2^2 + \cdots + a_n^2$$

$$= [a_1 \quad a_2 \quad \cdots \quad a_n] \cdot \begin{bmatrix} a_1 \\ a_2 \\ \cdots \\ a_n \end{bmatrix}$$

$$= AA^T$$

And similarly, the sum of multiplication can also be calculated by dot product or multiplication, this is another often used formular:

$$\sum_{i=1}^{n} a_i b_i = a_1 b_1 + a_2 b_2 + \cdots + a_n b_n$$

$$= [a_1 \quad a_2 \quad \cdots \quad a_n] \cdot \begin{bmatrix} b_1 \\ b_2 \\ \cdots \\ b_n \end{bmatrix}$$

$$= AB^T$$

Either `np.dot()` or `np.matmul()` can be used for this purpose, for example:

```
1  A = np.array([3, -1, 2, -6, 2, -3])
2  B = np.array([1, 2, 3, 2, -1, 5])
3  print("Sum of square:", np.matmul(A, np.transpose(A)))
4  print("Sum of multiply:", np.dot(A, np.transpose(B)))
```

```
Sum of square: 63
Sum of multiply: -22
```

Properties of Matrix Multiplication

1. $(AB)C = A(BC)$

2. $AB \neq BA$

3. $A(B+C) = AB+AC$

4. $(A+B)C = AC+BC$

Scalar Multiplication

Similar to scalar addition and subtraction, the matrix can be multiplied by a scalar number, the resulting matrix is same size as the original matrix, and each element of the matrix is multiplied by the scalar.

$$
\begin{aligned}
C_{(m \times n)} &= \lambda A_{(m \times n)} \\[2ex]
&= \lambda \cdot \begin{bmatrix} a_{11} & a_{12} & \cdots & a_{1n} \\ a_{21} & a_{22} & \cdots & a_{2n} \\ \cdots & \cdots & \cdots & \cdots \\ a_{m1} & a_{m2} & \cdots & a_{mn} \end{bmatrix} \\[2ex]
&= \begin{bmatrix} \lambda a_{11} & \lambda a_{12} & \cdots & \lambda a_{1n} \\ \lambda a_{21} & \lambda a_{22} & \cdots & \lambda a_{2n} \\ \cdots & \cdots & \cdots & \cdots \\ \lambda a_{m1} & \lambda a_{m2} & \cdots & \lambda a_{mn} \end{bmatrix}
\end{aligned}
$$

In Python the scalar multiplication is simple and straightforward,

```
1  A = np.array([[3, -1, 2], [-16, 2, -3]])
2  k = 3
3  print ("A =\n", A)
4  print ("\nk =", k)
5  C = k * A
6  print ("\nC = k * A =\n", C)
```

```
A =
   [[   3   -1    2]
    [-16    2   -3]]
k = 3
C = k * A =
   [[   9   -3    6]
    [-48    6   -9]]
```

3.1.10 Identity Matrix, Inverse and Transpose of Matrices

What is Identity Matrix

An identity matrix is a square matrix where its diagonal elements have the value of one, while the rest of the matrix elements are zero. I.e.

$$I = \begin{bmatrix} 1 & 0 & \cdots & 0 \\ 0 & 1 & \cdots & 0 \\ \cdots & \cdots & 1 & \cdots \\ 0 & 0 & \cdots & 1 \end{bmatrix}$$

In Python, `numpy.identity()` function is used to initialize an identity matrix. E.g. below code defines a 5×5 identity matrix:

```
1   I = np.identity(5)
2   print("I=\n", I)
```

```
I = [[1. 0. 0. 0. 0.]
     [0. 1. 0. 0. 0.]
     [0. 0. 1. 0. 0.]
     [0. 0. 0. 1. 0.]
     [0. 0. 0. 0. 1.]]
```

What is the Inverse of Matrix

The inverse of a matrix A, also called a reciprocal matrix, is a matrix denoted as A^{-1}, such as a reciprocal of number 5 is $1/5$.

A number multiplied by its reciprocal gets result of 1,

$$5 \times \frac{1}{5} = 1$$

Similarly, a matrix multiplied by its inverse gets identity matrix,

$$A A^{-1} = I$$

Hopefully this explains the inverse of a matrix. It's complicated to calculate the inverse from math, and sometimes there is no inverse for some matrices. It's beyond the scope of this book to calculate the inverse of matrices. Fortunately Python provide function `numpy.linalg.inv()` to calculate the inverse.

For example:

```
1   A = np.array([[3, -1, 2], [-16, 2, -3], [8, 1, 6]])
2   A_1 = np.linalg.inv(A)
3   I = np.matmul(A, A_1)
4   print("A=\n", A)
5   print("\nInverse of A_1 = \n", A_1)
6   print("\nA multiply by A_1:\n", I)
7   print("\nCheck A multiply by A_1 with Identity:\n",
        np.isclose(I, np.identity(3)))
```

```
A=
 [[  3  -1   2]
  [-16   2  -3]
  [  8   1   6]]

Inverse of A_1 =
 [[-0.16483516 -0.08791209  0.01098901]
  [-0.79120879 -0.02197802  0.25274725]
  [ 0.35164835  0.12087912  0.10989011]]
A multiply by A_1:
 [[ 1.00000000e+00  5.55111512e-17  2.77555756e-17]
  [ 1.66533454e-16  1.00000000e+00  1.38777878e-17]
  [-3.33066907e-16  0.00000000e+00  1.00000000e+00]]
Check A multiply by A_1 with Identity:
 [[ True  True  True]
  [ True  True  True]
  [ True  True  True]]
```

There is no concept of matrix division, however the inverse can be used for this purpose. For example, there is:

$$XA = B$$

Here we know A and B, and want to find X.

First, multiply both sides by A^{-1}:

$$XAA^{-1} = BA^{-1}$$

Since $AA^{-1} = I$ then we have:

$$XI = BA^{-1}$$

And because $XI=X$, so finally have:

$$X = BA^{-1}$$

What is the Transpose of a Matrix

The transpose is simply switching its rows with columns, it's denoted as A^T. For example,

$$A = \begin{bmatrix} 3 & -1 & 2 \\ -16 & 2 & -3 \end{bmatrix}$$

The transpose of A is,

$$A^T = \begin{bmatrix} 3 & -16 \\ -1 & 2 \\ 2 & 3 \end{bmatrix}$$

In Python, numpy.transpose() is used for calculating transpose.

```
1   A = np.array([[3, -1, 2], [-16, 2, -3]])
2   A_t = np.transpose(A)
3   print("A=\n", A)
4   print("\nTranspose = \n", A_t)
```

```
A = [[  3  -1   2]
     [-16   2  -3]]
Transpose =
     [[  3 -16]
```

```
   [ -1    2]
   [  2   -3]]
```

3.1.11 Determinant

The determinant is a number that can be calculated from a square matrix. The matrix must be square which means it has the same number of rows as columns. It's denoted as:

$$\det(A) = |A| = \begin{vmatrix} a_{11} & a_{12} & \cdots & a_{1n} \\ a_{21} & a_{22} & \cdots & a_{2n} \\ \cdots & \cdots & \cdots & \cdots \\ a_{n1} & a_{n2} & \cdots & a_{nn} \end{vmatrix}$$

How to calculate the determinant?

First it must be a square matrix to calculate the determinant. Let's begin with a 2 x 2 matrix:

$$\det(A) = |A| = \begin{vmatrix} 3 & -1 \\ 5 & 2 \end{vmatrix} = 3 \times 2 - (-1) \times 5 = 11$$

numpy.linalg.det() function is provided for calculating determinant:

```
1   A = np.array([[3, -1], [5, 2]])
2   A_det = np.linalg.det(A)
3   print("A=\n", A)
4   print("\nDeterminant = \n", A_det)
```

```
A= [[ 3 -1]
    [ 5  2]]
Determinant = 11.0
```

To calculate the determinant of a 3×3 matrix:

$$\det(A) \quad = \quad |A| \quad = \quad \begin{bmatrix} 3 & -1 & 2 \\ -16 & 2 & -3 \\ 8 & 1 & 6 \end{bmatrix}$$

$$= \quad 3 \times \begin{bmatrix} 2 & -3 \\ 1 & 6 \end{bmatrix} - (-1) \times \begin{bmatrix} -16 & -3 \\ 8 & 6 \end{bmatrix} + 2 \times \begin{bmatrix} -16 & 2 \\ 8 & 1 \end{bmatrix}$$

$$= \quad 3 \times (2 \times 6 - (-3) \times 1)$$
$$-(-1) \times ((-16) \times 6 - (-3) \times 8)$$
$$+2 \times ((-16) \times 1 - 2 \times 8)$$

$$= \quad 3 \times 15 - (-1) \times (-72) + 2 \times (-32)$$

$$= \quad -91$$

In Python:

```
1   A = np.array([[3,-1,2], [-16,2,-3], [8,1,6]])
2   A_det = np.linalg.det(A)
3   print("A=\n", A)
4   print("\nDeterminant = \n", A_det)
```

```
A = [[  3  -1   2]
     [-16   2  -3]
     [  8   1   6]]
 Determinant = -90.999
```

It's complicated to calculate the determinant of matrices more than *3x3*, and it's beyond the scope of this book. Fortunately it can always be calculated by Python `numpy.linalg.det()` function.

In previous section the inverse of matrices is introduced, and it's mentioned some matrices do not have inverse. In fact, if the determinant of a matrix is zero, then it does not have an inverse, the matrix is then said to be *singular*. Only non-singular matrices have inverses, which means a matrix has an inverse only if its determinant is not zero.

3.1.12 Eigenvectors/Eigenvalues and Singular Value Decomposition (SVD)

What are Eigenvectors and Eigenvalues

If there are a square matrix A, a scaler λ and a non-zero vector v, they satisfy the following relation,

$Av = \lambda v$

Then λ is *Eigenvalue*, and v is *Eigenvector* of matrix A.

Eigenvector must be non-zero, it's not considered a zero vector to be an eigenvector, although *Eigenvalues* may be zero.

`numpy.linalg.eig()` is used to calculate *Eigenvalue* and *Eigenvector* in Python.

```
1   import numpy as np
2   a = np.array([[3, 1], [2, 2]])
3   eigenvalue, eigenvector = np.linalg.eig(a)
4   print("Eigenvalue = ", eigenvalue)
5   print("Eigenvector = \n", eigenvector)
```

```
Eigenvalue = [4. 1.]
Eigenvector =
 [[ 0.70710678 -0.4472136 ]
  [ 0.70710678  0.89442719]]
```

In the above example, the eigenvalue has two values `4.0` and `1.0`, means there are two eigenvalues for the matrix; there are also two eigenvectors, the first column `[0.70710678, 0.70710678]` is the first eigenvector, and the second column `[-0.4472136, 0.89442719]` is the second eigenvector.

To verify the relationship of $Av = \lambda v$:

```
1   print("Verify first eigenvector:",
2          np.allclose(np.dot(a,eigenvector[:,0]),
              np.dot(eigenvalue[0],eigenvector[:,0]))
3          )
4   print("Verify second eigenvector:",
5          np.allclose(np.dot(a,eigenvector[:,1]),
```

```
            np.dot(eigenvalue[1],eigenvector[:,1]))
6        )
```

```
Verify first eigenvector: True
Verify second eigenvector: True
```

The Eigenvector returned by `numpy.linalg.eig()` function is normalized, means the norm (or length) of the vector is 1. Below code snippets are to print the norm of each eigenvector and verify it's normalized.

```
1   print("norm of first eigenvector:",
            np.linalg.norm(eigenvector[:,0]))
2   print("norm of second eigenvector:",
            np.linalg.norm(eigenvector[:,1]))
```

```
norm of first eigenvector:   0.999999
norm of second eigenvector:  0.999999
```

What is Singular Value Decomposition (SVD)

A matrix can be factorized as three matrices, which is denoted as:

$$A = U\Sigma V^T$$

Where:

A is $m{\times}n$ matrix.

U is $m{\times}m$ orthogonal matrix, means $U^T U = I_{m{\times}m}$.

Σ is $m{\times}n$ diagonal matrix, the singular values are in its diagonal, and all other elements are zero.

V is $n{\times}n$ orthogonal matrix, means $V^T V = I_{n{\times}n}$.

This is called *Singular Value Decomposition (SVD)*, it has some algebraic properties and a lot of applications in data science and machine learning. Here we do not deep dive into math details and not prove it from math perspective, because it's beyond the scope of this book. We will introduce how to use Python to calculate it.

In Python *scipy.linalg* package provides the function to calculate *svd*.

```
1   from scipy.linalg import svd
```

```
2    A = np.array([[1, 2], [3, 4], [5, 6]])
3    print("A=\n", A)
4    # Calculate SVD
5    U, s, VT = svd(A)
6    sigma = np.zeros((A.shape[0], A.shape[1]))
7    sigma[:A.shape[1], :A.shape[1]] = np.diag(s)
8    print("\nU=\n", U)
9    print("\nSigma=\n", sigma)
10   print("\nV^T=\n", VT)
```

```
A=
 [[1 2]
  [3 4]
  [5 6]]
U=
 [[-0.2298477   0.88346102  0.40824829]
  [-0.52474482  0.24078249 -0.81649658]
  [-0.81964194 -0.40189603  0.40824829]]
Sigma=
 [[9.52551809 0.         ]
  [0.         0.51430058]
  [0.         0.         ]]
V^T=
 [[-0.61962948 -0.78489445]
  [-0.78489445  0.61962948]]
```

In line 5, the `svd()` function is invoked and the returned value in the middle s is the singular values, sorted in descending order means biggest at the top, it's a vector with size of $min[m, n]$. In the above example it's a vector of 2 (which is $min[3, 2]$). So this returned value s is not in the format of Σ as defined above, which should be diagonal matrix in $m \times n$. In fact, the singular values in returned s should be in the diagonal of Σ. Line 6 and 7 in above code are to reformat s into Σ.

Now we have the three matrices U, Σ, and V^T, the below Python codes will reconstruct the original matrix A,

```
1    A_1 = (U.dot(sigma)).dot(VT)
2    print("Re-construct A from SVD:\n", A_1)
```

```
Re-construct A from SVD:
  [[1. 2.]
   [3. 4.]
   [5. 6.]]
```

3.1.13 Rank of Matrices

The rank of a matrix describes the *Linear Dependence* between its rows or columns. If a row in matrix is made of other rows by multiplying a scaler, then that row is dependent on other rows and not count towards the rank. If a row or column can count to the rank, it's called *linearly independent* row or column of the matrix, the rank of the matrix is the maximal number of *linearly independent* rows or columns.

For example:

$$A = \begin{bmatrix} 3 & -1 & 2 \\ 6 & -2 & 4 \end{bmatrix}$$

The numbers in second row are made of the first row by multiplying 2. So the rank of this matrix is 1 not 2, and the number of linearly independent rows is 1.

Look at the columns of matrix A, the second column is made of first column by multiplying *-1/3*, and the third column is also made of first column by multiplying *2/3*, so the rank is also 1 from column perspective, and the number of linearly independent columns is also 1.

Another example, look at an identity matrix I,

$$I = \begin{bmatrix} 1 & 0 & 0 & 0 \\ 0 & 1 & 0 & 0 \\ 0 & 0 & 1 & 0 \\ 0 & 0 & 0 & 1 \end{bmatrix}$$

The rank is 4, because all rows and columns are independent, and not relying on others. In another word, all rows or columns are *linearly independent*. The rank of an identity matrix is always its size, which is 4.

The rank will be always equal or smaller than the smallest dimension of a matrix, it can not be larger than that. For example, the rank will not be larger than 3 for a 3×5 matrix. If it's 3 then called *full rank*.

Why to find the rank? Normally a matrix represents the relationships between variables, the number of columns means the number of variables. The rank of the matrix tells whether there is a unique solution to solve all the variables, if the rank equals the number of variables, then there is a unique solution.

Then how to calculate rank? It's highly recommended to use Python provided `numpy.linalg.matrix_rank()` function:

```
1   a = np.array([[3,-1,2], [6,-2,4]])
2   print('A = ', a)
3   print('\nRank of A = ', p.linalg.matrix_rank(a))
```

```
A = [[ 3 -1  2]
     [ 6 -2  4]]
Rank of A = 1
```

The second example:

```
1   I = np.identity(4)
2   print('I = ', I)
3   print('\nRank = ',np.linalg.matrix_rank(I))
```

```
I = [[1. 0. 0. 0.]
     [0. 1. 0. 0.]
     [0. 0. 1. 0.]
     [0. 0. 0. 1.]]
Rank = 4
```

Alternatively, for a square matrix the determinant (see section 3.1.11) can also help, if the determinant is non-zero, it means all rows/columns are *linearly independent*, so it's full-rank matrix, meaning its rank equals the number of rows (or columns).

3.1.14 Cosine Similarity

Cosine similarity is a metric to measure the similarity of two vectors, it measures the cosine of the angle between the two vectors. Figure 3.11 shows two vectors $\vec{v}$ and $\vec{u}$ in 2-dimensional space, the angle between them is θ.

Cosine similarity is defined as the dot product of both vectors divided by the product of their norms, which are the lengths of the vectors:

$$\text{Cosine similarity} = \cos(\theta) = \frac{\vec{v} \cdot \vec{u}}{\|\vec{v}\| \cdot \|\vec{u}\|}$$

If θ is near zero degree, the two vectors are almost in the same direction, then the cosine similarity is near 1, which means the two vectors are similar.

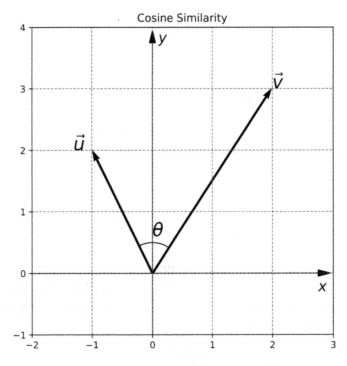

Figure 3.11 Cosine Similarity
Generated by source code at Vectors.ipynb

If θ is 90 degree, the two vectors are perpendicular to each other, their dot product is equal to zero, then the cosine similarity is 0, which means the two vectors are dissimilar.

If θ is 180 degree, the two vectors are in opposite direction, the cosine similarity is -1.

Section 3.1.3 introduces *Euclidean distance*, which is one of the methods to measure the similarity between two vectors by calculating the distance of them. If the two points are near, they are similar in terms of Euclidean distance. However, the cosine similarity does not care about distances, it only considers the directions. If two vectors are far away but in the same direction, meaning the lengths of them are very different, the cosine similarity still considers them as similar. For example, if the length of one vector is 100, the length of another is 1, both are in the same direction, then the cosine similarity considers them as similar, although Euclidean distance considers them as dissimilar.

In Python, cosine similarity can be calculated as:

```
1    import numpy as np
2    v = np.array([2,3])
3    u = np.array([-1,2])
4    cos_sim = np.dot(v, u) /
5                (np.linalg.norm(v)*np.linalg.norm(u))
6    print("Cosine Similarity is:", cos_sim)
```

```
Cosine Similarity is: 0.4961
```

Alternatively, `sklearn` package provides a pairwise calculation for cosine similarity, the output is a matrix:

```
1    from sklearn.metrics.pairwise import cosine_similarity
2    cos_sim2 = cosine_similarity([v, u])
3    print("Cosine Similarity matrix:\n", cos_sim2)
```

```
Cosine Similarity matrix:
 [[1.      0.496]
  [0.496  1.   ]]
```

The result is the pairwise value of cosine similarity. The number in upper-left corner is the similarity of vector $\vec{v}$ vs itself, the value is 1 meaning a vector is always similar to itself; the upper-right value is the similarity of vectors $\vec{v}$ vs $\vec{u}$, which is 0.49613894, same as the previous result.

The lower-left value is the similarity of vectors $\vec{u}$ vs $\vec{v}$, which is same as the upper-right value; and the last one lower-right value is the similarity of vector $\vec{u}$ vs itself.

3.2 Calculus

3.2.1 Functions and Derivatives

What is Derivative?

A derivative is the slope, or rate of change, of two points in a function. Say there is a function $y = f(x)$, $P1$ and $P2$ are two points in the function, as shown in Figure 3.12, the difference in x-axis is Δx, and the difference in y-axis is Δy, the slope of the difference is defined as $\Delta y/\Delta x$.

If move $P2$ towards $P1$, the Δx approaches to 0, then the derivative at $P1$, denoted as $f'(x)$, is defined as below, it's the slope of a tangent line at point $P1$.

$$f'(x) = \lim_{\Delta x \to 0} \frac{\Delta y}{\Delta x}$$

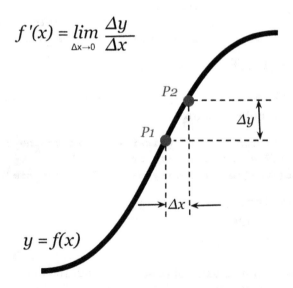

Figure 3.12 Derivative

As an example, in physics, the Velocity is the derivative of the Displacement (distance traveled) with respect to Time.

The derivative $f'(x)$ is actually a function, it has different values at different points in $y = f(x)$. The above discussion is about the point P_1, in fact every point in $f(x)$ has its derivative, which is the slope of tangent line at that point.

There is a function $f(x) = 2x^2 + x + 1$, as an example, let's find out its derivative,

$$\frac{\Delta y}{\Delta x} = \frac{f(x + \Delta x) - f(x)}{\Delta x}$$

$$= \frac{(2(x + \Delta x)^2 + (x + \Delta x) + 1) - (2x^2 + x + 1)}{\Delta x}$$

$$= \frac{(2(x^2 + 2x\Delta x + \Delta x^2) + (x + \Delta x) + 1) - (2x^2 + x + 1)}{\Delta x}$$

$$= \frac{2x^2 + 4x\Delta x + 2\Delta x^2 + x + \Delta x + 1 - 2x^2 - x - 1)}{\Delta x}$$

$$= \frac{4x\Delta x + 2\Delta x^2 + \Delta x}{\Delta x}$$

$$= 4x + 2\Delta x + 1$$

$$= 4x + 1$$

The last step above is because Δx is approaching 0, i.e. $\Delta x = 0$

As the result the derivative of function

$$f(x) = 2x^2 + x + 1$$

is:

$$f'(x) = 4x + 1.$$

Then what does it mean? It means at any point of function $f(x)=2x^2+x+1$, the slope or rate of change is $4x + 1$.

Derivatives for some common functions

Here we do not prove it from mathematics, but just introduce the conclusion of some common derivatives:

$f(x) = x$	$f'(x) = 1$
$f(x) = x^2$	$f'(x) = 2x$
$f(x) = x^3$	$f'(x) = 3x^2$
$f(x) = x^n$	$f'(x) = nx^{n-1}$
$f(x) = e^x$	$f'(x) = e^x$
$f(x) = a^x$	$f'(x) = ln(a)\,a^x$
$f(x) = sin(x)$	$f'(x) = cos(x)$
$f(x) = cos(x)$	$f'(x) = -sin(x)$

Multivariate functions

What is a *multivariate function*? Simply put, it's a function with more than one independent variables.

A single variable function is called *univariate function*, its output depends on the input variable, and it can be visualized in a two-dimensional space, meaning it can be drawn in a plane with x-axis as input variable and y-axis as output of the function.

On the other hand, the output of a multivariate function depends on the multiple input variables, which can be organized as a vector of the variables. A function with two variables can be visualized in a three-dimensional space, with x-axis and y-axis as input variables, and z-axis as the output. It's difficult to visualize functions with more than two variables, they are normally mathematically analyzed with the help of vectors and matrices.

Here is a multivariate function with two variables,

$$f(x_1, x_2) = \frac{1}{2}x_1^2 + x_2^2 + x_1 + x_2$$

This function can be drawn in the three-dimensional space, as Figure 3.13,

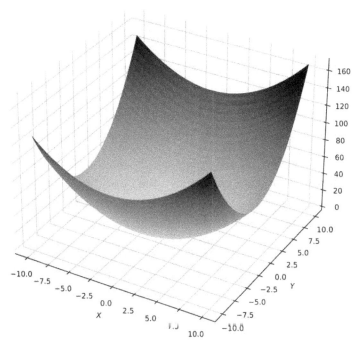

Figure 3.13 3D View of a Multivariate Function

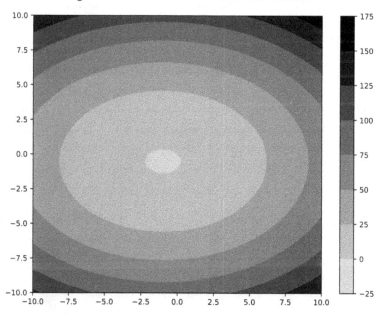

Figure 3.14 Contour View of a Multivariate Function
Generated by source code at Function_Derivatives.ipynb

The 3-D view in Figure 3.13 is a bowl-shaped plot, the x-axis and y-axis in the bottom plane represent the input variable x_1 and x_2, and the ranges of both are from 10.0 to -10.0, z-axis represents the output of the function, which is from 0 to 160.

In addition to the above 3D view, the function can also be visualized in the contour view, as Figure 3.14, which is excellent when presenting the functions with two input variables and one output.

The horizontal and vertical axes represent the input variable x_1 and x_2, the colors and lines in the contour represent the output of the function, the vertical bar in the right side shows the measure of each color, for example the light color at the very bottom represents the value of -25 to 0, so this color appears in the middle of the contour, meaning the values in that area are between -25 to 0. And the dark color at the top represents 150 to 175, which appears in the four corners of the contour.

Derivatives for Multivariate Functions

Then how to calculate derivatives for multivariate functions? As explained above the derivative is the slope of tangent line of a function at any point, it's same for the multivariate functions, the difference is a point for multivariate is specified by multiple variables instead of one.

Then we consider one variable at a time and hold others constant, this is called *partial derivative*. Say when consider partial derivative with respect to x_1, hold x_2 as constant, and all other variables if any, as constant. This is called *partial derivative* of x_1, simply because it's a derivative for one variable only, it's denoted as below, the symbol is ∂ instead of d.

$$\frac{\partial}{\partial x_1} f(x_1, x_2)$$

Since x_2 is held as constant here, the derivative of a constant is zero, so this partial derivative only has x_1 as its variable. For the example of above multivariate function of two variables:

$$f(x_1, x_2) = \frac{1}{2}x_1^2 + x_2^2 + x_1 + x_2$$

We do not prove it mathematically here, just give a conclusion of it's partial derivatives,

$$\frac{\partial}{\partial x_1} f(x_1, x_2) = x_1 + 1$$

And

$$\frac{\partial}{\partial x_2} f(x_1, x_2) = 2x_2 + 1$$

Next section will introduce how to obtain the derivatives with Python, since Python provides libraries and functions to do it. Therefore, you don't need to worry about the mathematical details.

3.2.2 Derivatives in Python

SymPy is a Python library for symbolic mathematics, it will display the symbolic mathematics expressions.

Univariate Functions

Here we use *SymPy* to obtain the derivative of a function. Take the same function as above section, $f(x) = 2x^2 + x + 1$, *SymPy* can give us a symbolic expression of its derivative.

```
1  import sympy as sym
2  def function(x):
3      return 2*x**2 + x + 1
4  x = sym.Symbol('x')
5  f = function(x)
6  f_derivative = sym.diff( f )
7  print("The function:  ", f)
8  print("The derivative:", f_derivative)
```

Line 1 is to import the *SymPy* library. It must be installed by PIP tool as described in section 2.5, otherwise it will cause an error.

Line 2 and 3 are to define the function as $2x^2 + x + 1$.

Line 4 is to create a symbol called x.

Line 5 is to obtain its derivative by calling `sympy.diff()`, this is the symbolic expression.

Line 7 and 8 are to print out the function and its derivative.

The result of above code snippets,

```
The function:    2*x**2 + x + 1
The derivative: 4*x + 1
```

Look at another example, replace Line 2 and 3 with below codes to define $f(x) = sin(x)$

```
2    def function(x):
3            return sym.sin(x)
```

Run the code, the result is:

```
The function:    sin(x)
The derivative: cos(x)
```

One more example: $f(x) = cos(x)$

```
2    def function(x):
3            return sym.cos(x)
```

The result:

```
The function:    cos(x)
The derivative: -sin(x)
```

In order to calculate the value of derivatives at any given point of x, Python provides function in *scipy* library. *SymPy* is to provide the symbolic expression, while *scipy* is to provide actual calculation.

Below code snippets show how to use it,

```
1    from scipy.misc import derivative
2    def function(x):
3            return 2*x**2 + x + 1
4    def deriv(x):
5            return derivative(function, x)
```

This function can be used to calculate and plot the function and its derivative, as below.

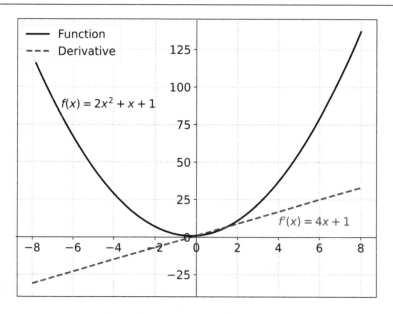

Figure 3.15 Function and Derivative
Generated by source code at Function_Derivatives.ipynb

Multivariate Functions

For multivariate functions, *SymPy* will also help to obtain the symbolic expression of partial derivatives.

Look at this function:

$$f(x_1, x_2) = \frac{1}{2}x_1^2 + x_2^2 + x_1 + x_2$$

```
1    def multivariate_function(x1, x2):
2        return 0.5*x1**2 + x2**2 + x1 + x2
3    x1, x2 = sym.symbols('x1 x2')
4    f = multivariate_function(x1, x2)
5    df1 = sym.diff(f, x1)
6    df2 = sym.diff(f, x2)
7    print("The function:", f)
8    print("Partial derivative of x1:", df1)
9    print("Partial derivative of x2:", df2)
```

Line 1 and 2 define the multivariate function. Line 3 specifies the symbols of x_1 and x_2. Line 5 and 6 obtain the partial derivatives using `sym.diff()`

function, same as described above for univariate function. Then Line 7 to 9 print out the symbolic expressions for function itself and the partial derivatives, the result shows:

```
The function: 0.5*x1**2 + x1 + x2**2 + x2
Partial derivative of x1: 1.0*x1 + 1
Partial derivative of x2: 2*x2 + 1
```

3.2.3 Differential

In calculus, the differential is defined as:

$$dy = f'(x)\, dx$$

as shown in Figure 3.16, there is a function $f(x)$, and $P1$ is a point in the function, MN is the tangent line at $P1$. As described in section 3.2.1, the derivative is the slope of the tangent line and is defined as:

$$f'(x) = \frac{\Delta y}{\Delta x} \quad \text{where } \Delta x \to 0$$

Note, $\Delta x = dx$, which is a small increment in x-axis, as it is increasing from x_o to $x_o + \Delta x$, the increment of $f(x)$ in y-axis is Δy.

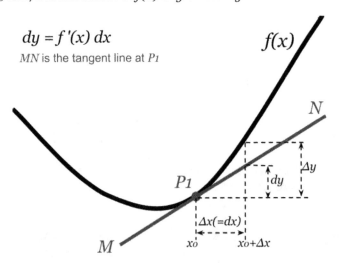

Figure 3.16 Differential

But Δy is not the differential, it is used to decide the slope of the tangent line. The differential is dy, which is the increment in y-axis of the tangent line. Figure 3.16 shows the differences between Δy and dy.

Basically, the differential dy is the linear part of the increment of $f(x)$, which is not exactly same as the increment of $f(x)$. But when dx, or Δx, is approaching to 0, then dy is considered equal to Δy, which means dy is almost same as the increment of $f(x)$. Therefore, the differential is a linear approximation to the increment of a function.

In summary, to simply put, the derivative is the slope of the tangent line at a point in $f(x)$; the differential is the increment in y-axis alone the tangent line, it's the linear part of the increment of $f(x)$.

3.2.4 Gradient Descent

Gradient descent is widely used optimization algorithm in machine learning to find the minima of a function, it's an iterative process.

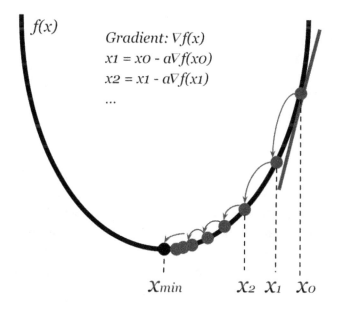

Figure 3.17 Gradient Descent

There is a function $f(x)$, its minimum value is at x_{min}, the purpose of gradient descent is to find x_{min}.

The *gradient* of a function is denoted as $\nabla f(x)$, consider the gradient is same as derivative for now, and it's the slope of tangent.

Now start from any initial point x_0, and try to move x_0 towards x_{min} little by little, then find next point x_1 by the following rule,

$$x_1 = x_0 - \alpha \nabla f(x_0)$$

α is called learning rate, its value is something like 0.01 or so. If the slope of tangent, gradient $= \nabla f(x)$ here, is a positive value, meaning the function is increasing when x increases, then x_1 will minus a small amount of $\alpha \nabla f(x)$ and the function will decrease a little from the previous point.

On the other hand, if the slope of tangent is a negative value, meaning the function is decreasing when x increases, this is the left part of Figure 3.17, then $x_0 - \alpha \nabla f(x)$ is actually plus a small amount, then the function will also decrease a little from the previous point.

This process will be repeated again and again until x is approaching x_{min} which is the target point at the minima of the function.

Which means the next point is:

$$x_2 = x_1 - \alpha \nabla f(x_1)$$

$$x_3 = x_2 - \alpha \nabla f(x_2)$$

... and so on.

In practice, a tolerance value ε is defined as criteria to terminate this iterative process, if $(x_n - x_{n-1}) < \varepsilon$, then it's deemed that no more changes in x, then x_{min} is reached. And also, a maximum number of iterations is defined, if the tolerance is not meet but it reaches the maximum of iteration, the process is also terminated. This is useful when sometimes for some reasons the algorithm does not converge to the x_{min}, this can avoid the infinite loop when something goes wrong.

If the learning rate α is selected too small, it will take long to reach the target; but if it's too big, it might not be able to converge at the target, the entire process might mean nothing, in this case the defined maximum value of iteration takes effect to terminate the process. Therefore, it's important to carefully select the learning rate α.

Take a function $f(x) = 2x^2 + x + 1$, as an example. The gradient is:

$$\nabla f(x) = \frac{d}{dx} f(x) = 4x + 1$$

Then the gradient descent rule is:

while $(x_{current} - x_{previous}) < \varepsilon$ and iteration $<$ `max_iters` {

$x_{current} = x_{previous} - \alpha \nabla f(x_{previous})$

}

ε is the tolerance, it's considered that the target is reached when:

$(x_{current} - x_{previous}) < \varepsilon$

And a maximum iteration number is defined as *max_iters*, when the iteration reaches this maximum number, the process will be terminated no matter it reaches the target or not.

The below Python codes define $\varepsilon = 1e-6$ (`0.000001`), and `max_iters` =`10000`.

```
1    def function(x):
2        return 2*x**2 + x + 1
3    def gradient(x):
4        return derivative(function, x)
5        # return (4*x + 1)
6
7    cur_x = -2.0
8    prev_x = 0
9    alpha = 0.01
10   epsilon = 1e-6
11   max_iters = 10000
12   iters = 0
13   x_value = []
14   iteration = []
15   while abs(cur_x - prev_x) > epsilon and
16           iters < max_iters:
17       x_value.append(cur_x)
```

```
18          iteration.append(iters)
19          prev_x = cur_x
20          cur_x = cur_x - alpha * gradient(prev_x)
21          iters = iters+1
22   print("The minima at", cur_x)
23   print("Minima of function", function(cur_x))
24   print("Iterations", iters)
```

Line 1 and 2 define the function of $f(x) = 2x^2 + x + 1$; line 3 and 4 define the gradient, you might think to use the method described in 3.2.2 to find out the derivative with `scipy.misc.derivative()` without worrying about the mathematical details. Line 7 to 12 is to define and initialize some variables, like learning rate α, termination criteria ε and max iteration, as well as the initial x_0 point. Line 13 and 14 are used to collect the data during gradient descent process and plot Figure 3.18. Line 15 to 21 run the gradient descent. Finally print the result:

```
The minima at -0.2500233145552139
Minima of function 0.8750000010871369
Iterations 275
```

The minimum value is at point $x = -0.25$, and the minimum of function is 0.875, the process runs 275 iterations.

The below two figures show how x is approaching the target. Figure 3.18 shows the horizontal axis is the iteration and vertical axis is x value, at the beginning $x = -2.0$, it gradually moves to the target of -0.25 as iteration going on, finally it reaches to the target and terminate the process when iteration is 275.

Figure 3.19 shows the gradient descent process starts from the initial point at $x = -2$, and moves along the blue line as the iteration is going on, the x is moving gradually down to the target point at bottom which is the minima of the function.

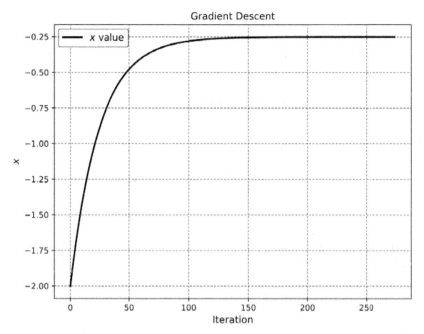

Figure 3.18 Gradient Descent Process, x vs Iteration

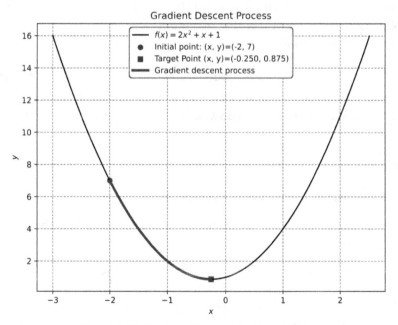

Figure 3.19 Gradient Descent Process, x vs y

Generated by source code at Gradient_Descent.ipynb

The above code snippets are used for illustrating the concept of gradient descent, in a real machine learning project it's highly recommended to use the Python provided function `scipy.optimize.minimize()` to calculate the minimum of function, it's simple and straightforward:

```
1    from scipy import optimize
2    x0 = -2.0
3    epsilon = 1e-6
4    minima = optimize.minimize(function,
5                               x0,
6                               method = 'CG',
7                               #  jac = gradient,
8                               tol=epsilon)
9    print(minima.message)
10   print(minima.fun)
11   print(minima.x)
```

```
Optimization terminated successfully.
0.8750000000000004
[-0.25000002]
```

There are several attributes inside its return value, `.message` tells successful or not, `.fun` shows the minimum value of function and `.x` shows the corresponding x value.

You don't have to provide the gradient function to `minimize()`, it will calculate by itself. However if you are confident to write the gradient function, you can pass it to `minimize()` as Line 7 above, it's optional.

Reference for details at
https://docs.scipy.org/doc/scipy/reference/generated/scipy.optimize.minimize.html

Gradient Descent for Multivariate Functions

The gradient for univariate functions is its derivative, but how about multivariate functions?

There is a multivariate function,

$$f(x_1, x_2, \dots, x_n)$$

The gradient is a vector of the partial derivative of each variable of the function, reference section 3.2.1 for partial derivatives.

$$\nabla f(x_1, x_2, \cdots, x_n) = \begin{bmatrix} \dfrac{\partial}{\partial x_1} f(x_1, x_2, \cdots, x_n) \\ \dfrac{\partial}{\partial x_2} f(x_1, x_2, \cdots, x_n) \\ \cdots \\ \dfrac{\partial}{\partial x_n} f(x_1, x_2, \cdots, x_n) \end{bmatrix}$$

The gradient descent rule is same as univariate functions,

$$X_1 = X_0 - \alpha \nabla f(X_0)$$

Where X_0 and X_1 are vectors of all variables.

As an example, use the same multivariate function as section 3.2.1, where its 3D view and contour view are shown in Figure 3.13 and Figure 3.14.

$$f(x_1, x_2) = \frac{1}{2}x_1^2 + x_2^2 + x_1 + x_2$$

Its gradient is:

$$\nabla f(x_1, x_2) = \begin{bmatrix} \dfrac{\partial}{\partial x_1} f(x_1, x_2) \\ \dfrac{\partial}{\partial x_2} f(x_1, x_2) \end{bmatrix} = \begin{bmatrix} x_1 + 1 \\ 2x_2 + 1 \end{bmatrix}$$

Its gradient descent rule is:

$$X_1 = X_0 - \alpha \nabla f(X_0) = X_0 - \alpha \begin{bmatrix} x_1 + 1 \\ 2x_2 + 1 \end{bmatrix}$$

Below is the Python code to define the multivariate function and its gradient:

```
1   def multivariate_function(x):
2       x1, x2 = x
3       return 0.5*x1**2 + x2**2 + x1 + x2
4   def multivariate_gradient(x):
5       grad = np.empty(len(x))
6       grad[0] = x[0] + 1
7       grad[1] = 2*x[1] + 1
8       return grad
```

The parameter of both functions above is vector of 2, meaning:

$$x = [\, x_1 \ x_2 \,]$$

The `multivariate_function(x)` returns a scaler and the gradient function `multivariate_gradient(x)` will return a vector of 2 elements, because the gradient for multivariate function is a vector, and each element is a partial derivative.

Same as above, run the gradient descent for this two-variable function:

```
1    cur_x = np.array([2, -2])
2    prev_x = np.zeros(len(cur_x))
3    alpha = 0.01
4    epsilon = 1e-6
5    max_iters = 10000
6    iters = 0
7    x1_value, x2_value, iteration = [],[],[]
8    while abs(cur_x[0] - prev_x[0]) > epsilon and
9            iters < max_iters:
10       x1_value.append(cur_x[0])
11       x2_value.append(cur_x[1])
12       iteration.append(iters)
13       prev_x = cur_x
14   cur_x = cur_x - alpha *
                     multivariate_gradient(prev_x)
15       iters = iters+1
16   print("The minima at", cur_x)
17   print("Minima of function",
                     multivariate_function(cur_x))
18   print("Iterations", iters)
```

Here are the results, after 1027 iterations the target point is at $[-1, -0.5]$, and the minimum of the function is -0.75.

```
The minima at [-0.99990127 -0.5]
Minima of function -0.7499999951258126
Iterations 1027
```

Figure 3.20 shows how the x $[x_1, x_2]$ is approaching to the target. x_1 moves from 2.0 to -1.0 and converge around 500 iterations; x_2 goes from -2.0 to -0.5 and converge around 200 iterations, the process terminates after 1027 iterations.

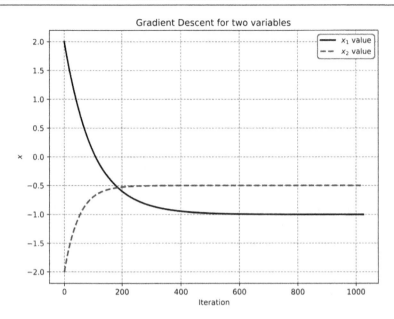

Figure 3.20 Gradient Descent for Two-Variable Function
Generated by source code at Gradient_Descent.ipynb

And again, it's highly recommended to use the Python provided function `scipy.optimize.minimize()` in a real world machine learning project. Just take above code example as illustration of the ideas of gradient descent.

Here is how to use `scipy.optimize.minimize()` for multivariate function,

```
1    from scipy import optimize
2    epsilon = 1e-6
3    x0 = (2.0, -2.0)
4    result =
5           optimize.minimize(multivariate_function,
6                             x0,
7                             method='CG',
8                             tol=epsilon)
9    print(result.message)
10   print(result.fun)
11   print(result.x)
```

```
Optimization terminated successfully.
```

```
-0.7499999999999969
[-1.00000005 -0.49999996]
```

Basically, everything is same as that for univariate function, except the x0 and `result.x` are arrays, because this is multivariate function which parameter is vector of variables.

About Learning Rate

How the learning rate affects the gradient descent process. Let's look at the iterative process with different α values, change the α value and execute the above code, here is the summary:

α	# of iterations	Minima	Target
0.001	8004	-0.7499	[-0.999 -0.5]
0.005	1920	-0.7499	[-0.999 -0.5]
0.01	1027	-0.7499	[-0.999 -0.5]
0.05	234	-0.7499	[-0.999 -0.5]
0.1	121	-0.7499	[-0.999 -0.5]
0.5	22	-0.7499	[-0.999 -0.5]
1.0	--	Not converge	Not converge
1.5	--	Not converge	Not converge
2.0	--	Not converge	Not converge

The smaller the α is, the more iterations it will take to reach the target. However, if the α is too big, in this case $\alpha \geq 1.0$, the process will not converge to target.

3.3 Advanced Functions

This section introduces some commonly used functions as well as their derivatives, they are widely used for machine learning and data sciences.

3.3.1 Identity (or Linear) Function

The identity function, also called linear function, is very simple and always returns the same value that was used as its argument. It's defined as:

$$f(x) = x$$

and its derivative is defined as:

$$f'(x) = 1$$

This is a linear transformation and quite simple but is limited in its capacity to learn complex functional mappings and solve complex problems. The reason is because no matter how many layers of the linear function, they behave just like a single layer because summing up all the layers will give another linear function, which exactly same as a single layer of the linear function.

Another problem is that its derivative is a constant, it has no relation to the input data x, the constant value loses the information of the input data and then not able to provide any better calculation.

```
1    def linear(x):
2        return x
3    x = sym.Symbol('x')
4    function = linear(x)
5    derivative = sym.diff( function )
6    plot_function_derivative(
7            function,
8            derivative,
9            xlim = [-4.0, 4.0],
10           ylim = [-4.0, 4.0])
```

The result is shown in Figure 3.21, the black solid line is the function, the blue dashed line is its derivative.

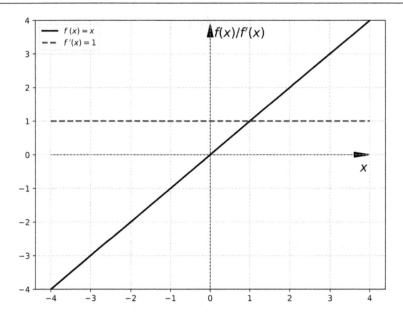

Figure 3.21 Identity or Linear Function
Generated by source code at Advanced_Functions.ipynb

As explained in previous section, *SymPy* library is used here to draw the function figure. Line 1 and 2 define the function, line 3 and 4 define the symbol as *x*, and line 5 obtains the symbolic expression of its derivative. Then line 6 to 10 call `plot_function_derivative()` function to draw the figure.

Please reference the source code at *Advanced_Functions.ipynb* for the details of `plot_function_derivative()` function, its self-explanative and easy to understand. Also reference the *SymPy* plotting module at https://docs.sympy.org/latest/modules/plotting.html.

3.3.2 Sigmoid (or Logistic) Function

Different from the above Identity function, the Sigmoid, or Logistic, is a non-linear function and defined as:

$$f(x) = \frac{1}{(1 + e^{-x})}$$

and its derivative is defined as:

$$f'(x) = f(x)(1 - f(x))$$

$$= \frac{e^{-x}}{(1 + e^{-x})^2}$$

The Sigmoid function is one of the most widely used non-linear functions, it gives an "S" shaped curve between 0 and 1, which means it transforms the input values into the range between 0 and 1. The output is assumed to be 1 if it's near 1, (say >=0.95); and 0 if it's near 0, (say <= 0.05). This function is often used for classification problems in machine learning and data sciences.

As shown in Figure 3.22, the black solid line is Sigmoid function, the blue dashed line is its derivative.

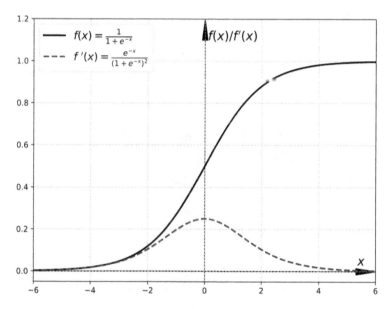

Figure 3.22 Sigmoid or Logistic Function
Generated by source code at Advanced_Functions.ipynb

The below code snippets generate Figure 3.22,

```
1   def sigmoid(x):
2       return 1/(1+sym.exp(-x))
3   x = sym.Symbol('x')
4   function = sigmoid(x)
5   derivative = sym.diff( function )
```

```
6    plot_function_derivative(
7            function,
8            derivative,
9            xlim = [-6.0, 6.0],
10           ylim = [0.0, 1.0] )
```

3.3.3 Tanh Function

Tanh, or hyperbolic tangent, function is another non-linear function, it's similar to Sigmoid and gives an "S" shaped curve but zero centered between -1 to 1.

It's defined as:

$$f(x) = \frac{\sinh(x)}{\cosh(x)}$$
$$= \frac{e^x - e^{-x}}{e^x + e^{-x}}$$
$$= \frac{e^{2x} - 1}{e^{2x} + 1}$$

Where $sinh(x)$ is hyperbolic sine function, and $cosh(x)$ is hyperbolic cosine function, which are defined as below:

$$\sinh(x) = \frac{e^x - e^{-x}}{2}$$
$$\cosh(x) = \frac{e^x + e^{-x}}{2}$$

The derivative of tanh function is:

$$f'(x) = 1 - f(x)^2$$
$$= sech(x)^2$$

Where $sech(x)$ is Hyperbolic Secant function, it's defined as:

$$sech(x) \quad = \quad \frac{1}{\cosh(x)}$$

$$= \quad \frac{2}{e^x + e^{-x}}$$

$$= \quad \frac{2e^x}{e^{2x} + 1}$$

The below code snippets define the tanh function and use the same method as above to obtain the derivative and draw the functions.

```
1  def tanh(x):
2      return (sym.exp(x)  -  sym.exp(-x))/
3              (sym.exp(x)  +  sym.exp(-x))
4  x = sym.Symbol('x')
5  function = tanh(x)
6  derivative = sym.diff( function )
```

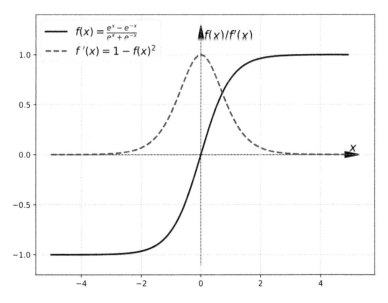

Figure 3.23 Tanh, or Hyperbolic Tangent Function
Generated by source code at Advanced_Functions.ipynb

3.3.4 ReLU (Rectified Linear Unit) Function

ReLU, or Rectified Linear Unit, is a partial linear function, it's same as identity function when input is positive, otherwise it will output zero.

It is defined as:

$$f(x) \ = \ max(\ o\ ,x\ )$$

Its derivative is:

$$f'(x) = \begin{cases} 1 & : \quad x > 0 \\ 0 & : \quad x < 0 \end{cases}$$

ReLU function is simple and computationally efficient, it's very quick to converge. However, it's not good for negative input data because it always returns 0 when input data is negative.

Figure 3.24 shows the ReLU function and its derivative.

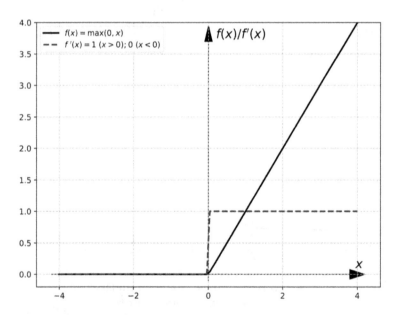

Figure 3.24 ReLU, or Rectified Linear Unit Function
Generated by source code at Advanced_Functions.ipynb

The below code snippets define the ReLU function; and use the same method to obtain the derivative and draw the function.

```
1  def relu(x):
2     return sym.Max(0, x)
3  x = sym.Symbol('x')
4  function = relu(x)
5  derivative = sym.diff( function )
```

3.3.5 Leaky ReLU Function

Leaky ReLU is a variation of ReLU, it is defined as:

$$f(x) = \max(x, \varepsilon x)$$

where ε is something like 0.1 or 0.01.

The derivative is:

$$f'(x) = \begin{cases} 1 & : \quad x > 0 \\ \varepsilon & : \quad x < 0 \end{cases}$$

Figure 3.25 shows the Leaky ReLU function and its derivative:

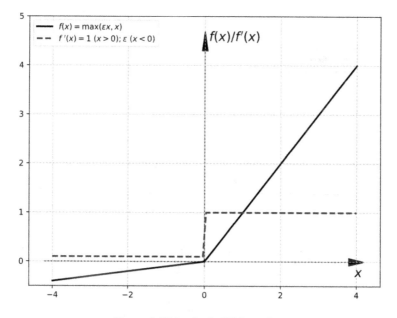

Figure 3.25 Leaky ReLU Function
Generated by source code at Advanced_Functions.ipynb

The below code snippets define the Leaky ReLU function; and use the same method to obtain the derivative and draw the function.

```
1    def leaky_relu(x, epsilon):
2        return sym.Max(epsilon*x, x)
3    x = sym.Symbol('x')
4    function = leaky_relu(x)
5    derivative = sym.diff( function )
```

3.3.6 Gaussian Function

Gaussian function is also a non-linear function, it's widely used in many areas of science, engineering, data analysis and machine learning.

The simplest form of gaussian function is defined as:

$$f(x) = e^{-x^2}$$

and its derivative is:

$$f'(x) = -2xe^{-x^2}$$

Figure 3.26 shows the Gaussian function and its derivative:

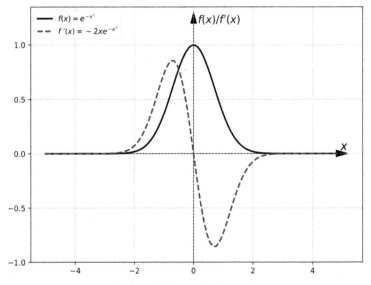

Figure 3.26 Gaussian Function

Generated by source code at Advanced_Functions.ipynb

The below code snippets define the Gaussian function; and use the same method to obtain the derivative and draw the function.

```
1   def gaussian(x):
2       return sym.exp(-x**2)
3   x = sym.Symbol('x')
4   function = gaussian(x)
5   derivative = sym.diff( function )
```

3.3.7 Normal Distribution

Normal distribution, also known as Gaussian distribution, is the application of Gaussian function, it's widely used in many areas such as data sciences, machine learning, statistical analysis as well as engineering.

In general, the data can be distributed in many different ways, in the "normal distribution" the data is distributed symmetrically from a center point and follow some rules. It forms a bell-shaped curve.

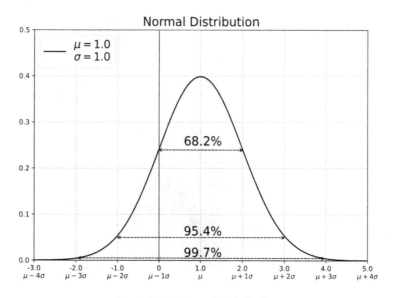

Figure 3.27 Normal Distribution
Generated by source code at Advanced_Functions.ipynb

Normal distribution is defined as:

$$p(x) = \frac{1}{\sigma\sqrt{2\pi}} e^{-\frac{(x-\mu)^2}{2\sigma^2}}$$

x is the variable that represent input data, the parameter μ is the *mean* or *expectation* of the normal distribution, it is also called *median*; the parameter σ is the *standard deviation* of the normal distribution.

Figure 3.27 shows a normal distribution with $\mu=1.0$ and $\sigma=1.0$; the mean or μ is the center of the data, and the data is distributed symmetrically from the μ at point *1.0*, meaning half of the data is in the left side of μ, and half in the right side.

The standard deviation σ is used to measure how the data is distributed, it is following some rules, as shown in above Figure 3.27, 68.2% of the data is in the area between μ-1σ and μ+1σ, meaning the area under the curve and between μ-1σ and μ+1σ is 68.2%; and $\mu\pm2\sigma$ is 95.4%, $\mu\pm3\sigma$ is 99.7%, $\mu\pm4\sigma$ is 99.99% and so on.

Figure 3.28 also depicts the data distribution rules in a different way, 34.1% between μ and μ+1σ, and another 34.1% between μ and μ-1σ; 13.6% between μ+1σ and μ+2σ, and another 13.6% between μ-1σ and μ-2σ; 2.1% between μ+2σ and μ+3σ, and another 2.1% between μ-2σ and μ-3σ; finally, 0.1% beyond μ+3σ and μ-3σ respectively.

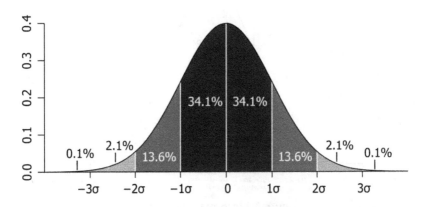

Figure 3.28 Normal Distribution, σ vs probabilities

By M. W. Toews - Own work, based (in concept) on figure by Jeremy Kemp, on 2005-02-09, CC BY 2.5, https://commons.wikimedia.org/w/index.php?curid=1903871

The famous Six Sigma theory is coming from the idea that there are 3.4 per million outside of $\mu \pm 6\sigma$.

Depends on the different values of μ and σ, the shape of the normal distribution curve might be different, it could be wider or narrower, taller or lower, but the bell-shaped curve will not change, and the rule will not change either.

Python provides `norm.pdf()` function in `scipy.stats` package to calculate the normal distribution, it's efficient and easy to use, the code snippets show how to invoke this function.

```
1    from scipy.stats import norm
2    mu = 1.0
3    sigma = 1.0
4    y = norm.pdf(x, mu, sigma)
```

In most of case you should use this function, however in this section we do a little deep dive, define a normal distribution function from scratch based on the math formula shown above.

The Python codes are shown as below, the function take three parameters, x for input variable, mu for μ, and sigma for σ. The `np.pi` inside the function is for π, and `np.e` for e. This function uses basic Python operations without any functions from any packages.

```
1    def normal_distribution(x, mu, sigma):
2        c = 1 / ( sigma * (2 * np.pi)**0.5 )
3        e = ( (x-mu)/sigma )**2
4        return c * np.e**(-0.5 * e)
```

To test this function, we have below codes that invoke both our function and `scipy.stats.norm.pdf()` function with same parameters and compare the results.

```
5    mu = 1.0
6    sigma = 0.5
7    x = np.random.uniform(size=(10))
8    y1 = normal_distribution(x, mu, sigma)
9    y2 = norm.pdf(x, mu, sigma)
10   for i in range(len(x)):
11     print("x =", round(x[i],6),
12             "\ty1 =", round(y1[i],6),
```

```
13                    ";\ty2 =", round(y2[i],6),
14                    ";\ty1==y2?",np.isclose(y1[i], y2[i])
```

Line 8 invokes the function defined in line 1 to 4, and line 9 invokes `scipy.stats.norm.pdf()` function, line 10 to 14 print x as input data and both results:

```
x = 0.175656 y1 = 0.204973; y2 = 0.204973; y1==y2? True
x = 0.846663 y1 = 0.761233; y2 = 0.761233; y1==y2? True
x = 0.409697 y1 = 0.397442; y2 = 0.397442; y1==y2? True
x = 0.415349 y1 = 0.402756; y2 = 0.402756; y1==y2? True
x = 0.948779 y1 = 0.793709; y2 = 0.793709; y1==y2? True
...
```

The above function is an example and for illustration purpose as a deep dive into normal distribution. It's recommended to use the function of `scipy.stats.norm.pdf()` in the real machine learn projects as they are optimized.

3.3.8 Multivariate Normal Distribution

The previous section discussed one-dimensional normal distribution, meaning x is one-dimensional variable, μ and σ are also scaler number. But how about multi-dimensional normal distribution, meaning x could be multi-dimensional variables?

The Multivariate Normal Distribution defined as:

$$p(x; \mu, \Sigma) = \frac{1}{\sqrt{(2\pi)^n |\Sigma|}} exp\left(-\frac{1}{2}(x-\mu)^T \Sigma^{-1}(x-\mu)\right)$$

where, n is the dimension,

x is an n-dimensional vector, $x = [\, x_1 \ x_2 \ \ldots \ x_n\,]$

μ is the *mean*, an n-dimensional vector, $\mu = [\, \mu_1 \ \mu_2 \ \ldots \ \mu_n\,]$

Σ is covariance matrix in the size of $n \times n$.

This section will focus on the 2-dimensional normal distribution, in this case the input x is a 2-dimensional vector, μ is also a 2-dimensional vector,

Σ is a matrix of 2×2. As an example, the parameters of a normal distribution are as below:

$$\mu = \begin{bmatrix} 1.0 & 2.0 \end{bmatrix}$$

$$\Sigma = \begin{bmatrix} 9.0 & 2.0 \\ 4.0 & 8.0 \end{bmatrix}$$

There are two figures shown below, Figure 3.29 is in the 3D space, x and y at the bottom plane are the 2-dimensional input data, p in the vertical axis shows the output of the normal distribution.

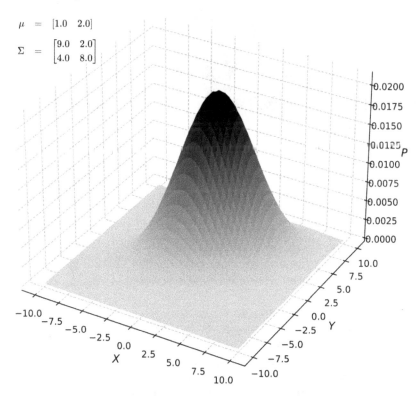

Figure 3.29 Multivariate Normal Distribution, 3D View

Figure 3.30 is its contour diagram. A contour diagram is an efficient way to describe functions with a two-dimensional input and a one-dimensional output. The color bar in the right shows the density of the output as well as its mapping in the x-y plane.

Similarly to one-dimensional normal distribution, Python provides `multivariate_normal`.**pdf ()** function in **scipy.stats** package to calculate the multivariate normal distribution, it's efficient and easy to use, below code snippets show how to invoke this function.

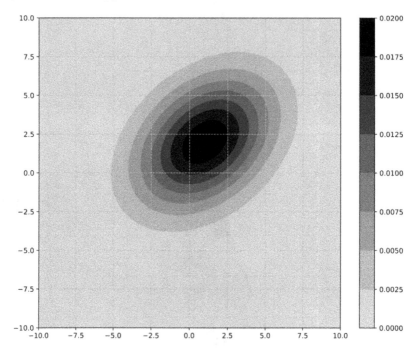

Figure 3.30 Multivariate Normal Distribution, Contour View
Generated by source code at Advanced_Functions.ipynb

```
1    import numpy as np
2    from scipy.stats import multivariate_normal
3    x = np.random.uniform(size=(10, 2))
4    mu = np.array([1.0, 2.0])
5    Sigma = np.array([[9.0, 2.0], [4.0, 8.0]])
6    z = multivariate_normal.pdf(x, mu, Sigma)
```

In this section we also do some deep dive to define a two-dimensional normal distribution function from scratch based on the math formula shown above. This is a math and Python practice, please feel free to skip this part if you are not interested and go to next section.

The function will be defined as,

```
def normal_distribution_2d(x, y, mu, Sigma):
```

The input parameters are:

- x and y are the two variables for the two-dimensional normal distribution.
- mu is the mean value for μ, a 2-D vector.
- Sigma is the covariances for Σ, a 2 × 2 matrix.

The math formula is as below, it's 2-dimensional which means $n=2$:

$$p(x; \mu, \Sigma) = \frac{1}{\sqrt{(2\pi)^n |\Sigma|}} exp\left(-\frac{1}{2}(x - \mu)^T \Sigma^{-1}(x - \mu)\right)$$

There are two steps:

1. To implement the first part of the formula:

$$\frac{1}{\sqrt{(2\pi)^n |\Sigma|}}$$

   The three lines of codes below will do the job. $np.linalg.det()$ function is used to calculate the determinant of $|\Sigma|$, which is the input parameter $Sigma$, a 2 × 2 matrix. See section 3.1.11 for matrix determinant.

```
n = 2
sigma_det = np.linalg.det(Sigma)
c = 1.0 / ((2 * np.pi)**n * sigma_det)**0.5
```

2. To implement the second part:

$$\left(-\frac{1}{2}(x - \mu)^T \Sigma^{-1}(x - \mu)\right)$$

   a) First calculate Σ^{-1}, it's the inverse of Σ, which is the input parameter $Sigma$, a 2 × 2 matrix. $np.linalg.inv()$ function is used to calculate the inverse, the result is also a 2 × 2 matrix. See section 3.1.10 for matrix inverse.

```
sigma_inv = np.linalg.inv(Sigma)
```

b) Next, $(x - \mu)$ is a 2-D vector, because x and y are passed as input parameter and μ is also a 2-D vector from input parameter, then $(x - \mu)$ is:

$$\begin{bmatrix} x - \mu_0 \\ y - \mu_1 \end{bmatrix},$$

And $(x - \mu)^T = \begin{bmatrix} x - \mu_0 & y - \mu_1 \end{bmatrix}$

c) $(x - \mu)^T \Sigma^{-1}$ is the dot product of above two matrices, and the result is a 2-D row vector:

$$(x - \mu)^T \Sigma^{-1}$$

$$= \begin{bmatrix} x - \mu_0 & y - \mu_1 \end{bmatrix} \cdot \begin{bmatrix} \Sigma_{00}^{-1} & \Sigma_{01}^{-1} \\ \Sigma_{10}^{-1} & \Sigma_{11}^{-1} \end{bmatrix}$$

$$= \begin{bmatrix} (x - \mu_0)\Sigma_{00}^{-1} + (y - \mu_1)\Sigma_{10}^{-1} & (x - \mu_0)\Sigma_{01}^{-1} + (y - \mu_1)\Sigma_{11}^{-1} \end{bmatrix}$$

d) Lastly, calculate $(x - \mu)^T \Sigma^{-1} (x - \mu)$, which is again the dot product of two vectors, the first one is the result of above step c) which is a 2D vector, and the second one is another 2D vector in above step b), the result of this dot product will be a scalar.

$$(x - \mu)^T \Sigma^{-1} (x - \mu)$$

$$= \begin{bmatrix} (x - \mu_0)\Sigma_{00}^{-1} + (y - \mu_1)\Sigma_{10}^{-1} & (x - \mu_0)\Sigma_{01}^{-1} + (y - \mu_1)\Sigma_{11}^{-1} \end{bmatrix} \cdot \begin{bmatrix} x - \mu_0 \\ y - \mu_1 \end{bmatrix}$$

$$= ((x - \mu_0)\Sigma_{00}^{-1} + (y - \mu_1)\Sigma_{10}^{-1})(x - \mu_0) +$$
$$((x - \mu_0)\Sigma_{01}^{-1} + (y - \mu_1)\Sigma_{11}^{-1})(y - \mu_1)$$

$$= (x - \mu_0)^2\Sigma_{00}^{-1} + (y - \mu_1)\Sigma_{10}^{-1}(x - \mu_0) +$$
$$(x - \mu_0)\Sigma_{01}^{-1}(y - \mu_1) + (y - \mu_1)^2\Sigma_{11}^{-1}$$

$$= (x - \mu_0)^2\Sigma_{00}^{-1} + (y - \mu_1)(x - \mu_0)(\Sigma_{10}^{-1} + \Sigma_{01}^{-1}) + (y - \mu_1)^2\Sigma_{11}^{-1}$$

Finally, it is implemented as line 6 to 10 in below code snippets.

Here is the code for 2D normal distribution:

```
1    def normal_distribution_2d(x, y, mu, Sigma):
```

```
2      n = 2
3      sigma_det = np.linalg.det(Sigma)
4      c = 1.0 / ((2 * np.pi)**n * sigma_det)**0.5
5      sigma_inv = np.linalg.inv(Sigma)
6      e = ( ( x-mu[0] )**2 * sigma_inv[0,0] +
7             ( y-mu[1] )**2 * sigma_inv[1,1] +
8             ( x-mu[0] ) * ( y-mu[1] ) *
9             (sigma_inv[0,1] + sigma_inv[1,0])
10          )
11     return c * np.e ** (-0.5 * e)
```

As testing, the below code snippets compare this function with `scipy.stats.multivariate_normal.pdf()` using same parameters,

```
12   mu = np.array([1.0, 2.0])
13   Sigma = np.array([[9.0, 2.0], [4.0, 8.0]])
14   x = np.random.uniform( size=(10, 2) )
15   y1 = normal_distribution_2d(x[:,0], x[:,1], mu, Sigma)
16   y2 = multivariate_normal.pdf(x, mu, Sigma)
17   for i in range(len(x)):
18     print(x[i], "--->\t",
19            round(y1[i],3),
20            round(y2[i],3),
21            np.isclose(y1[i], y2[i], atol=1e-2) )
```

Here are the testing results

```
[0.7622258  0.62222023] ---> 0.018 0.019 True
[0.45095468 0.36975292] ---> 0.017 0.018 True
[0.68569495 0.4159305 ] ---> 0.017 0.018 True
[0.09560973 0.03193154] ---> 0.016 0.017 True
[0.83099717 0.66698751] ---> 0.018 0.019 True
...
```

And again, the function we created above is an example and for illustration purpose only. It's recommended to use Python provided `scipy.stats.multivariate_normal()` and related functions in the real machine learn projects as they are optimized.

3.3.9 Softmax Function

Softmax is another type of probability distribution function, it transforms the input vector of n to a same size vector and sum up all its elements to 1. Each element of the output vector is between the range of [0, 1] and all the elements sum up to 1.

Softmax is also called *multinomial logistic regression*, each element in its output vector is the probability of that class. Will discuss it in detail in logistic regression section later.

Softmax function is defined as:

$$\sigma(x)_j = \frac{e^{x_j}}{\sum\limits_{i=1}^{n} e^{x_i}}$$

It works like Figure 3.31, the input is a vector of $[\,2 \;\; 5 \;\; 3\,]$, the output is a vector of same size $[\,0.042 \;\; 0.843 \;\; 0.114\,]$. The sum of all elements of output is 1, each element of the output represents the probability of that item.

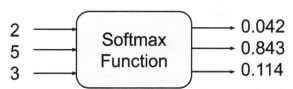

Figure 3.31 Softmax Function

This is the Python implementation:

```
1   def softmax(x):
2       return(np.exp(x)/np.exp(x).sum())
3   x = np.array([2, 5, 3])
4   print("x =", x)
5   print("softmax(x):", softmax(x))
```

```
x = [2 5 3]
softmax(x): [0.04201007 0.84379473 0.1141952 ]
```

4. Machine Learning

T his chapter will introduce Machine Learning (ML) and Deep Learning (DL) which include many mathematical algorithms and implementation techniques. Machine learning is a part of artificial intelligence, and deep learning is a part of machine learning. Both machine learning and deep learning will automatically "learn" the patterns from the massive amount of data with mathematical algorithms and will apply those patterns to the new data to make predictions and decisions without human interference.

What exactly is the Machine Learning? Based on the wikipedia:

> Machine learning (ML) is a field of inquiry devoted to understanding and building methods that 'learn', that is, methods that leverage data to improve performance on some set of tasks. It is seen as a part of artificial intelligence.
>
> Machine learning algorithms build a model based on sample data, known as training data, in order to make predictions or decisions without being explicitly programmed to do so.[2] Machine learning algorithms are used in a wide variety of applications, such as in medicine, email filtering, speech recognition, agriculture, and computer vision, where it is difficult or unfeasible to develop conventional algorithms to perform the needed tasks
>
> from https://en.wikipedia.org/wiki/Machine_learning

There are two key parts of machine learning,

1. To find patterns from the data
2. Make predictions for future new data.

How to find patterns from the data? For example, there is a dataset as below table, each row represents the statistics of housing data for a specific community.

Housing Median Age	Total Rooms	Total Bedrooms	Population	Households	Median Income	Median House Value
41	880	129	322	126	8.3252	452,600
21	7099	1106	2401	1138	8.3014	358,500
52	1467	190	496	177	7.2574	352,100
52	1274	235	558	219	5.6431	341,300
52	1627	280	565	259	3.8462	342,200
52	919	213	413	193	4.0368	269,700
52	2535	489	1094	514	3.6591	299,200
52	3104	687	1157	647	3.12	241,400
...	...	...	...	...	...	...

The left six columns are input data, i.e., housing median age, total rooms, total bedrooms, population, households and median income; the last column at the right is the output which is the median house value of the community. Machine learning will learn from the dataset and find out the patterns of how the input data is related to the output, it will use the mathematical algorithms to effectively identify the patterns.

After it learned from thousands or even millions of the data records, it will make predictions for future new data, for example there is a new community with following input data, what will be the median house value (the output) for that community?

Housing Median Age	Total Rooms	Total Bedrooms	Population	Households	Median Income	Median House Value
52	3503	752	1504	734	3.2705	?

The machine learning will predict the value as 241,800 after applying the new data to the learned machine learning model.

Then what a machine learning specialist or developer will do? Basically, there are two things to do:

1. The data
2. The algorithm

The quality of *data* is important for machine learning projects, in real-world projects lots of efforts are needed for preparing the datasets, like cleanup the data, ensuring the accuracy of the data, removing blank records etc. For example, the date field should have all dates in the same format, if most dates are in format of "2021/06/21", but some are "Jun 21, 2021", this will cause error when processing the dataset.

In most of cases these activities should also be working together with the subject-matter experts who have the expertise in the domain, like healthcare data needs to be reviewed with health experts to ensure the accuracy; housing data to review with real estate experts, and so on.

In this book, however, almost all the datasets are from the Python packages, like `scikit-learn` and `tensorflow`, they are well-prepared and ready to use, no need for the efforts such as data clean-up etc.

The *algorithm* is another aspect of machine learning, a good algorithm will help it to better learn from the data. This chapter will introduce 12 different algorithms, from linear regression to neural networks, which have different characteristics for different purposes.

The neural networks are deep learning; and those other than neural networks are machine learning. Normally the neural networks are more complicated than those without neural networks and require bigger datasets to learn and need more computational resources.

There are two types of machine learning algorithm, *Supervised Learning* and *Unsupervised Learning*. The former learns from the labeled data, which means the algorithm knows what the data is, for example, the algorithm receives a picture, and is told the picture is a dog, then the algorithm tries to map the picture to the dog. The latter learns from the data without labels, for example the algorithm receives a picture but doesn't know what this picture is, it works on its own to discover the information of the data, and explore the patterns and classifications etc.

The algorithms introduced in this chapter starts from the simplest one, and are grouped as below:

- Supervised learning
  - · 4.1 Linear Regression
  - · 4.2 Logistic Regression
  - · 4.3 Multinomial Logistic Regression
  - · 4.6 Support Vector Machine (SVM)
  - · 4.7 K-Nearest Neighbors
  - · 4.9 Artificial Neural Network (ANN)
  - · 4.10 Convolutional Neural Network (CNN)
- Unsupervised learning
  - · 4.4 K-Means Clustering
  - · 4.5 Principal Component Analysis (PCA)
  - · 4.8 Anomaly Detection
  - · 4.11 Recommendation System
  - · 4.12 Generative Adversarial Network

This chapter will introduce the algorithms not only using the functions provided by the advanced packages and libraries, but also implementing them from scratch. Then why from scratch?

Today's programming environments have numerous packages, libraries and frameworks that make the jobs easier by providing straightforward and reusable functions to build machine and deep learning models with a variety of algorithms. However, having a deep understanding of how things work behind the scenes and how the models perform using various mathematical algorithms and formula is a skill on its own.

By learning the fundamentals of creating the machine/deep learning models from scratch using basic libraries like numpy, without the help of any advanced packages, you will gain a deeper understanding of the models, and will be able to better apply those advance libraries in real machine learning projects.

Enjoy the Machine Learning!

4.1 Linear Regression

Linear regression is a commonly used model of machine learning, it's one of the simplest algorithms. The basic idea is to predict the value of an output variable based on the input variables. The output variable to predict is also known as *dependent variable*; The input variables are called the *independent variables*. The data for linear regression is quantitative scalar, meaning something like length, height, weight, price, population, etc.

Linear regression is supervised learning, both the data (input independent variables) and the label (output dependent variable) are needed for the learning process. The algorithm finds out the relationship between the input and output.

In order to predict the output variable based on the inputs, the liner regression process is trying to draw a line that best fit all input data, the line is the result of the linear regression, and it will be used for future predictions.

4.1.1 Introduction

The simplest form of linear regression is,

$$y = \theta_0 + \theta_1 x$$

x is the independent variable, only one variable in this case; θ_0 and θ_1 are parameters; y is the output variable, it's dependent on x, θ_0 and θ_1.

It is called *hypothesis function*, and it is a line. θ_0 is a constant and called *intercept* or *bias*, and it's the y value when the line crosses the y-axis when $x=0$. θ_1 is the slope of the line, it's called *coefficients*. The process of linear regression is to find out the intercept θ_0 and coefficient θ_1 so that the line best fit the data. After the best intercept and coefficient are found, the hypothesis function can be used for predictions.

To visualize the data and the hypothesis function, there is a sample dataset, each data has a x value and a y value, it can be drawn in the x-y

plane, the linear regression is to find a line that best fit all the sample data, as shown in Figure 4.1.

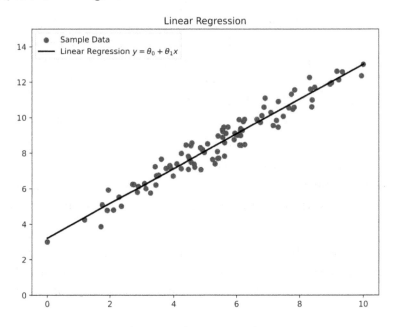

Figure 4.1 Linear Regression

Generated by source code at Linear_Regression_Introduction.ipynb

The Sample Dataset

`sklearn.datasets.make_regression()` function can be used to generate a sample dataset for a variety of purposes, here we use it to generate the dataset for linear regression.

```
1  X, y = datasets.make_regression(n_samples=100,
2                                   n_features=1,
3                                   noise=10,
4                                   random_state=0)
```

n_samples is to specify how many data points in the sample dataset; n_features means how many variables for the dataset, in this case only one variable; noise is to specify how far the data away from a target line, if zero then all data points are along a line, a bigger value will make the data points far away from the target line. random_state determines random number generated for the dataset, a value specified here means the same outcome is reproducible every time this function is called.

As the notation in this book, an uppercase X is used to denote the independent variable(s), a lowercase y is to denote the dependent output variable.

y in the sample data is called true label, it depends on X, the process is to find out the relationships between them.

Optionally, we can also format the data a little bit, it moves the data to a different range, but not affect the linear regression process. We scale the X and y to range of $[0, 10]$, and add a bias (or intercept) of 3.0 to y.

```
5    bias = 3.0
6    X = np.interp(X, (X.min(), X.max()), (0, 10))
7    y = np.interp(y, (y.min(), y.max()), (0, 10))
8    y = y + bias
```

This generates the sample dataset shown in Figure 4.1.

Linear Regression with Sklearn

`sklearn` library provides functions for linear regression,

```
9     from sklearn.linear_model import
      LinearRegression
10    model = LinearRegression(fit_intercept=True)
11    model.fit(X, y)
12    score = model.score(X, y, sample_weight=None)
13    print("Score:", score)
14    print("Coefficient (theta_1):", model.coef_)
15    print("Intercept (theta_0):", model.intercept_)
```

Line 9 is to import the library; line 10 is to create a linear regression model; line 11 is to fit the model with input data X and the true label y.

Then the linear regression is done, the `model` has all the information of the results. The black line in Figure 4.1 is the result of linear regression, it is the best fit of all data, the key values of the result are like below,

```
Score: 0.9417294727711081
Coefficient (theta_1): [0.9796368]
```

```
Intercept (theta_0): 3.2119370881393365
```

The score measures how good the line fits all data, it's called R^2 *Score*, or *Coefficient of Determination*, it will be explained in detail later. The best value is 1.0, but it can be as bad as negative value. Here our result is *0.94* which is not bad.

The coefficient or θ_1 is *0.98*, which is the slope of the line; and intercept or θ_0 is *3.21*, which is the y value when the line crosses y-axis. Then the hypothesis function is:

$$y = 3.21 + 0.98x$$

This function will be used to predict X in the future.

In line 10 of above code snippets, `fit_intercept=True` is passed to the `LinearRegression()` function, this means the process is to find both intercept and coefficient; if `fit_intercept=False` the process will set intercept to zero, there will be no intercept in the result, which means the line will always pass through the origin point (x, y = $[0,0]$). Normally the intercept gives it more flexibility to make the line fits all data, so it's suggested to set `fit_intercept=True`.

The above example has one independent variable, so it's easy to plot the data and hypothesis function in a 2-D plane. In the case of multiple independent variables, it's basically same as single independent variable, although not easy to visualize, the coefficient is not a single value but a vector with its elements equal to the number of variables.

4.1.2 Diabetes Dataset

This is a dataset regarding to the diseases of diabetes, there are 10 diagnostic measurements in the dataset, and the objective is to predict whether a person has diabetes and the progress of the diabetes. The source and details of this dataset it available at the below link,

https://www.kaggle.com/datasets/mathchi/diabetes-data-set

There are totally 442 records and 11 columns in the dataset, first 10 columns are the diagnostic measurements, and the last one is the progression of diabetes one year after baseline. All columns are quantitative values, so this dataset is ideal for linear regression.

Below is the list of columns:

#	Column	Description
1	age	age in years
2	sex	gender
3	bmi	body mass index
4	bp	average blood pressure
5	s1	tc, total serum cholesterol
6	s2	ldl, low-density lipoproteins
7	s3	hdl, high-density lipoproteins
8	s4	tch, total cholesterol / HDL
9	s5	ltg, possibly log of serum triglycerides level
10	s6	glu, blood sugar level
11	target	a quantitative measure of disease progression one year after baseline

Column #1 to #10 are used as features or input variables, they are independent variables; Column #11 will be the output variable, it depends on the other columns.

This dataset comes with `sklearn.datasets` it's easy and straightforward to load it with Python,

```
1   from sklearn import datasets
2   diabetes = datasets.load_diabetes()
```

The dataset is loaded into the variable `diabetes`, then explore the details of the dataset by printing out its attributes,

```
3   print("Data:", diabetes.data.shape)
4   print("Target:", diabetes.target.shape)
5   print("Features:", diabetes.feature_names)
6   print("Description:", diabetes.DESCR)
7   print("Keys:", diabetes.keys())
```

```
Data: (442, 10)
Target: (442,)
```

```
Features: ['age', 'sex', 'bmi', 'bp', 's1', 's2',
's3', 's4', 's5', 's6']
Description:
Diabetes dataset
. . .
```

The data is presented in a matrix of 442×10, and the target is 442×1. In order to further process the data, load the data into a pandas dataframe,

```
8    import pandas as pd
9    diab = pd.DataFrame(diabetes.data)
10   diab.columns = diabetes.feature_names
11   diab['target'] = diabetes.target
```

pandas is Python library used for data analysis and manipulation, it can be used to better understand the data, and clean up the data if needed. Here print out the brief summary of the dataset, as below:

```
12   print(diab.head())
13   print(diab.describe())
```

And in order to better understand the dataset, pandas provides an useful tool called correlation matrix, it shows the correlation of columns in pairwise, from where we can understand how each columns related to others, and most important, it shows the linear relationship between columns. Seaborn, a Python data visualization library, is used here to visualize the correlation. The codes are like below:

```
14   import seaborn as sns
15   correlation_matrix = diab.corr()
16   plt.figure(figsize = (10, 8))
17   sns.heatmap(data=correlation_matrix.round(1),
                 annot=True)
```

As the result, the heatmap of correlation is displayed as Figure 4.2:

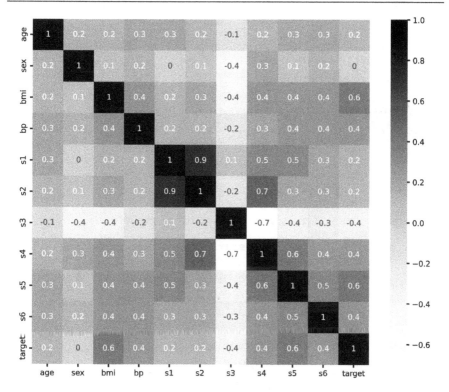

Figure 4.2 Diabetes Dataset Correlation Heatmap
Generated by source code at Linear_Regression_Introduction.ipynb

How to read the above heatmap? The first row is the feature *age*, the last column is the output variable *target*, the value of *0.2* is shown there (the top right corner of Figure 4.2), it means feature *age* has correlation of *0.2* with the *target*. The correlation value near *1* means a strong linear relationship, the value near *0* means no relationship, and *-1* means a strong negative linear relationship.

Now focus on the right column of above heatmap, which is the *target*, and look for which feature has the biggest correlation value, both *bmi* (in row 3) and *s5* (in row 9) have the value of 0.6, which has the most linear relationship with *target*. And also notice that the second row *sex* has a value of *0* meaning there are no relationship with *target*. And *s3* in row 7 is *-0.4* meaning a not-strong negative linear relationship.

4.1.3 Linear Regression on Diabetes Dataset

Since *bmi* and *s5* have the most correlation with *target*, this section will focus on these two features.

Take *bmi* as a single feature and do the linear regression. The dataset is already loaded into a pandas variable `diab` in the previous section, now load only one column from `diab` into X, and load the target into `y`.

```
1   X = diab.loc[:, ['bmi']].values
2   y = diabetes.target
```

Then create a linear regression model and fit the model with X and `y`:

```
3   model = LinearRegression(fit_intercept=True)
4   model.fit(X, y)
5   print("Coefficient:", model.coef_)
6   print("Intercept:", model.intercept_)
7   print("Score:", model.score(X1, y1))
```

The result of the `LinearRegression` model:

```
Coefficient:  949.43526038
Intercept:    152.1334841628967
Score:        0.3439237602253803
```

The coefficient is the slope of the line, and intercept is the *y* value when the line crosses the *y*-axis, the hypothesis function for the feature *bmi* is:

$$y = 152.13 + 949.44x$$

The score is 0.34, which doesn't sound like a good one, that's because the data is scattered far away from a line; another reason might be the dataset is small, if there is a large dataset of tens of thousand data the result could be better.

Figure 4.3 shows the data of *bmi* vs *target*, as well as the result of linear regression:

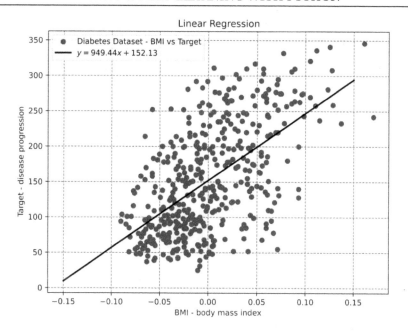

Figure 4.3 Linear Regression on BMI Feature

Generated by source code at Linear_Regression_Introduction.ipynb

Then look at another feature *s5*,

```
1  X2 = diab.loc[:, ['s5']].values
2  y2 = diabetes.target
3  model = LinearRegression(fit_intercept=True)
4  model.fit(X2, y2)
5  x2fit = np.linspace(-0.15, 0.15, 100)
6  print("Coefficients:", model.coef_)
7  print("Intercept:", model.intercept_)
8  print("Score:", model.score(X2, y2))
```

```
Coefficients: 916.13872282
Intercept:    152.13348416289628
Score:        0.32022405096453443
```

Figure 4.4 shows *s5* vs *target*, as well as the result of linear regression, the feature *s5* looks similar to the previous one *bmi*, and the score is also similar.

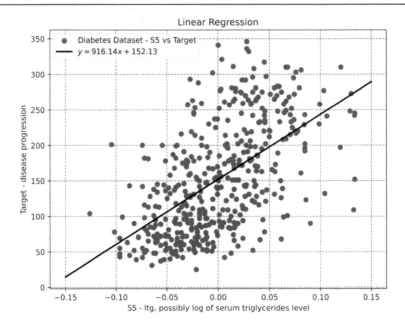

Figure 4.4 Linear Regression on S5 Feature
Generated by source code at Linear_Regression_Introduction.ipynb

The hypothesis function for the feature *s5* is:

$$y = 152.13 + 916.14x$$

So far, the linear regression is against single variable, or single feature. Now look at the multiple features, basically it's same as single one, but it's difficult or even not possible to visualize the data and results because one feature can be drawn in a 2-D plane, two features have to be drawn in 3-D space, and more then two features will not be able to draw.

The diabetes dataset has totally ten features, now load them all into the variable,

```
1  X3 = diab.loc[:, diabetes.feature_names].values
2  y3 = diabetes.target
```

diabetes.feature_names has the name of all features of the dataset -- ['age', 'sex', 'bmi', 'bp', 's1', 's2', 's3', 's4', 's5', 's6']. Line 1 will load all of them into X3, now it is a matrix of 442×10, meaning totally 442 data points, each has 10 features. And y3 is same as previous which has the *target* feature. The rest is same as previous, create a linear regression model and fit it with the data:

```
3    model = LinearRegression(fit_intercept=True)
4    model.fit(X3, y3)
5    coefficient = pd.Series(model.coef_)
6    coefficient.index = diabetes.feature_names
7    intercept = model.intercept_
8    print("Intercept:", intercept)
9    print("Coefficients:")
10   print(coefficient)
11   print("Score:", model.score(X3, y3) )
```

The result is a little different from previous, because this time there are 10 elements in coefficient, each corresponding to one feature,

```
Intercept: 152.1334841628965
Coefficients:
age      -10.012198
sex     -239.819089
bmi      519.839787
bp       324.390428
s1      -792.184162
s2       476.745838
s3       101.044570
s4       177.064176
s5       751.279321
s6        67.625386
Score: 0.5177494254132934
```

The score looks a little bit better than the previous single-feature ones. Now this time the hypothesis function is:

$$y = \theta_0 + \theta_1 x_1 + \theta_2 x_2 + \cdots + \theta_{10} x_{10}$$

Where θ_0 is the intercept and θ_1 to θ_{10} are coefficients.

In general, the hypothesis function for linear regression is defined as:

$$y = \theta_0 + \theta_1 x_1 + \theta_2 x_2 + \cdots + \theta_m x_m$$

Where m is the total number of features.

4.1.4 Train-Test Subsets and Evaluation

In the real machine learning project, instead of using the whole dataset to fit the model, it's a common practice to split the dataset into a *train set* and a *test set*. This is a technique for evaluating the performance of the model.

The procedure is to divide the dataset into two subsets, the first subset is called *train dataset* and is used to fit the model; the second subset is called *test dataset* which is not used to fit the model, instead it's used to make predictions and evaluate the model.

In summary:

- Train dataset is used to fit the machine learning model
- Test dataset is used to evaluate the machine learning model

The reason of doing this is because if use the whole dataset to fit the model, we don't know how the model is doing with new data, because the model has already seen all data. Now use train set, for example 75% of the dataset, to fit the model, the remaining 25% data is the "new data" to the model, the performance can be evaluated with this test set.

In Python the `sklearn` package provides the function to perform the train-test split.

```
1   from sklearn.model_selection import train_test_split
2   X_train, X_test, y_train, y_test =
3               train_test_split(X3, y3, train_size =.75)
```

The `train_test_split()` function will randomly split the data into train and test sets, the size can also be specified, line 3 above specifies train set as 75%. Then print the size of each dataset:

```
4   print(X_train.shape)
5   print(y_train.shape)
6   print(X_test.shape)
7   print(y_test.shape)
```

```
(331, 10)
(331,)
(111, 10)
```

```
(111,)
```

The total 442 records are split into 331 in train set and 111 to test set. The train set is used to fit the model,

```
8    model = LinearRegression(fit_intercept=True)
9    model.fit(X_train, y_train)
10   score = model.score(X_train, y_train)
11   print(score)
```

```
0.5360245327873312
```

The test set is used to make predictions and evaluate the score,

```
12   y_pred = model.predict(X_test)
13   score = model.score(X_test, y_test)
14   print(score)
```

```
0.442960870613316
```

The score on test set is less than that on train set, it's normal because the test set is "new data" to the model. And the score on test set is more reliable to describe the accuracy of the model.

The `train_test_split()` function split the data randomly, so each time running the code might get different data in each set, and the result might slightly different. If want the exact same result each time running the code, set `random_state` to an integer number and pass it to the function, it initializes a random seed using the given interger. Each time run the code with same seed, the split datasets are same.

The score is used many times in evaluating the results of linear regression, then what is the score and how it is calculates?

The score is called *Coefficient of Determination* of the prediction, it is noted as R^2, and also called *R2 Score*, which is defined as:

$$R^2 = \frac{\sum (y_{true} - y_{pred})^2}{\sum (y_{true} - y_{mean})^2}$$

Where y_{true} is the true label of the dataset, it's basically the y that comes with the dataset. y_{pred} is the prediction from the model and y_{mean} is the mean of the true label.

In addition to the `score()` function in the `LinearRegression` model, `sklearn.metrics.r2_score()` can also be used for calculating the R2 score,

```
15    from sklearn.metrics import r2_score
16    y_pred = model.predict(X_test)
17    score = r2_score(y_test, y_pred)
18    print(score)
```

0.442960870613316

The result are same as the `score()` function in the `LinearRegression` model.

4.1.5 Algorithm and Implementation, Part 1

This section and next will introduce the algorithm of linear regression behind the scenes, how it works and how it is implemented without using advanced packages of machine learning.

This section deals with single feature, or single variable, and next section for multiple features; instead of using the functions provided by `sklearn`, only basic Python functions and operations are used here.

Hypothesis Function for Single Variable

As described in previous sections, the purpose of linear regression is to find a hypothesis function that can best fit all data. For one single feature the hypothesis function is:

$$h_\theta(x) = \theta_0 + \theta_1 x$$

θ_1 is *coefficient* and θ_o is *intercept,* or *bias.* x is the independent variable. The objective of linear regression is to find θ_1 and θ_o to decide the hypothesis function based on a dataset of x and its true label y.

The hypothesis function can be implemented as:

```
1    def hypothesis(x, theta_1, theta_0):
2        y = theta_1 * X + theta_0
3        return(y)
```

Least Square Method

Then how to decide the hypothesis will "best fit" the data?

Least Squares Method is a mathematical method used to decide the best fit of a hypothesis function by minimizing the errors, or distances from each point to the function.

In most cases a data point might not just in the line, there is a distance to the line. The distance from a data point to the hypothesis line is the error of that data point. The error is shown in a vertical dashed line from the data point to the hypothesis line in Figure 4.5, for example look at the data point of x_9, the error or distance is shown as the vertical dashed line.

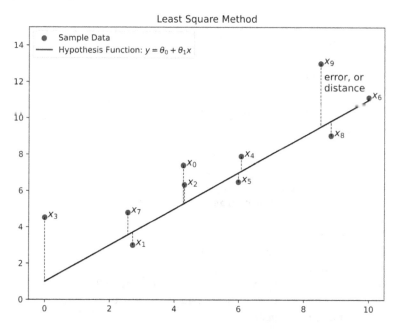

Figure 4.5 Least Square Method

Generated by source code at Linear_Regression_Algorithm_Implementation_1.ipynb

Some data points are above the hypothesis line, which errors are positive; some are below the line which errors are negative. So, the errors are squared and summed up for all data points, therefore it doesn't matter an error is positive or negative. The line with minimum value of the sum of square of errors is the best fit. The error is called *Mean Squared Error* (MSE), and this method is called *Least Square Method*.

Cost Function

Based on the Least Square Method, a cost function can be defined to calculate the Mean Squared Error (MSE), it is the sum of square of errors as discussed above. Its result is a scalar value:

$$J = \frac{1}{n} \sum_{i=1}^{n} \left(y^{(i)} - y_{pred}^{(i)} \right)^2$$

Where n is the number of sample data, i is the i-th sample data, $x^{(i)}$ is the i-th sample data and $y^{(i)}$ is its true value, $y_{pred}^{(i)}$ is the predicted value of i-th sample data.

Because:

$$y_{pred}^{(i)} = h_\theta(x^{(i)}) = \theta_0 + \theta_1 x^{(i)}$$

Then the cost function is:

$$J = \frac{1}{n} \sum_{i=1}^{n} \left(y^{(i)} - (\theta_0 + \theta_1 x^{(i)}) \right)^2$$

It is implemented as:

```
4    def cost(X, y, theta_1, theta_0):
5        y_pred = hypothesis(X, theta_1, theta_0)
6        sum = 0
7        n = len(y)
8        for i in range (0,n):
9            distance = y[i] - y_pred[i]
10           squared_distance = distance**2
11           sum = sum + squared_distance
12       return(sum/n)
```

The objective of linear regression is to find θ_1 and θ_0 in order to make the cost function minimum. Now the θ_1 and θ_0 become the variables of the cost function, the $x^{(i)}$ and $y^{(i)}$ are not variables in this case, because the sample data will provide values for them. This is why the sample data is used to train the model, meaning using $x^{(i)}$ and $y^{(i)}$ values to find out θ_1 and θ_0 to minimize the cost function.

The below two figures show how the cost changes when θ_1 and θ_0 change, both are inverted bell-shaped curve. From the left figure, the cost reaches minimum when θ_1 is around 1; and from the right figure, the cost reaches minimum when θ_0 around 3.

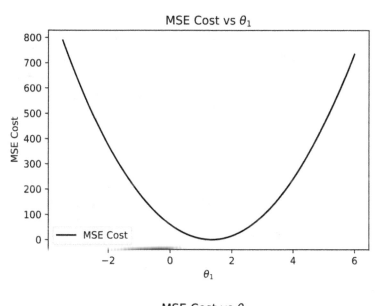

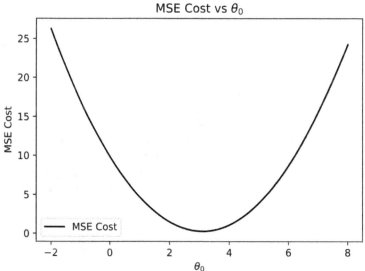

Generated by source code at Linear_Regression_Algorithm_Implementation_1.ipynb

Section 3.2.4 described gradient descent which is used to find the minimum value of a function, it's especially good at this type of inverted bell-shaped curve. In this case there are two variables θ_1 and θ_0, the multivariate function gradient descent is applicable.

As a quick review of the gradient descent for multivariate function, the gradient is a vector of the partial derivative of each variable of the function. The gradient of the cost function is:

$$\nabla J(\theta_0, \theta_1) = \begin{bmatrix} \dfrac{\partial}{\partial \theta_0} J(\theta_0, \theta_1) \\ \dfrac{\partial}{\partial \theta_1} J(\theta_0, \theta_1) \end{bmatrix} = \begin{bmatrix} \dfrac{2}{n} \sum_{i=1}^{n} \left(h(x^{(i)}) - y^{(i)} \right) \\ \dfrac{2}{n} \sum_{i=1}^{n} \left(h(x^{(i)}) - y^{(i)} \right) x^{(i)} \end{bmatrix}$$

We just give the conclusion without mathematically prove here, for details please see the #12 in Reference section at the end of this book.

The gradient descent rule is:

$$\theta = \theta - \alpha \, \nabla J(\theta_0, \theta_1)$$

Where α is the learning rate.

This can be implemented in Python,

```
13    def gradient_descent(X, y, epochs, alpha):
14        for i in range(epochs):
15            y_pred = predict(X)
16            n = len(X)
17            #Gradient of theta_1 and theta_0
18            grad_theta_1 = (2/n)*sum( X * (y_pred - y) )
19            grad_theta_0 = (2/n)*sum(y_pred -y )
20            #Apply gradient decent rules
21            theta_1 = theta_1 - alpha * grad_theta_1
22            theta_0 = theta_0 - alpha * grad_theta_0
```

X any y are the sample data, epochs is the maximum number of iterations, something like *10,000*; and alpha is the learning rate something like *0.001*.

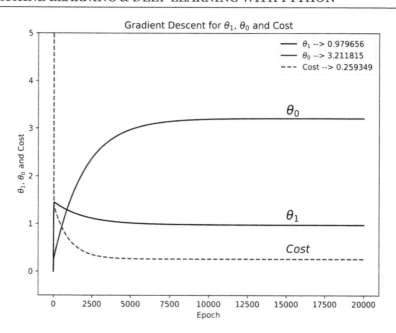

Figure 4.6 Linear Regression Gradient Descent

Generated by source code at Linear_Regression_Algorithm_Implementation_1.ipynb

Then use the same sample dataset in section 4.1.1 and pass it to the above `gradient_descent` function.

As shown in Figure 4.6, when the epoch (the number of iterations) approaches 20,000, θ_1 and θ_0 converge to the values where the cost reaches its minimum value, the cost is shown in the dashed line.

The full source code is at *Linear_Regression_Algorithm_Implementation_1 .ipynb,* all the above code snippets are put together in a Python class called `LinearRegression_SingleFeature`, like below,

```
1    class LinearRegression_SingleFeature:
2      def __init__(self, X , y):
3        self.X = np.hstack(X)
4        self.y = y
5        self.theta_1, self.theta_0 = 0, 0
6      def predict(self, X):
7        return (self.theta_1 * X + self.theta_0)
8      def fit(self, epochs, alpha):
9        #Gradient Descent process
```

```
10          for i in range(epochs):
11            y_pred = self.predict(self.X)
12            n = len(self.X)
13            #Gradient of theta_1 and theta_0
14            grad_theta_1 = (2/n)*sum( self.X * (y_pred - self.y) )
15            grad_theta_0 = (2/n)*sum(y_pred - self.y )
16            #Apply gradient decent rules
17            self.theta_1 = self.theta_1 - alpha * grad_theta_1
18            self.theta_0 = self.theta_0 - alpha * grad_theta_0
19        def cost(self):
20          y_pred = self.predict(self.X)
21          sum = 0
22          n = len(self.X)
23          for i in range (n):
24            distance = self.y[i] - y_pred[i]
25            squared_distance = distance**2
26            sum = sum + squared_distance
27          return(sum/n)
28        def score(self):
29          y_pred = self.predict(self.X)
30          y_mean = np.mean(self.y)
31          u, v = 0, 0
32          for i in range (len(self.y)):
33            u = u + (self.y[i] - y_pred[i])**2
34            v = v + (self.y[i] - y_mean)**2
35          return( 1 - (u/v))
```

Line 2 to 5 are to initialize the class and set X and y into internal variables and set initial θ_1 and θ_0 to zero. Line 6 and 7 define the hypothesis function called `predict()` here. Line 8 to 18 perform the gradient descent which is called `fit()`. Line 19 to 27 calculate the cost and line 28 to 35 calculate the score.

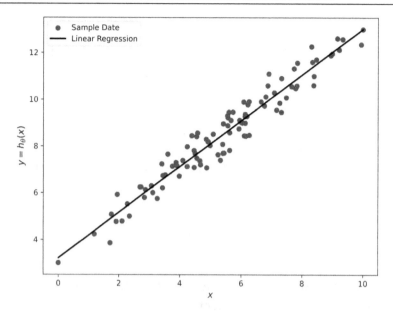

Figure 4.7 Linear Regression Result for Single Feature
Generated by source code at Linear_Regression_Algorithm_Implementation_1.ipynb

Now invoke the class, pass the sample data, run the `fit()` function for gradient descent:

```
36   lrsf = LinearRegression_SingleFeature(X,y)
37   lrsf.fit(20000 , 0.002)
38   print("theta_1 =", lrsf.theta_1)
39   print("theta_0 =", lrsf.theta_0)
40   print("cost =", lrsf.cost())
41   print("score =", lrsf.score())
```

Then print out the results:

```
theta_1 = 0.9796564563102947
theta_0 = 3.2118151850339762
cost     = 0.2593486896016992
score    = 0.9417294723385957
```

The result of linear regression is shown in Figure 4.7:

Finally, compare the results with the `LinearRegression` model in `sklearn`:

```
42    from sklearn.linear_model import
      LinearRegression
43    model = LinearRegression(fit_intercept=True)
44    model.fit(X, y)
45    print("theta_1 =", model.coef_)
46    print("theta_0 =", model.intercept_)
47    print("cost =",
48          mean_squared_error(y, model.predict(X)) )
49    print("score =",
50          model.score(X, y, sample_weight=None))
```

```
coef_       = 0.9796368
intercept_  = 3.2119370881393365
cost        = 0.25934868767668634
score       = 0.9417294727711081
```

The results of `sklearn` model are very close to that of our implementation. `coef_` is coefficient and is `theta_1` in our code; `intercept_` is intercept and is `theta_0` in our code.

In real machine learning project, it's recommended to use `sklearn` models because it's optimized and well-tested. Our code is for the purpose of better understanding what's happening behind the scenes.

4.1.6 Algorithm and Implementation, Part 2

Last section introduced how the one-feature linear regression works, the variables dealt with are one independent input variable X, one dependent output variable y also known as true label, θ_1 and θ_0, they were all scalar values and easy to deal with.

This section is to introduce multi-feature linear regression, the input variable X is no longer a single variable, if there are m-features, X has m variables; y has one output variable; coefficient will be same as the size of X, meaning m elements; intercept will have one element. In order to calculate them efficiently, vectors and matrices operations will be used for multi-features linear regression. Revisit section 3.1 for vectors and matrices if necessary.

Notations

m	Number of features
n	Number of data samples
X	Input data, or independent variables, in matrix of $n \times m$
y	target value, or dependent output variable, or true label, in matrix of $n \times 1$
$x^{(i)}, y^{(i)}$	i-th sample data and true label
$y_{pred}^{(i)}$	i-th predicted value
x_j	j-th feature, where $j \in [1, m]$
θ	Intercept and coefficient, where θ_0 is intercept; θ_j is j-th element of coefficient and $j \in [1, m]$

Hypothesis Function

The hypothesis function for m-feature linear regression is defined as:

$$h_\theta(x) = \theta_0 + \theta_1 x_1 + \theta_2 x_2 + \cdots + \theta_m x_m$$

θ_1 to θ_m are coefficient and θ_0 is intercept. x_1 to x_m are the independent variables.

X can be presented by a vector:

$$X = \begin{bmatrix} 1 & x_1 & x_2 & \cdots & x_m \end{bmatrix}$$

And θ can also be presented by a vector:

$$\theta = \begin{bmatrix} \theta_0 \\ \theta_1 \\ \theta_2 \\ \cdots \\ \theta_m \end{bmatrix}$$

Note, the intercept θ_0 is together with coefficient, so the size of θ is $m+1$; and a 1 is added to X to make the intercept for hypothesis function.

Then the hypothesis function can be rewritten as:

$$
\begin{aligned}
h_\theta(X) &= \theta_0 + \theta_1 x_1 + \theta_2 x_2 + \cdots + \theta_m x_m \\[2mm]
&= \begin{bmatrix} 1 & x_1 & x_2 & \cdots & x_m \end{bmatrix} \cdot
\begin{bmatrix} \theta_0 \\ \theta_1 \\ \theta_2 \\ \cdots \\ \theta_m \end{bmatrix} \\[2mm]
&= X \cdot \theta
\end{aligned}
$$

It ends up with dot product of two vectors/matrices. The data in X normally comes with multiple data points, instead of a vector, it's normally a matrix. Say if there are n data points, each has m features, then X is $n \times m$ matrix.

The hypothesis function is implemented using matrix multiplication in Python,

```
1   def hypothesis(X, theta):
2           return np.matmul(X, theta)
```

X is a $n \times m$ matrix, meaning it has n data points and m features or variables, while `theta` is $m \times 1$ matrix, as explained in section 3.1.9, the result of multiplication of matrices of size $(n \times m)$ and $(m \times 1)$ is $(n \times 1)$, so the result of hypothesis function is $n \times 1$ matrix, which is the same size of y. And the result is actually a prediction of y.

What is *fit_intercept*?

In above hypothesis function, θ_o is the intercept and a 1 is added to X, when all X equal to zero the output is the intercept θ_o which is not zero; in another word, the hypothesis function will not pass through the origin point. In this case the linear regression will fit the intercept.

Otherwise, if don't add 1 to X and no θ_o, the intercept is zero, when all X equal to zero the output is also zero, the hypothesis function will always pass through the origin point, in this case the linear regression will not fit the intercept.

If not `fit_intercept`, X is normally like this:

$$
X = \begin{bmatrix} x_1 & x_2 & \cdots & x_m \end{bmatrix}
$$

If `fit_intercept` in the calculation, need to add one column with value of 1, then X becomes:

$$X = \begin{bmatrix} 1 & x_1 & x_2 & \cdots & x_m \end{bmatrix}$$

The size of X was $n \times m$, now m becomes $m+1$ in case of `fit_intercept`. Later we still use m to describe the size of X, just remember when fit intercept, it becomes $m+1$.

```
3    X = np.hstack((np.ones((X.shape[0],1)), X))
4    theta = np.ones((X.shape[1], 1))
```

Line 3 is to add 1 to the first column of X; Line 4 is to initialize `theta` to make it same size as number of columns of X. Here use `np.ones()` to initialize all elements of `theta` with value of 1, it doesn't matter to use `np.zeros()` to set them to 0.

Data Scaling

When dealing with multiple features, the data ranges for some features are totally different from others, for example in the housing dataset the feature of bedroom number could be ranging from 1 to 6, while the feature of area in square feet could be ranging from 500 to 5000. This difference could cause imbalance and inaccurate when performing the mathematical calculations, and sometimes could cause data type overflow in the calculation.

For these reasons, it's always a best practice to scale the data for each feature so that all features are all within the same range, for example -1 to 1, or 0 to 1.

There are a variety of methods to scale the data, here introduce the *Standard Scalar*, it's defined as:

$$X_{scaled} = \frac{X_{raw} - \mu}{\sigma}$$

Where X_{raw} is the original raw data, X_{scaled} is the scaled data. μ is the mean of the raw data, and σ is the standard deviation or the raw data.

```
5    def scale(X):
6        mu = np.mean(X, axis=0)
7        sigma = np.std(X, axis=0)
```

```
8       return (X - mu)/sigma
```

The result is same size as X, which is a $n \times m$ matrix

Cost Function

The cost function is basically same as that in one-feature linear regression,

$$J(\theta) = \frac{1}{n}\sum_{i=1}^{n}\left(y^{(i)} - y^{(i)}_{pred}\right)^2$$

$$= \frac{1}{n}\sum_{i=1}^{n}\left(y^{(i)} - h_\theta(X)\right)^2$$

It's implemented considering the matrix operations:

```
9    def cost(X, y, theta):
10       y_pred = hypothesis(X, theta)
11       return(np.average((y - y_pred)**2, axis=0))
```

The result is a scaler value.

Gradient

The same gradient descent method will be used here. The gradient is a vector, each element is the partial derivative of a feature/variable. The size of gradient is same as that of θ, for fit-intercept the size is $m+1$; for non-intercept the size is m.

$$\nabla J(\theta) = \begin{bmatrix} \frac{\partial}{\partial\theta_0}J(\theta) \\ \frac{\partial}{\partial\theta_1}J(\theta) \\ \dots \\ \frac{\partial}{\partial\theta_m}J(\theta) \end{bmatrix} = \begin{bmatrix} \frac{1}{n}\sum_{i=1}^{n}\left(h_\theta(x^{(i)}) - y^{(i)}\right) \\ \frac{1}{n}\sum_{i=1}^{n}\left(h_\theta(x^{(i)}) - y^{(i)}\right)x_1^{(i)} \\ \dots \\ \frac{1}{n}\sum_{i=1}^{n}\left(h_\theta(x^{(i)}) - y^{(i)}\right)x_m^{(i)} \end{bmatrix}$$

It's implemented in Python as below,

```
12   def gradient(X, y, theta):
13       n = X.shape[0]
14       d = hypothesis(X, theta) - y
15       return( (2/n) * np.dot(np.transpose(X), d) )
```

Line 14 calculates $(h(x^{(i)}) - y^{(i)})$, and the result d is $n \times 1$ matrix. Line 15 calculates the sum of $(h(x^{(i)}) - y^{(i)}) x^{(i)}$, it performs calculation for all features of x in one go, instead of one by one. x is $n \times m$ matrix, the transpose of x is $m \times n$, d is $n \times 1$, the dot product of the two is $m \times 1$, this is the size of gradient, so each feature has one gradient.

The size of m discussed above does not include the intercept; if intercept is added the m becomes $m+1$.

The gradient descent rule is:

$$\theta = \theta - \alpha \, \nabla J(\theta)$$

Where α is the learning rate.

Below is the full code of LinearRegression class, each individual function above is rewritten as Python class here,

```
1    class LinearRegression:
2      def __init__ (self, X , y, fit_intercept=True):
3        self.y = y.reshape(-1, 1)
4        self.X = self.scale(X)
5        if fit_intercept:
6          self.X = np.hstack(
7                          (np.ones((self.X.shape[0],1)),
8                          self.X))
9        self.theta = np.ones((self.X.shape[1], 1))
10       self.fit_intercept = fit_intercept
11     def scale(self, X):
12       return (X - np.mean(X, axis=0))/np.std(X, axis=0)
13     def predict(self, X):
14       if self.fit_intercept:
15         X = np.hstack((np.ones((X.shape[0],1)), X))
16       return np.matmul(X, self.theta)
17     def __predict(self):
18       return np.matmul(self.X, self.theta)
19     def gradient(self):
20       n = self.X.shape[0]
21       d = self.__predict() - self.y
22       return( (2/n) * np.dot(np.transpose(self.X), d) )
23     def cost(self):
24       y_pred = self.__predict()
25       cost_ = np.average((self.y - y_pred) ** 2,
```

```
26                              axis=0)
27          return(cost_.item())
28      def fit(self, epochs, alpha):
29          for i in range(epochs):
30              y_pred = self.__predict()
31              self.theta = self.theta - alpha*self.gradient()
32      def score(self):
33          y_pred = self.__predict()
34          y_mean = np.average(self.y, axis=0)
35          u = ((self.y - y_pred) ** 2).sum(axis=0)
36          v = ((self.y - y_mean) ** 2).sum(axis=0)
37          score_ = 1 - (u/v)
38          return(score_.item())
```

Linear_Regression_Algorithm_Implementation_2.ipynb in the Github repository has the full source code.

Now generate sample data and give it a try, use the same `datasets.make_regression()` function and set `n_features=8` to create data with 8 features,

```
1   X, y = datasets.make_regression(n_samples=5000,
2                                   n_features=8,
3                                   noise=30,
4                                   random_state=0)
```

Then run the linear regression and print out the results:

```
5   lr = LinearRegression(X, y)
6   lr.fit(epochs=8000, alpha=0.0005)
7   theta = pd.Series(np.hstack(lr.theta))
8   print("Intercept:")
9   print(theta[0:1].to_string())
10  print("Coefficient:")
11  print(theta[1:].to_string())
12  print("Cost:", lr.cost())
13  print("Score:", lr.score())
```

```
Intercept:
0    -1.437462
Coefficient:
1    93.063535
2    54.814060
```

```
3      82.108192
4      71.601580
5       7.885793
6      37.073841
7      33.776433
8      45.269625
Cost:  878.4499520973873
Score: 0.9704361325795118
```

Then compare it with `sklearn` linear regression model,

```
14 model = inear_model.LinearRegression(fit_intercept=True)
15 model.fit(X, y)
16 # Print results
17 intc_ = pd.Series(model.intercept_)
18 coef_ = pd.Series(model.coef_)
19 coef_.index = coef_.index + 1
20 print("Intercept:")
21 print(intc_.to_string())
22 print("Coefficient:")
23 print(coef_.to_string())
24 print("Cost:",
25        metrics.mean_squared_error(y, model.predict(X)))
26 print("Score:", model.score(X, y) )
```

```
Intercept:
0       0.468012
Coefficient:
1      95.138104
2      55.724115
3      81.391803
4      72.601130
5       7.805795
6      36.949831
7      33.840377
8      45.218454
Cost:  878.4473847878311
Score: 0.9704362189812461
```

As the comparison, the cost and score are very close, although the coefficient and intercept have some discrepancies.

	Our function		sklearn function	
Intercept:	0	-1.437462	0	0.468012
Coefficient:	1	93.063535	1	95.138104
	2	54.814060	2	55.724115
	3	82.108192	3	81.391803
	4	71.601580	4	72.601130
	5	7.885793	5	7.805795
	6	37.073841	6	36.949831
	7	33.776433	7	33.840377
	8	45.269625	8	45.218454
Cost:		878.449952		878.447385
Score:		0.970436		0.970436

Figure 4.8 shows how the cost converges in the fit process of the gradient descent.

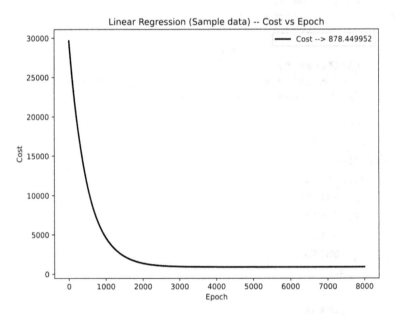

Figure 4.8 Linear Regression Cost vs Epoch

Generated by source code at Linear_Regression_Algorithm_Implementation_2.ipynb

Then compare the results on all features of diabetes dataset that described in section 4.1.2, here is the result,

	Our function	sklearn function
Intercept:	152.1334842	0.468011594
Coefficients:	age -0.470798	age -10.012198
	Sex -11.400935	sex -239.819089
	bmi 24.739992	bmi 519.839787
	bp 15.424315	bp 324.390428
	s1 -36.498399	s1 -792.184162
	s2 21.738619	s2 476.745838
	s3 4.277573	s3 101.044570
	s4 8.271220	s4 177.064176
	s5 35.294306	s5 751.279321
	s6 3.220959	s6 67.625386
Score:	0.517745422	0.517749425
Cost:	2859.714138	2859.690399

Again, the score and cost are very close, however the intercept and coefficients have differences. It could because the solutions are not unique for multiple features, different solutions could have the same score and cost. The result of linear regression is finally a line, even in the case of multiple features. The line is in multi-dimensional space, which can not be visualized, there could be different lines that achieve the same result, i.e., the minimum cost.

4.2 Logistic Regression

Logistic regression is also a supervised learning method. Basically, supervised learning resolves two types of problem, regression problem and classification problem.

The regression problem deals with the dependent output variables of quantitative values, such as length, height, weight, price, population, etc., this is resolved by linear regression in previous section 4.1.

The classification problem deals with the dependent output variables of classification values, like yes or no, a dog or not a dog, benign or malignant of a tumor, etc. The output values are binary, i.e. *0* or *1*. The logistic regression will solve this type of problems.

There are two types of logistic regression, binary and multinomial.

Binary logistic regression, the outcome is a binary value, *0* or *1*. The examples are like mentioned above, yes or no, etc.

Multinomial logistic regression, the outcome are multiple classes, for example the color of a car – red, blue, black or white. There are three or more predefined classes for the output.

4.2.1 Introduction

The input variables, or independent variables, are same as that in linear regression, for the binary logistic regression, the output is a binary value 0 or 1, as shown in Figure 4.9.

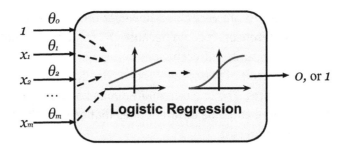

Figure 4.9 Logistic Regression

The multinomial logistic regression will be discussed in next section.

There are two steps involved in logistic regression, first step is linear regression on the input variables. Same as linear regression, the input variable X can be presented by a vector, *1* is added to the beginning of X to make the intercept:

$$X = \begin{bmatrix} 1 & x_1 & x_2 & \cdots & x_m \end{bmatrix}$$

And θ, intercept and coefficient, can also be presented by a vector:

$$\theta = \begin{bmatrix} \theta_0 \\ \theta_1 \\ \theta_2 \\ \cdots \\ \theta_m \end{bmatrix}$$

Then from the linear regression, there is:

$$z = X\theta = \theta_0 + \theta_1 x_1 + \theta_2 x_2 + \cdots + \theta_m x_m$$

The second step is to transform the above result z into a binary value. The sigmoid function, introduced in section 3.3.2, is used for this type of transformation.

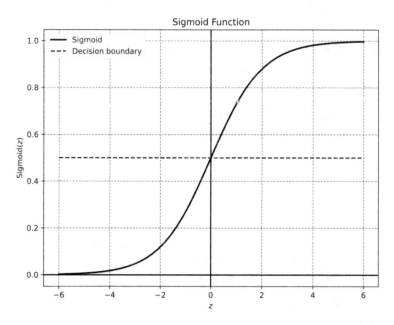

Figure 4.10 Sigmoid Function
Generated by source code at Logistic_Regression_Introduction.ipynb

As a recap of sigmoid function, it's defined as:

$$f(z) = \frac{1}{(1 + e^{-z})}$$

Its output, as shown in Figure 4.10, is between 0 to 1.

Now apply the sigmoid function to the output of linear regression,

$$h_\theta(X) \;=\; \frac{1}{(1+e^{-z})}$$

$$=\; \frac{1}{(1+e^{-(\theta_0+\theta_1 x_1+\theta_2 x_2+\cdots+\theta_m x_m)})}$$

$$=\; \frac{1}{(1+e^{-X\theta})}$$

This is the *hypothesis function* for logistic regression.

In Figure 4.10, the output is either near *0* or *1* if the input is far away from *0*, but if the input is near *0* the output is around *0.5*. In order to transform the output into binary value of *0/1*, a threshold is defined, say *0.5*, if the output is greater than the threshold then set it to *1*, otherwise *0*.

Draw a horizontal line at $y=0.5$ as the dashed line shown in Figure 4.10, if the output is above the line then it's *1*, if below the line then *0*, this line is called *decision boundary*.

Here use `sklearn.datasets.make_classification()` to generate some sample data for logistic regression:

```
1    X, y = datasets.make_classification(n_samples=100,
2                                   n_features=2,
3                                   n_redundant=0,
4                                   n_informative=2,
5                                   random_state=5,
6                                   n_clusters_per_class=1)
7    print("size of X", X.shape)
8    print("size of y", y.shape)

size of X (100, 2)
size of y (100,)
```

There are totally 100 data points are generated, so X has 100 rows and y also has 100 rows. There are two features meaning the input variables are x_1 and x_2, X has 2 columns, each corresponding to one feature.

There are two classes, the labels are *0* and *1* for the two classes, which means the values of y are either *0* or *1*. Figure 4.11 shows the sample data in two classes, it is drawn in x_1-x_2 plane, meaning horizontal axis is x_1, and vertical axis is x_2. The legend shows the label of the each class, the data points in • are labeled as *0*, the data in × are *1*.

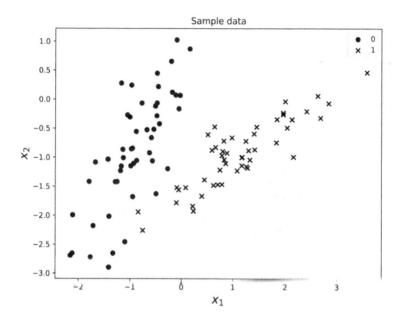

Figure 4.11 Sample Data for Logistic Regression
Generated by source code at Logistic_Regression_Introduction.ipynb

Python `sklearn` provides `LogisticRegression()` function, now apply the above dataset to it.

```
9    model = linear_model.LogisticRegression()
10   model.fit(X, y)
11   y_pred = model.predict(X)
12   print("Score:", model.score(X, y))
13   print("Intercept:", model.intercept_)
14   print("Coefficient:", model.coef_)
```

```
Score: 0.98
Intercept: [-1.37987521]
Coefficient: [[ 3.16162505 -1.57119877]]
```

As the result, the score is 0.98, intercept and coefficient are also obtained.

Figure 4.12 shows the result of *decision boundary* on the x_1-x_2 plane. All the data on one side of the decision boundary are predicted as class of 0, and all on other side are as class of 1.

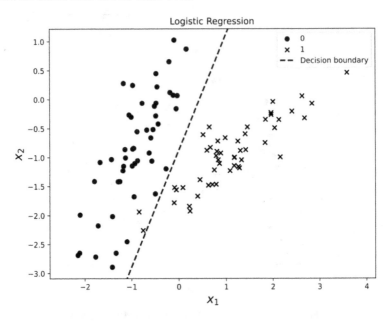

Figure 4.12 Logistic Regression on Sample Data
Generated by source code at Logistic_Regression_Introduction.ipynb

Will explain how to read the logistic regression results and understand the decision boundary in the following sections.

4.2.2 Decision Boundary

It was mentioned in Figure 4.10 of sigmoid function that the decision boundary is the horizontal line at $y=0.5$, however in Figure 4.12 the decision boundary is no longer a horizontal line. That's because it's transformed to the x_1-x_2 plane, the horizontal and vertical axes are changed.

Then how it's transformed?

Since the above sample data has two featuers, x_1 and x_2, and from the results of logistic regression, intercept is θ_0 and coefficient is (θ_1, θ_2).

The hypothesis function of logistic regression is:

$$h_\theta(X) = \frac{1}{(1 + e^{-z})}$$

$$= \frac{1}{(1 + e^{-(\theta_0 + \theta_1 x_1 + \theta_2 x_2)})}$$

The decision boundary is defined as the output of hypothesis being 0.5, which means:

$$h_\theta(X) = \frac{1}{(1 + e^{-(\theta_0 + \theta_1 x_1 + \theta_2 x_2)})} = \frac{1}{2}$$

Then:

$$1 + e^{-(\theta_0 + \theta_1 x_1 + \theta_2 x_2)} = 2$$

$$e^{-(\theta_0 + \theta_1 x_1 + \theta_2 x_2)} = 1$$

$$\theta_0 + \theta_1 x_1 + \theta_2 x_2 = 0$$

Finally,

$$x_2 = -\frac{\theta_1}{\theta_2} x_1 - \frac{\theta_0}{\theta_2}$$

This is the decision boundary in x_1-x_2 plain, θ_0, θ_1 and θ_2 can be retrieved from the results of the logistic regression model, then we can draw the decision boundary as in Figure 4.12.

The below code snippets will make the decision boundary:

```
1    def decision_boundary(x, intercept, coefficient):
2        theta_0 = intercept
3        theta_1, theta_2 = coefficient
4        c = -theta_0/theta_2
5        m = -theta_1/theta_2
6        return m * x + c
7    x_1 = np.array(-2.0, 2.0)
8    x_2 = decision_boundary(x_1,
9                            model.intercept_[0],
10                           model.coef_[0])
```

Weighted Decision Boundary

Sometimes the decision boundary at 0.5 is not appropriate to solve the problem, a weight should be added to one class to make it favorable, for example a weight of $w=2$ will make the decision boundary at $1/(w+1)$, i.e. $1/3$, instead of 0.5. The output above $1/3$ is classified as one class, and below $2/3$ as another class.

In this case, there is:

$$h_\theta(X) = \frac{1}{(1 + e^{-(\theta_0 + \theta_1 x_1 + \theta_2 x_2)})} = \frac{1}{w+1}$$

Then:

$$1 + e^{-(\theta_0 + \theta_1 x_1 + \theta_2 x_2)} = w + 1$$

$$e^{-(\theta_0 + \theta_1 x_1 + \theta_2 x_2)} = w$$

$$\theta_0 + \theta_1 x_1 + \theta_2 x_2 = -\log_e(w) = -\ln(w)$$

Finally,

$$x_2 = -\frac{\theta_1}{\theta_2} x_1 - \frac{\theta_0 + \ln(w)}{\theta_2}$$

This can be used to draw the weighted decision boundary line.

4.2.3 Evaluation

Accuracy Score

The accuracy score is used to measure the logistic regression results, the best value is 1.0, meaning all predicted values are correct; the worst possible value is 0.0 meaning none of predicted values are correct.

It's defined as:

$$\text{accuracy score} = \frac{1}{n} \sum_{i=1}^{n} 1\left(y^{(i)} = y_{pred}^{(i)}\right)$$

where n is the total number of sample data, $y^{(i)}$ is the true value of the i-th sample data, and $y_{pred}^{(i)}$ is the corresponding predicted value.

There are two ways to obtain the score of logistic regression, first, use the model's `score()` function, need to create a model and fit it.

```
1    score = model.score(X, y)
2    print("Score:", score)
```

In the example in above section, the score of the model is 0.98.

Second, use the `sklearn.metrics.accuracy_score()` function, also need to create a model, fit it and make prediction.

```
1    from sklearn import metrics
2    y_pred = model.predict(X)
3    score = metrics.accuracy_score(y, y_pred)
4    print("Accuracy Score:", score )
```

If run this code snippets against above example, the same score is displayed.

```
Accuracy Score: 0.98
```

Confusion Matrix

Confusion Matrix is used to measure the performance of the resolution of classification problems, it's not only used for logistic regression but also used for other classification algorithms.

In order to better understand it, first need to understand the below four concepts, true positives, true negatives, false positives and false negatives.

True Positives (TP)	Data is labelled as 1, and it's predicted as 1. (Correct). E.g., the color is predicted to be red, and it's actually red.
True Negatives (TN)	Data is labelled as 0, and it's predicted as 0. (Correct). E.g., the color is predicted not red, and it's actually not red.
False Positives (FP)	Data is not labelled as 1, but it's predicted as 1. (Error). E.g. the color is predicted to be red, but it's actually not red.
False Negatives (FN)	Data is not labelled as 0, but it is predicted as 0. (Error). E.g. the color is predicted not red, but it's actually red.

A confusion matrix is a tool to display the information in a matrix, like below table,

Predicted value

		0	1
True label	0	True Negatives (TN)	False Positives (FP)
	1	False Negatives (FN)	True Positives (TP)

The information shown in the diagonal are TN and TP which are correct results; the information other than diagonal, FP and FN, are errors.

Python `sklearn` has `confusion_matrix()` function to show it:

```
1    from sklearn import metrics
2    y_pred = model.predict(X)
3    cm = metrics.confusion_matrix(y, y_pred)
4    print("Confusion Matrix:", cm)
```

The results are shown as:

```
Confusion Matrix:
 [[50  0]
  [ 2 48]]
```

The True Negative (TN) is 50, True Positive (TP) is 48, False Positive (FP) is 0 and False Negative (FN) is 2.

The confusion matrix can be visualized in a heatmap as Figure 4.13. In order not to flip back and forth to previous pages, below Figure 4.14 is a duplication of Figure 4.12,

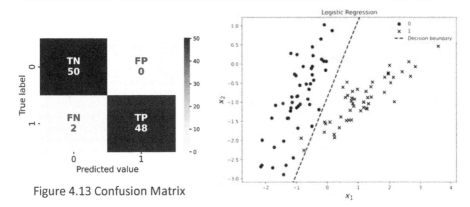

Figure 4.13 Confusion Matrix

Figure 4.14 Logistic Regression Results

In Figure 4.13, the upper-left shows 50 as TN (true negative), from Figure 4.14 the ● shaped data are labeled as O, and they are all in the left side of the decision boundary line meaning predicted as O, so the result is all 50 ● shaped data are labeled as O and predicted as O, they are true negatives (TN).

The lower-right shows 48 as TP (true positive), because there are 48 × shaped data in the right side of decision boundary, the true value is 1 and predicted as 1. So they are true positives (TP).

The above two cases are in the diagonal of the confusion matrix, they are correctly predicted.

The lower-left of matrix shows 2 as FN (false negative), from Figure 4.14 there are two × shaped data (true label is 1) in the left side of the line, meaning they are predicted as O. Therefore they are false negatives (FN).

The upper-right of the matrix shows 0, meaning there are no false positives, because there are no ● shaped data (true label is O) in the right side of the line, and predicted as 1.

The confusion matrix is very useful tool to evaluate the result of classification algorithms, it will be used in later this book.

4.2.4 Breast Cancer Dataset

This is a dataset coming with `sklearn` for classification purpose. There are two classes in the output, so it's ideal for binary logistic regression algorithm. There is totally $n=569$ sample date, and $m=30$ features, the output is 0 for malignant or 1 for benign.

Now load the data and print out the details of the dataset,

```
1  from sklearn import datasets
2  data = datasets.load_breast_cancer()
3  print("Data:", data.data.shape)
4  print("Target:", data.target.shape)
5  print("Features:", data.feature_names)
6  print("Description:", data.DESCR)
7  print("Keys:", data.keys())
```

```
Data:    (569, 30)
Target: (569,)
...
```

The features are listed below,

#	Feature	Min Value	Max Value
1	radius (mean):	6.981	28.11
2	texture (mean):	9.71	39.28
3	perimeter (mean):	43.79	188.5
4	area (mean):	143.5	2501
5	smoothness (mean):	0.053	0.163
6	compactness (mean):	0.019	0.345
7	concavity (mean):	0	0.427
8	concave points (mean):	0	0.201
9	symmetry (mean):	0.106	0.304
10	fractal dimension (mean):	0.05	0.097
11	radius (standard error):	0.112	2.873
12	texture (standard error):	0.36	4.885

13	Perimeter (standard error):	0.757	21.98
14	area (standard error):	6.802	542.2
15	Smoothness (standard error):	0.002	0.031
16	compactness (standard error):	0.002	0.135
17	concavity (standard error):	0	0.396
18	concave points (standard error):	0	0.053
19	symmetry (standard error):	0.008	0.079
20	fractal dimension (standard error):	0.001	0.03
21	radius (worst):	7.93	36.04
22	texture (worst):	12.02	49.54
23	perimeter (worst):	50.41	251.2
24	area (worst):	185.2	4254
25	smoothness (worst).	0.071	0.223
26	compactness (worst):	0.027	1.058
27	concavity (worst):	0	1.252
28	concave points (worst):	0	0.291
29	symmetry (worst):	0.156	0.664
30	fractal dimension (worst):	0.055	0.208

By looking at the minimum and maximum values of each feature, it's noticed that some features are ranging from 0 to less than 1, and some features are ranging from hundreds to thousands, e.g. feature #24. So it's important to scale the data before using it, see section 4.1.6 for data scaling. sklearn provides StandardScaler() function for data scaling,

```
11   from sklearn import preprocessing
12   scaler = preprocessing.StandardScaler()
13   X1 = scaler.fit_transform(data.data)
14   y1 = data.target
15   print(X1.shape)
16   print(y1.shape)
```

Line 12 and 13 scale the data so that all feature are within the similar ranges. Now split the data into train and test subsets, see section 4.1.4 for details.

```
21   X_train, X_test, y_train, y_test = \
22          train_test_split(X1, y1, random_state=2,
23                              train_size = .75)
24   print("X_train:", X_train.shape)
25   print("y_train:", y_train.shape)
26   print("X_test: ", X_test.shape)
27   print("y_test: ", y_test.shape)
```

```
X_train:  (426, 30)
y_train:  (426,)
X_test:   (143, 30)
y_test:   (143,)
```

Now the train set has 426 sample data and test set has 143.

Create a logistic regression model and use the train set to fit it:

```
31   from sklearn import linear_model
32   model = linear_model.LogisticRegression()
33   model.fit(X_train, y_train)
```

And then use test set to make prediction and evaluation:

```
34   y_pred = model.predict(X_test)
35   ascore = metrics.accuracy_score(y_test, y_pred)
36   cmatrix = metrics.confusion_matrix(y_test, y_pred)
37   print("Accuracy Score:\n", ascore)
38   print("Confusion Matrix:\n", cmatrix)
```

```
Accuracy Score:
 0.972027972027972
Confusion Matrix:
 [[55  1]
  [ 3 84]]
```

The accuracy score is 0.97, and Figure 4.15 visualizes the confusion matrix.

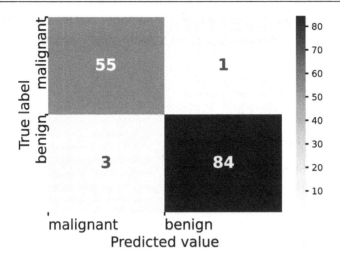

Figure 4.15 Confusion Matrix

There are 55 malignant are predicted as malignant; 84 benign predicted as benign. They are correctly predicted values.

However, there is 1 malignant predicted as benign, and 3 benign as malignant. These are errors.

Please note, it's important to scale the data before applying the dataset to logistic regression. If the data is not scaled, it will give an error something like below:

```
/usr/local/lib/python3.7/dist-
packages/sklearn/linear_model/_logistic.py:818:
ConvergenceWarning: lbfgs failed to converge
(status=1):
STOP: TOTAL NO. of ITERATIONS REACHED LIMIT.

Increase the number of iterations (max_iter) or scale
the data as shown in …
```

4.2.5 Algorithm and Implementation of Logistic Regression

This section will introduce the algorithms for logistic regression behind the scenes, the implementation will only use the basic Python operations without the advanced machine learning packages and libraries. This section will focus on binary logistic regression only, meaning 2-classes output.

Notations

m	Number of features
n	Number of data samples
X	Input data, or independent variables, in matrix of $n \times m$
y	target value, or dependent output variable, or true label, in matrix of $n \times 1$
$x^{(i)}, y^{(i)}$	i-th sample data and true label
$y_{pred}^{(i)}$	i-th predicted value
x_j	j-th feature, where $j \in [1, m]$
θ	Intercept and coefficient, where θ_o is intercept; θ_j is j-th element of coefficient and $j \in [1, m]$

Hypothesis Function

As explained in section 4.2.1, the hypothesis function for logistic regression is defined as:

$$h_\theta(X) = \frac{1}{(1 + e^{-z})}$$

$$= \frac{1}{(1 + e^{-(\theta_0 + \theta_1 x_1 + \theta_2 x_2 + \cdots + \theta_m x_m)})}$$

$$= \frac{1}{(1 + e^{-X\theta})}$$

where:

$$z = X\theta = \theta_0 + \theta_1 x_1 + \theta_2 x_2 + \cdots + \theta_m x_m$$

Same as linear regression, if fit-intercept then θ_o is added, otherwise $\theta_o = 0$.

It's implemented as:

```
1   def sigmoid(z):
```

```
2          return 1/(1 + np.exp(-z))
3    def hypothesis(X, theta):
4          z = np.dot(X, theta)
5          return sigmoid(z)
```

The output of hypothesis function is between 0 and 1. A threshold is normally set to 0.5, it could be a weighted value though, if the output is greater than the threshold then set it to 1, otherwise set it to 0, the final output is either 0 or 1.

Cost Function

The cost function is used to measure the difference between the predicted value and the true value. Linear regression in previous section uses Mean Squared Error (MSE) to calculate the cost. Logistic Regression uses *Cross Entropy* to calculate the cost. And the objective of the regression process is to find θ that makes the cost minimum.

The cross-entropy function is defined as following:

$$J(\theta) = \begin{cases} -\log(h_\theta(x)) & : y = 1 \\ -\log(1 - h_\theta(x)) & : y = 0 \end{cases}$$

It could be implemented in Python as:

```
1    def cross_entropy(x, y):
2          h = sigmoid(x)
3          if y == 1:
4              return -np.log(h)
5          else:
6              return -np.log(1 - h)
```

The plot of this function looks like Figure 4.16, when $y = 1$, the cost is very big if the output of $h_\theta(X)$ is near 0; and gradually becomes smaller when the output is approaching 1; and reach minimum value when the output is 1. This is because when $y = 1$ and $h_\theta(X)$ is 0, the difference is big and then the cost is big; when $y = 1$ and $h_\theta(X)$ is also 1, the difference is 0, and the cost is also 0.

In the other hand, when $y = 0$, the cost starts from 0 when $h_\theta(X)$ is 0, and gradually increases when y is approaching to 1.

The above cost functions are separated for $y=1$ and $y=0$, it can be combined and rewritten as:

$$J(\theta) = -\frac{1}{n} \sum_{i=1}^{n} \left(y^{(i)} \log(h_\theta(x^{(i)})) + (1 - y^{(i)}) \log(1 - h_\theta(x^{(i)})) \right)$$

Figure 4.16 shows the cross entropy cost function:

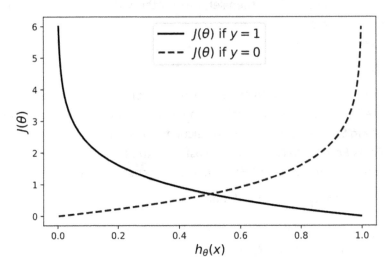

Figure 4.16 Cross Entropy Cost Function

Generated by source code at Logistic_Regression_Algorithm_Implementation.ipynb

It's implemented as:

```
1   def cross_entropy(x, y):
2       h = sigmoid(x)
3       return (-y*np.log(h)-(1-y)*np.log(1-h)).mean()
```

Gradient

Same as linear regression, the gradient descent method will be used to find the minimum value of the cost function. The gradient is a vector, each element is the partial derivative of a feature/variable. The size of gradient is same as that of θ.

The conclusion is given here without mathematical proofs, please reference the materials #13, #14 and #15 in References section for details. The gradient vector for cross entropy function is as below:

$$\nabla J(\theta) = \begin{bmatrix} \dfrac{\partial}{\partial \theta_0} J(\theta) \\[2ex] \dfrac{\partial}{\partial \theta_1} J(\theta) \\[2ex] \ldots \\[2ex] \dfrac{\partial}{\partial \theta_m} J(\theta) \end{bmatrix} = \begin{bmatrix} \dfrac{1}{n} \sum\limits_{i=1}^{n} \left(h_\theta(x^{(i)}) - y^{(i)} \right) \\[2ex] \dfrac{1}{n} \sum\limits_{i=1}^{n} \left(h_\theta(x^{(i)}) - y^{(i)} \right) x_1^{(i)} \\[2ex] \ldots \\[2ex] \dfrac{1}{n} \sum\limits_{i=1}^{n} \left(h_\theta(x^{(i)}) - y^{(i)} \right) x_m^{(i)} \end{bmatrix}$$

It's implemented in Python as,

```
4    def gradient(X, y, theta):
5        n = X.shape[0]
6        h = hypothesis(X, theta):
7        return ((1/n)*np.dot(np.transpose(X),(h-y)))
```

Here uses dot product to perform the sum of multiplication, see section 3.1.9 and 3.1.5 if not familiar with dot product. Also need to transpose X before applying dot product. Please note X is $n \times m$ matrix, the transpose of X is $m \times n$, h and y are $n \times 1$ matrix. So the result of gradient() is a $m \times 1$ matrix, which is the same as the size of θ.

Please also note, if fit-intercept, then θ_o is added and m is 1 plus number of feathers, if not fit-intercept the m is the number of features.

The gradient descent rule is same as linear regression,

$$\theta = \theta - \alpha \, \nabla J(\theta)$$

Where α is the learning rate.

Below is the full code of LogisticRegression class, each individual function defined above is rewritten as Python class,

```
1    class LogisticRegression:
2        def __init__(self, X, y, fit_intercept=True):
3            self.y = y.reshape(-1, 1)
4            self.X = self._scale(X)
5            if fit_intercept:
6                self.X = np.hstack(
7                        (np.ones((self.X.shape[0],1)),self.X))
8            self.theta = np.zeros((self.X.shape[1], 1))
9            self.fit_intercept = fit_intercept
```

```
10      def _scale(self, X):
11          return (X - np.mean(X, axis=0))/np.std(X, axis=0)
12      def _sigmoid(self, z):
13          return 1/(1 + np.exp(-z))
14      def hypothesis(self, X, theta):
15          z = np.dot(X, theta)
16          return self._sigmoid(z)
17      def cross_entropy_cost(self, h, y):
18          return (-y*np.log(h)-(1-y)*np.log(1-h)).mean()
19      def gradient(self, X, h, y):
20          return np.dot(np.transpose(X),(h-y))/y.shape[0]
21      def fit(self, epochs, alpha):
22          for i in range(epochs):
23              h = self.hypothesis(self.X, self.theta)
24              cost = self.cross_entropy_cost(h, self.y)
25              grad = self.gradient(self.X, h, self.y)
26              self.theta -= alpha * grad
27      def predict(self, X, treshold=0.5):
28          if self.fit_intercept:
29              X = np.hstack((np.ones((X.shape[0],1)), X))
30          pred = self.hypothesis(X, self.theta)
31          return (pred >= treshold).astype(int).reshape(-1)
```

Similar to linear regression, the initializer __init__() takes X and y, then add intercept to X if `fit_intercept=True`, and initialize `theta` to the same size as X.

The class has a built-in _scale() function, it doesn't matter if the data X is not scaled. There are _sigmoid(), hypothesis(), gradient() and cross_entropy_cost() functions defined. fit() runs the gradient descent process, and predict() make predictions with default threshold of 0.5.

Now generate sample data to test LogisticRegression class,

```
1   from sklearn import datasets
2   X, y = datasets.make_classification(
3                   n_samples=1000,
4                   n_features=12,
5                   n_redundant=0,
6                   n_informative=2,
7                   random_state=1,
```

```
 8                       n_clusters_per_class=1)
 9    print("X size:", X.shape)
10    print("y size:", y.shape)
11    print("y classes:", np.unique(y))
```

```
X size:      (1000, 12)
y size:      (1000,)
y classes: [0 1]
```

The sample dataset has *1000* data points and *12* features, so X is *1000* ×
12 matrix, y is *1000* × *1*, and the classes in y have *0* and *1* values.

Then split the data into train and test subsets,

```
12    X_train, X_test, y_train, y_test = \
13            train_test_split(X, y,
14                             train_size = .75,
15                             random_state=1)
```

Apply the datasets to LogisticRegression class, use the train set to fit
it and use test set to evaluate it,

```
21    regressor = LogisticRegression(X_train, y_train)
22    regressor.fit(epochs=6000, alpha=0.01)
23    y_pred = regressor.predict(X_test)
24    a_score = metrics.accuracy_score(y_test, y_pred)
25    c_matrix = metrics.confusion_matrix(y_test, y_pred)
26    print("Accuracy Score:\n", a_score)
27    print("\nConfusion Matrix:\n", c_matrix)
```

```
Accuracy Score:
 0.888
```

```
Confusion Matrix:
 [[112    4]
  [ 24 110]]
```

The confusion matrix shows there are 112 *0*'s and 110 *1*'s are correctly
identified, the accuracy score is 0.888. And Figure 4.17 shows the Cost vs
Epoch during the gradient descent process.

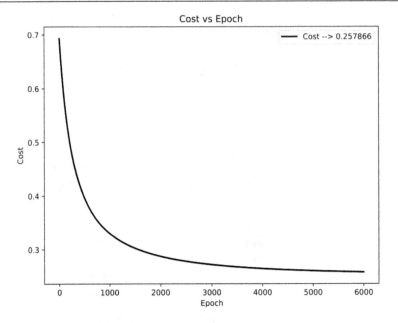

Figure 4.17 Logistic Regression Cost vs Epoch
Generated by source code at Logistic_Regression_Algorithm_Implementation.ipynb

Then as testing, compare the `sklearn` logistic regression model with the same sample dataset,

```
1    from sklearn import linear_model
2    model = linear_model.LogisticRegression()
3    model.fit(X_train, y_train)
4    y_pred_ = model.predict(X_test)
5    a_score = metrics.accuracy_score(y_test, y_pred)
6    c_matrix = metrics.confusion_matrix(y_test, y_pred)
7    print("Accuracy Score:", a_score)
8    print("\nConfusion Matrix:\n", c_matrix)
```

```
Accuracy Score:
 0.888

Confusion Matrix:
 [[112    4]
  [ 24 110]]
```

As one more test, apply the breast cancer dataset to both and compare the results,

```
21    from sklearn import datasets
22    data = datasets.load_breast_cancer()
23    scaler = preprocessing.StandardScaler()
24    X1 = scaler.fit_transform(data.data)
25    y1 = data.target
26    X_train, X_test, y_train, y_test = \
27            train_test_split(X1, y1,
28                                 train_size = .75,
29                                 random_state=2)
30    regressor = LogisticRegression(X_train, y_train)
31    regressor.fit(epochs=5000, alpha=0.01)
32    y_pred = regressor.predict(X_test)
33    a_score = metrics.accuracy_score(y_test, y_pred)
34    c_matrix = metrics.confusion_matrix(y_test, y_pred)
35    print("Accuracy Score:", a_score)
36    print("\nConfusion Matrix:\n", c_matrix)
```

```
Accuracy Score:    0.9790209790209791
Confusion Matrix:
 [[54  2]
  [ 1 86]]
```

Then the `sklearn` model:

```
41    from sklearn import linear_model
42    model = linear_model.LogisticRegression()
43    model.fit(X_train, y_train)
44    y_pred = model.predict(X_test)
45    a_score = metrics.accuracy_score(y_test, y_pred)
46    c_matrix = metrics.confusion_matrix(y_test, y_pred)
47    print("Accuracy Score:", a_score)
48    print("\nConfusion Matrix:\n", c_matrix)
```

```
Accuracy Score: 0.972027972027972
Confusion Matrix:
 [[55  1]
  [ 3 84]]
```

By comparing the results of both, it looks both are similar although there are little discrepancies.

4.3 Multinomial Logistic Regression

Multinomial logistic regression is used for multi-classes categorical problems, the difference from logistic regression discussed in section 4.2 is the multi-classes output. As shown in Figure 4.18, left side is same as that in binary logistic regression, but the right side has multiple output values. For example, the colors, the models of cars, the languages, the type of plants and so on. They are no longer a yes-no problem.

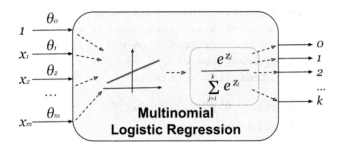

Figure 4.18 Multinomial Logistic Regression

4.3.1 Introduction

Similar to the binary logistic regression, there are also two steps. The first step is same, apply linear regression on the input variables:

$$z = X\theta = \theta_0 + \theta_1 x_1 + \theta_2 x_2 + \cdots + \theta_m x_m$$

The second step is different, the binary logistic regression uses sigmoid function, but multinomial uses softmax function which outputs multiple values, see section 3.3.9.

Softmax function is defined as:

$$\sigma(z_j) = \frac{e^{z_j}}{e^{z_1} + e^{z_2} + \cdots + e^{z_k}}$$

where $j \in [\,1, k\,]$.

The output of softmax function will be k values, each of them is between 0 and 1, the sum of all values is 1. Therefore, the output can be interpreted as probabilities, if the input value is small or negative then the softmax turns it into a small probability, if the input is large then output is a large probability.

Generate sample data,

```
1    from sklearn import datasets
2    X, y = datasets.make_classification(
3                      n_samples=1000,
4                      n_features=12,
5                      n_informative=3,
6                      n_classes=6,
7                      n_clusters_per_class=1,
8                      random_state=1)
9    print("X size:    ", X.shape)
10   print("y size:    ", y.shape)
11   print("y classes:", np.unique(y))
```

```
X size:     (1000, 12)
y size:     (1000,)
y classes:  [0 1 2 3 4 5]
```

The dataset has 1000 sample data, $n = 1000$; there are 12 features, $m = 12$; the size of X is $m \times n = 1000 \times 12$; the size of y is $m \times 1 = 1000 \times 1$, and the unique values of y are $0, 1, 2, 3, 4, 5$, meaning there are 6 classes.

Split the data into train and test sets:

```
21   from sklearn import model_selection
22   X_train, X_test, y_train, y_test = \
23           model_selection.train_test_split(X, y,
24                              train_size = .75,
25                              random_state = 2)
26   print("X_train size:", X_train.shape)
27   print("y_train size:", y_train.shape)
28   print("y_train classes:", np.unique(y))
29   print("X_test size:", X_test.shape)
30   print("y_test size:", y_test.shape)
31   print("y_test classes:", np.unique(y))
```

```
X_train size:    (750, 12)
y_train size:    (750,)
y_train classes:[0 1 2 3 4 5]
```

```
X_test size:      (250, 12)
y_test size:      (250,)
y_test classes:   [0 1 2 3 4 5]
```

The sample data X is split into X_train/y_train and X_test/y_test, train-set has 750 and test-set has 250. The features and classes are kept same.

Now create a multi-class logistic regression with sklearn package, the function is same as previous binary logistic regression, but explicitly pass a parameter multi_class='multinomial'. Actually, the function is smart enough to detect the classes of the sample data and process it accordingly.

```
41   from sklearn import linear_model
42   model = linear_model.LogisticRegression(
43                          multi_class='multinomial')
44   model.fit(X_train, y_train)
45   y_pred = model.predict(X_test)
46   a_score = metrics.accuracy_score(y_test, y_pred)
47   c_matrix = metrics.confusion_matrix(y_test, y_pred)
48   print("Accuracy Score:", a_score)
49   print("Confusion matrix:\n", c_matrix)
```

```
Accuracy Score: 0.792

Confusion matrix:
 [[27  0  1  9  0  0]
 [ 3 36  0 15  0  0]
 [ 0  1 42  1  2  0]
 [ 2  3  0 28  0  3]
 [ 5  0  1  0 30  0]
 [ 2  0  1  0  3 35]]
```

Because there are 6 classes in this example, the confusion matrix is different from previous example, which was 2 by 2 matrix, now it's 6 by 6 matrix. Figure 4.19 visualizes the confusion matrix,

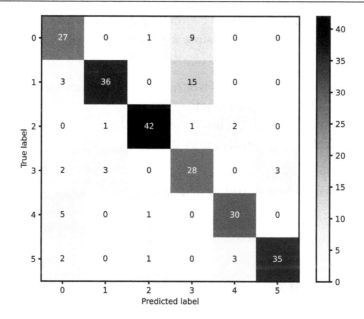

Figure 4.19 Confusion Matrix of Multinomial Logistic Regression
Generated by source code at Multinomial_Regression_Introduction.ipynb

Look at the first row of the confusion matrix, there are 27 zeros are correctly predicted, but 1 mistakenly predicted as 2, and 9 predicted as 3.

Similarly in the second row, there are 36 ones are correctly predicted, but 3 are predicted as 0, and 15 are predicted as 3. And so on.

The confusion matrix is very useful tool to evaluate the performance of logistic regression, not only the binary one but also the multinomial one.

4.3.2 One-hot Encoding

One-hot encoding is a technique when resolving the categorical data problem. Then what is one-hot encoding?

Consider the example of color, suppose there are four colors: 0 is for red, 1 for green, 2 for blue and 3 for yellow. This is a typical categorical data. As the comparison, consider an example of the quantitative data, say the number of bedrooms of a house, there are 0 bedroom, 1 bedroom, 2 bedrooms and 3 bedrooms. The 0, 1, 2, and 3 for colors are different from that of bedrooms, because the 3 bedrooms significantly add values to a house than the 1 bedroom, therefore 3 is more than 1 when doing the calculation.

However, in the case of colors, 3 which is for yellow does not add more value than 1 which is for green, both green and yellow are equal in their value, and there are no relationships between them, so it might confuse the categorical algorithm if pass the value of 0, 1, 2 and 3.

Therefore, the one-hot encoding is used for dealing with this situation. Because there are four classes for the color, then use a vector of four to represent it,

Class	red	green	blue	yellow	One-hot Encoding
0: red	1	0	0	0	[1 0 0 0]
1: green	0	1	0	0	[0 1 0 0]
2: blue	0	0	1	0	[0 0 1 0]
3: yellow	0	0	0	1	[0 0 0 1]

By one-hot encoding, the categorical features are turned into binary features, there are no relationships between each class, and each class is equally weighted. The real-world objects are described accurately in this way, and it will not confuse the algorithm.

`sklearn` provides function for one-hot encoding,

```
1    color = np.array([[0], [1], [2], [3]])
2    ohe = preprocessing.OneHotEncoder()
3    color_onehot = ohe.fit_transform(color)
4    print("Color:\n", color)
5    print("Color in one-hot\n", color_onehot.toarray())
```

```
Color:
 [[0]
  [1]
  [2]
  [3]]

Color in one-hot
```

```
[[1.  0.  0.  0.]
 [0.  1.  0.  0.]
 [0.  0.  1.  0.]
 [0.  0.  0.  1.]]
```

Below code snippets do the one-hot encoding without using any advanced Python packages/libraries, it helps to understand what's happen behind the scenes, the result is same as above.

```
1   def one_hot(y):
2       n_classes = len(np.unique(y))
3       oh = np.zeros((len(y), n_classes))
4       for i, val in enumerate(y):
5           oh[i, val] = 1.0
6       return oh
7   oh = one_hot(color)
8   print("Color:\n", color)
9   print("Color in one-hot\n", oh)
```

To reverse one hot encoding is an opposite operation, it can be accomplished by `numpy.argmax()` function,

```
11  def reverse_one_hot(one_hot):
12      result = np.argmax(one_hot, axis=1)
13      return result.reshape(-1,1)
14  roh = reverse_one_hot(oh)
15  print("One-hot:\n", oh)
16  print("Reverse One-hot:\n", roh)
```

```
One-hot:
 [[1.  0.  0.  0.]
  [0.  1.  0.  0.]
  [0.  0.  1.  0.]
  [0.  0.  0.  1.]]

Reverse One-hot:
 [[0]
  [1]
  [2]
  [3]]
```

4.3.3 Classification Report

In addition to the confusion matrix, a *classification report* is another method to measure the performance and quality of predictions from a classification algorithm. It tells how many predictions are correct and how many are not. This is also a useful tool for resolving classification problems.

There are three concepts in the classification report, precision, recall and F1 score.

What are Precision and Recall

Based on the explanation of wikipedia:

> *Precision (also called positive predictive value) is the fraction of relevant instances among the retrieved instances, while recall (also known as sensitivity) is the fraction of relevant instances that were retrieved. Both precision and recall are therefore based on relevance.*
>
> From https://en.wikipedia.org/wiki/Precision_and_recall

Section 4.2.3 has introduced the concepts of True Positives (TP), True Negatives (TN), False Positives (FP) and False Negatives (FN). In order to better understand the *precision* and *recall*, see Figure 4.20.

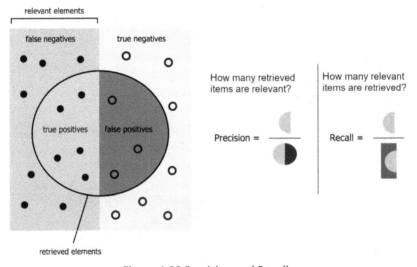

Figure 4.20 Precision and Recall

The true label of dataset consists of two parts: the True Positives (left half circle) and False Negatives (left part rectangle); and the false label also consists of two parts: the False Positives (right half circle) and True Negatives (right part rectangle).

The Predicted Positives is the whole circle in the middle and consists of True Positives and False Positives.

As shown in the lower part of Figure 4.20, the *Precision* is defined as the percentage of True Positives against all Predicted Positives. Simply put, precision is how many positives are real out of all predicted positives. Precision demonstrates the ability to distinguish the negatives, a higher value of precision means it can effectively distinguish the positives from the negatives.

While the *recall* is the percentage of true positives against all actual positives. Simply put, recall is how many positives are predicted out of all real positives. Recall demonstrates the ability to recognize the positives in the dataset, a higher recall value means it can effectively recognize the positives.

For example, when diagnose a disease, a high precision score means a smaller number of mistakes in the positive results, most positive results are real positives, only a small number of positive results are actually negative. A high recall score means most of actual positives are diagnosed as positive, only small number of actual positives are not correctly diagnosed.

As a summary, the **precision** and **recall** are calculated by True Positives (TP), True Negatives (TN), False Negatives (FN), they are defined as:

$$\text{precision} = \frac{TP}{TP + FP}$$

$$\text{recall} = \frac{TP}{TP + FN}$$

What is F_1 Score

F_1 score is a measure of the accuracy, it's a balance of precision and recall, it's defined as:

$$F_1 = \frac{2 \cdot \text{precision} \cdot \text{recall}}{\text{precision} + \text{recall}}$$

$$= \frac{TP}{TP + \frac{1}{2}(FP + FN)}$$

The highest F_1 score is 1.0, indicating a perfect precision and recall. While the lowest possible value is 0, when either the precision or recall is zero.

The Classification Report

After the classification model is built, fit and predicted, the results can be used to create a classification report.

Now use the results of the example in section 4.3.1 to generate a classification report,

```
1  from sklearn.metrics import classification_report
2  c_report = classification_report(y_test, y_pred)
3  print(c_report)
```

	precision	recall	f1-score	support
0	0.69	0.73	0.71	37
1	0.90	0.67	0.77	54
2	0.93	0.91	0.92	46
3	0.53	0.78	0.63	36
4	0.86	0.83	0.85	36
5	0.92	0.85	0.89	41
accuracy			0.79	250
macro avg	0.81	0.80	0.79	250
weighted avg	0.82	0.79	0.80	250

The report shows the precision, recall and F_1 score for each class. For example, for class 0, the precision is 0.69; recall is 0.73 and F_1 score is 0.71. The last column of the report shows "support", it's the number of data samples in that class. For example, there are 37 data points in class 0.

The last three rows of the report show the accuracy, macro average and weighted average. The macro average is the mean average of each class, and weighted average is calculated by adding the number of data in each class as the weight.

4.3.4 Hand-written Digits Dataset

This data set contains 8×8 pixels images of hand-written digits, the total number is 1797, there are 10 classes, where each class refers to a digit from 0 to 9. Since each image has 8×8 pixels, and each pixel is a feature, there are 64 features. Therefore, $n = 1797, m = 64, k = 10$.

The dataset can be loaded from `sklearn.datasets`, and the details can be obtained from the attributes of the dataset.

```
1   from sklearn import datasets
2   digits = datasets.load_digits()
3   print("Data:", digits.data.shape)
4   print("Target:", digits.target.shape)
5   print("Features:", digits.feature_names)
6   print("Description:", digits.DESCR)
7   print("Keys:", digits.keys())
```

```
Data: (1797, 64)
Target: (1797,)
Features: ['pixel_0_0', 'pixel_0_1', 'pixel_0_2'...
...
```

Then retrieve the data from the dataset, and print out the size of the data,

```
8    X = digits.data
9    y = digits.target
10   print(X.shape)
11   print(y.shape)
12   print(np.unique(y))
```

```
(1797, 64)
(1797,)
[0 1 2 3 4 5 6 7 8 9]
```

The size of X is 1797 × 64, and size of y is 1797, the unique values in y are from 0 to 9, meaning there are 10 classes.

Then scale the data and split it into train and test sets,

```
21   from sklearn import preprocessing
22   from sklearn import model_selection
23   scaler = preprocessing.StandardScaler()
24   X = scaler.fit_transform(X)
25   X_train, X_test, y_train, y_test = \
26   model_selection.train_test_split(X, y,
27                                    train_size = .75,
28                                    random_state=2)
```

Create a multinomial logistic regression model, fit it with train dataset, and make prediction with test dataset,

```
31   from sklearn import linear_model
32   model = linear_model.LogisticRegression(
33                     multi_class='multinomial')
34   model.fit(X_train, y_train)
35   y_pred = model.predict(X_test)
```

Then print out the results of accuracy score, confusion matrix and Classification Report,

```
41   from sklearn.metrics import accuracy_score
42   from sklearn.metrics import confusion_matrix
43   from sklearn.metrics import classification_report
44   a_score = accuracy_score(y_test, y_pred)
45   c_matrix = confusion_matrix(y_test, y_pred)
46   c_report = classification_report(y_test, y_pred)
47   print("Accuracy Score:", a_score)
48   print("Confusion matrix:\n", c_matrix)
49   print("Classification Report:\n", c_report)
```

```
Accuracy Score: 0.9666666666666667

Confusion matrix:
 [[37  0  0  0  0  0  0  0  0  0]
 [ 0 40  0  0  0  0  0  0  2  1]
 [ 0  0 43  1  0  0  0  0  0  0]
 [ 0  0  0 44  0  0  0  0  1  0]
 [ 0  0  0  0 37  0  0  1  0  0]
 [ 0  0  0  0  0 46  0  0  0  2]
```

```
[ 0  1  0  0  0  0 51  0  0  0]
[ 0  0  0  0  1  0  0 47  0  0]
[ 0  3  1  0  0  0  0  0 44  0]
[ 0  0  0  0  0  1  0  0  0 46]]
```

```
Classification Report:
                precision    recall  f1-score   support
           0       1.00      1.00      1.00        37
           1       0.91      0.93      0.92        43
           2       0.98      0.98      0.98        44
           3       0.98      0.98      0.98        45
           4       0.97      0.97      0.97        38
           5       0.98      0.96      0.97        48
           6       1.00      0.98      0.99        52
           7       0.98      0.98      0.98        48
           8       0.94      0.92      0.93        48
           9       0.94      0.98      0.96        47
    accuracy                           0.97       450
   macro avg       0.97      0.97      0.97       450
weighted avg       0.97      0.97      0.97       450
```

4.3.5 Algorithm and Implementation of MLR

This section will introduce the algorithms for multinomial logistic regression behind the scenes, the implementation will only use the basic Python operations without the advanced packages and libraries.

Notations

m	Number of features
n	Number of data samples
k	Number of classes
X	Input data, or independent variables, in matrix of $n \times m$
y	target value, or dependent output variable, or true label, in matrix of $n \times 1$
$x^{(i)}, y^{(i)}$	i-th sample data and true label
$y_{pred}^{(i)}$	i-th predicted value
x_j	j-th feature, where $j \in [1, m]$
θ	Intercept and coefficient, the size is $m \times k$.

Hypothesis Function

As explained in section 4.3.1 softmax function is use for multinomial logistic regression, it's defined as:

$$\sigma(z_l) = \frac{e^{z_l}}{e^{z_1} + e^{z_2} + \cdots + e^{z_k}}$$

$$= \frac{e^{z_l}}{\sum_{l=1}^{k} e^{z_l}}$$

where:

$$z = \theta_0 + \theta_1 x_1 + \theta_2 x_2 + \cdots + \theta_m x_m = X\theta, \text{ and } l \in [1, k]$$

The output of softmax function is a vector of size k, the same number of the classes, they are the probability of each input value. And the output is normalized, meaning the sum of all elements is 1, and each element is between 0 and 1.

The Hypothesis function for multinomial logistic regression is:

$$h_\theta(X) = \frac{1}{\sum_{l=1}^{k} e^{X\theta^{(l)}}} \begin{bmatrix} e^{X\theta^{(1)}} \\ e^{X\theta^{(2)}} \\ \cdots \\ e^{X\theta^{(k)}} \end{bmatrix}$$

Where θ is a matrix of $m \times k$, its columns are classes and denoted by $\theta^{(k)}$, its rows are features which is same as the binary logistic regression. Therefore it can be denoted as,

$$\theta = \begin{bmatrix} | & | & | & | \\ \theta^{(1)} & \theta^{(2)} & \cdots & \theta^{(k)} \\ | & | & | & | \end{bmatrix}$$

θ has m rows which corresponding to the features. Compare with the θ for binary logistic regression, it has m rows but only one column.

And X is $n \times m$, (meaning n data points, and each data point has m features), θ is $m \times k$, then $z = X\theta$, z is $n \times k$. Compare with that for binary logistic regression, z was $n \times 1$.

In order to implement softmax function in Python for z as $n \times k$ matrix, we need to make some changes mathematically to the softmax function, because the original formula is not good at handling matrices.

$$\sigma(z_l) = \frac{e^{z_l}}{\sum\limits_{l=1}^{k} e^{z_l}}$$

$$= \frac{e^{\max(z)} \cdot e^{z_l}}{e^{\max(z)} \cdot \sum\limits_{l=1}^{k} e^{z_l}}$$

$$= \frac{e^{(z_l - \max(z))}}{\sum\limits_{l=1}^{k} e^{(z_l - \max(z))}}$$

Therefore the softmax function can be implemented as:

```
1  def softmax(z):
2      z_max = np.amax(z, axis=1, keepdims=True)
3      exp_shifted = np.exp(z - z_max)
4      return exp_shifted / np.sum(exp_shifted,
5                                  axis=1,
6                                  keepdims=True)
```

`axis=1` is to calculate along the columns, meaning both sum and max are calculated along columns, the columns are representing classes, then the sum and max are calculated against all classes. If the calculation is along the wrong direction the results will not be correct.

Then implement hypothesis function,

```
7  def hypothesis(X, theta):
8      z = np.dot(X, theta)
9      return (softmax(-z))
```

Cost Function

The cost function is used to measure the difference between the predicted value and the true value. Same as binary logistic regression, the *Cross Entropy* cost function is used here. The objective of the regression process is to find θ that makes the cost minimum.

The cross-entropy function for multinomial logistic regression is:

$$J(\theta) = -\frac{1}{n} \sum_{i=1}^{n} \sum_{l=1}^{k} 1\left\{y^{(i)} = k\right\} \log\left(h_\theta(x^{(i)})\right)$$

$$\text{where: } 1\left\{\cdots\right\} = \begin{cases} 1 & : \text{when } \{true\} \\ 0 & : \text{when } \{false\} \end{cases}$$

It is implemented as:

```
11    def cost(X, y, theta):
12        h = hypothesis(X, theta)
13        return (-np.mean(np.sum(np.log(h)*(y),axis=1)))
```

The mean is calculated as default which is along rows and against n i.e., all data points, this implements the first summation sign i.e., $1/n$ sum for i from 1 to n; the sum is calculated as `axis=1`, along columns and against k (all classes), i.e, sum for l from 1 to k.

The result of cross-entropy cost function is a scaler value.

Gradient

The gradient descent method will be used to find the minimum value of the cost function. The gradient is a vector, each element is the partial derivative of a feature/variable. The size of gradient is same as that of θ.

The conclusion is given here without mathematically proving, please reference the materials #16 in References section for details. The gradient for multinomial logistic regression is defined as:

$$\nabla J(\theta) = \begin{bmatrix} \dfrac{\partial}{\partial \theta_0} J(\theta) \\[2mm] \dfrac{\partial}{\partial \theta_1} J(\theta) \\[1mm] \dots \\[1mm] \dfrac{\partial}{\partial \theta_m} J(\theta) \end{bmatrix} = \begin{bmatrix} \dfrac{1}{n} \sum\limits_{i=1}^{n} \left(y^{(i)} - h_\theta(x^{(i)}) \right) \\[3mm] \dfrac{1}{n} \sum\limits_{i=1}^{n} \left(y^{(i)} - h_\theta(x^{(i)}) \right) x_1^{(i)} \\[1mm] \dots \\[1mm] \dfrac{1}{n} \sum\limits_{i=1}^{n} \left(y^{(i)} - h_\theta(x^{(i)}) \right) x_m^{(i)} \end{bmatrix}$$

It's implemented in Python as,

```
1    def gradient(X, y, theta):
2        h = hypothesis(X, theta)
3        return np.dot(np.transpose(X), (y - h))/y.shape[0]
```

It's very similar to the gradient of logistic regression, see section 4.2.5.

Below is the full code of `MultinomialLogisticRegression` class, each individual function defined above is rewritten as Python class,

```
1    class MultinomialLogisticRegression:
2        def __init__(self, X, y, fit_intercept=True):
3            self.X = X
4            self.y = self.one_hot(y.reshape(-1,1))
5            if fit_intercept:
6                self.X=np.hstack((np.ones((self.X.shape[0], 1)),
7                                  self.X))
8            self.theta = np.zeros((self.X.shape[1],
9                                   self.y.shape[1]))
10           self.fit_intercept = fit_intercept
11       def one_hot(self, y):
12           n_classes = len(np.unique(y))
13           oh = np.zeros((len(y), n_classes))
14           for i, val in enumerate(y):
15               oh[i, val] = 1.0
16           return oh
17       def softmax(self, z):
18           z_max = np.amax(z, axis=1, keepdims=True)
19           exp_shifted = np.exp(z - z_max)
20           return exp_shifted / np.sum(exp_shifted, axis=1,
                                           keepdims=True)
21       def hypothesis(self, X):
22           z = np.dot(X, self.theta)
```

```
23        return (self.softmax(-z))
24    def cost(self, h, y):
25        return (-np.mean(np.sum(np.log(h) * (y), axis=1)))
26    def gradient(self, X, h, y):
27        return np.dot(np.transpose(X), (y - h)) /
28                        y.shape[0]
29    def fit(self, epochs=5000, alpha=0.01):
30        for i in range(epochs):
31            h = self.hypothesis(self.X)
32            cost = self.cost(h, self.y)
33            grad = self.gradient(self.X, h, self.y)
34            self.theta -= alpha * grad
35    def predict(self, X):
36        if self.fit_intercept:
37            X = np.hstack((np.ones((X.shape[0], 1)), X))
38        h = self.hypothesis(X)
39        return np.argmax(h, axis=1)
```

Now apply the hand-written digits dataset to this class and evaluate the results,

```
41    from sklearn import metrics
42    from sklearn import preprocessing
43    from sklearn import datasets
44    from sklearn import model_selection
45    digits = datasets.load_digits()
46    scaler = preprocessing.StandardScaler()
47    X = scaler.fit_transform(digits.data)
48    y = digits.target
49    X_train, X_test, y_train, y_test = \
50    model_selection.train_test_split(X, y,
51                                        train_size = .75,
52                                        random_state=0)
53    regressor = MultinomialLogisticRegression(X_train,
54                                                y_train)
55    regressor.fit(epochs=10000, alpha=0.01)
56    y_pred = regressor.predict(X_test)
57    a_score = accuracy_score(y_test, y_pred)
58    c_matrix = confusion_matrix(y_test, y_pred)
59    c_report = classification_report(y_test, y_pred)
60    print("Accuracy Score:", a_score)
61    print("Confusion matrix:\n", c_matrix)
62    print("Classification Report:\n", c_report)
```

The results are:

```
Accuracy Score: 0.9622222222222222
Confusion matrix:
[[37  0  0  0  0  0  0  0  0  0]
 [ 0 40  0  0  1  0  1  0  0  1]
 [ 0  0 44  0  0  0  0  0  0  0]
 [ 0  0  0 44  0  0  0  0  1  0]
 [ 0  0  0  0 36  0  0  2  0  0]
 [ 0  0  0  0  0 47  0  0  0  1]
 [ 0  1  0  0  0  0 51  0  0  0]
 [ 0  0  0  0  2  0  0 46  0  0]
 [ 0  3  1  0  0  1  0  0 43  0]
 [ 0  0  0  0  0  1  0  1  0 45]]
```

Classification Report:

	precision	recall	f1-score	support
0	1.00	1.00	1.00	37
1	0.91	0.93	0.92	43
2	0.98	1.00	0.99	44
3	1.00	0.98	0.99	45
4	0.92	0.95	0.94	38
5	0.96	0.98	0.97	48
6	0.98	0.98	0.98	52
7	0.94	0.96	0.95	48
8	0.98	0.90	0.93	48
9	0.96	0.96	0.96	47
accuracy			0.96	450
macro avg	0.96	0.96	0.96	450
weighted avg	0.96	0.96	0.96	450

Compare these results with that in section 4.3.4 where the same dataset applied to `sklearn` model, although not exact same, we got similar results.

The full source code is located at *MLR_Algorithm_Implementation.ipynb*, feel free to play with it and test it with other datasets.

It's recommended to use Python provided advanced machine learning libraries and packages in the real projects. The above codes are used for better understanding the algorithm only.

Figure 4.21 shows the cost vs epoch during the training process, the cost is larger than 2.0 at the beginning, and then it reduces significantly when epoch increases.

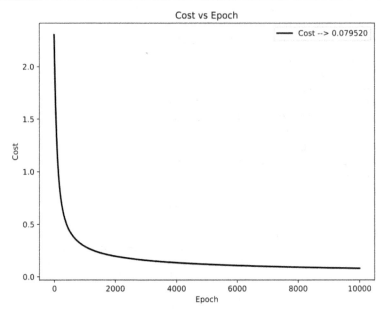

Figure 4.21 Multinomial Logistic Regression, Cost vs Epoch
Generated by source code at MLR_Algorithm_Implementation.ipynb

4.4   K-Means Clustering

4.4.1   What is K-Means Clustering

K-means clustering is one of the unsupervised machine learning algorithms, and one of the popular methods of clustering unlabeled data into k clusters. Unlabeled data means the data without defined categories or groups. The objective of K-Means algorithm is to find out clusters or groups in the data, with the number of clusters represented by k. The algorithm works iteratively to assign each data point to one of the clusters based on the features that are provided. Data points are clustered based on feature similarity. It automatically categorizes the data and finds a number of *centroids*, each representing a cluster of data. A *centroid* is the arithmetic mean position, or average position, of a cluster of data.

Unsupervised machine learning means the system will learn from the data by itself, rather than explicitly telling it what is true and what is false. Therefore K-Means does not need y from the dataset.

The results of K-means are:

- The centroids of the K clusters
- Labels for the data

As a real-world example, a T-shirt maker wants to make the products fitting for a wide range of people with different heights and weights. The maker will make the T-shirts in three sizes: L, M and S for different people, meaning choose one size for the people in L group, one for M group and another for S group. The three sizes are called *centroids* in the terminology of K-means clustering, each *centroid* represents a group, or a cluster, of people.

K-Means is an effective algorithm to resolve this type of problems, it will find out the three centroids for size of L, M and S from the data collected from people with different heights and weights. Figure 4.22 shows this concept, x-axis represents height of people and y-axis for weight, the data points represent the people in different height and weight, and the data can be grouped in three clusters as S, M and L.

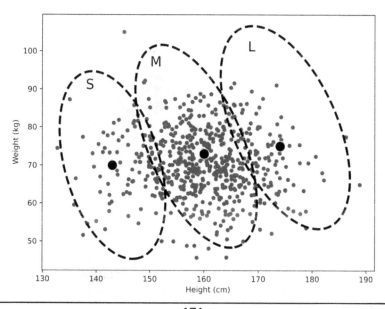

Figure 4.22 K-Means Introduction, T-Shirts Example
Generated by source code at K-Means_Clustering_Introduction.ipynb

The arithmetic mean (average) position of each group is the *centroid* and located near the center of each group. The maker will make the T-shirts use the size of the centroids that will fit most of people.

K-means is one of the unsupervised learning methods because it will find the results from the data itself by calculation, don't need a label marked for each data.

In the contrary, the supervised learning will need a label for each data, say some data are marked with L, some M and some S, the algorithm will learn from the data and the true labels.

Now generate sample data for K-Means:

```
1   from sklearn.datasets import make_blobs
2   X, _ = make_blobs(n_samples=1000, n_features=2,
3               centers=[[-1,-1], [0,0], [1,1], [2,2]],
4               cluster_std=[0.4, 0.3, 0.3, 0.3],
5               random_state = 9)
```

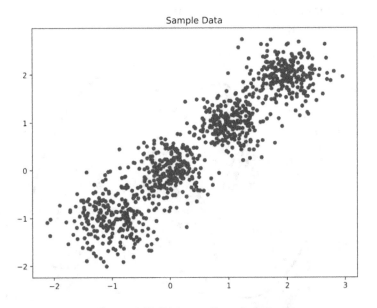

Figure 4.23 K-Means, Sample Data
Generated by source code at K-Means_Clustering_Introduction.ipynb

The generated data has two features, so we can easily visualize it as shown in Figure 4.23. We don't take y from the dataset, because the labels in y are not needed.

By looking at the data, it looks like there are four clusters, so apply the K-Means model with $k=4$ by passing n_clusters=4 as parameter. Next section will discuss how to decide the number of clusters.

```
11    from sklearn.cluster import KMeans
12    model = KMeans(n_clusters=4,
13                   init='k-means++',
14                   random_state=9)
15    y_pred = model.fit_predict(X)
16    centroids = model.cluster_centers_
17    labels = model.labels_
```

After a K-Means model is created and fit with the dataset, the attribute of model.cluster_centers_ has the centroids of k clusters, it's size is $m \times k$, m is the number of features of the dataset.

The attribute of model.labels_ has the labels of the dataset, it's size is $n \times 1$, n is the number of data points in the dataset.

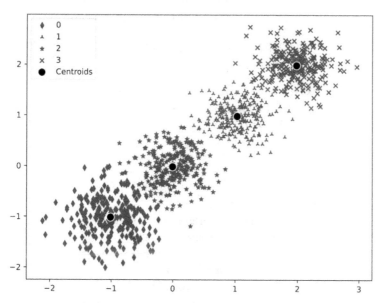

Figure 4.24 K-Means Clustering, the Results
Generated by source code at K-Means_Clustering_Introduction.ipynb

173

K-Means algorithm has calculated the centroids and labels, the results are plotted as Figure 4.24

There are four clusters are identified, 0, 1, 2 and 3, each in a different shape in Figure 4.24; and the centroid for each cluster is also identified.

4.4.2 How to Find the Number of Clusters

When create a K-Means model, the clusters k is a user-defined input parameter, the model will not calculate it. In the previous example we plot the sample data in Figure 4.23, and manually find out the number of clusters is 4 by looking at the figure.

However, in the real-world projects it's not easy to manually identify the number of clusters, and in most cases it's not possible to visualize the data when the features are more than 3.

The *Elbow method* is a technique to help us to find out the number of clusters, the idea is to run multiple K-Means processes with different k, say from 1 to 10, and calculate the sum of squared distances for each k value. The sum of squared distances, also called *Distortion*, is the sum of squared distances from each data point to its assigned centroid.

Then plot the distortions vs k, typically the curve looks like an arm, and the elbow is the best value of k.

```
1   from sklearn.cluster import KMeans
2   Sum_of_squared_distances = []
3   K = range(1, 15)
4   for k in K:
5       model = KMeans(n_clusters=k,
6                      init='k-means++',
7                      random_state=42)
8       model = km.fit(X)
9       Sum_of_squared_distances.append(model.inertia_)
10  fig = plt.figure(figsize=(8, 6))
11  plt.plot(K, Sum_of_squared_distances, 'bo-')
12  plt.xlabel(r'Clusters $k$')
13  plt.ylabel('Sum of Squared Distances')
14  plt.title('Elbow Method For K-Means')
15  plt.show()
```

The above code snippets use k from 1 to 15 and run K-Means for each. In the results of the K-Means model, the attribute `model.inertia_` has the distortion (or sum of squared distances) value, it is used for visualizing purpose.

Figure 4.25 is the result, it shows the distortion against k. The distortion is over *2500* when $k = 1$, it drops to less than *1000* when $k = 2$, and drops again to less than *500* when $k = 3$. And then $k = 4$ is the "elbow" point, because the distortion is not dropping much more when k increases from that point. Finally, 4 is selected as the number of clusters k.

This is the *Elbow* method.

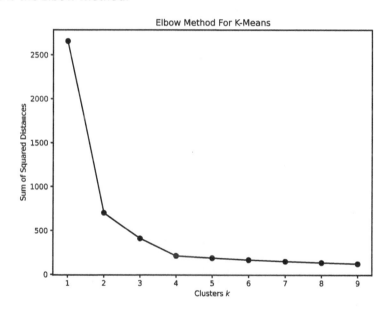

Figure 4.25 K-Means Clustering, Elbow Method
Generated by source code at K-Means_Clustering_Introduction.ipynb

4.4.3 Algorithm and Implementation of K-Means

The objective of the algorithm is to minimize the distortion (or sum of squared distances) between the data points and their assigned centroids.

Euclidean Distance

The Euclidean distance is defined as the distance between two points. In 2-dimentional space it's defined as:

$$d = \sqrt{(x_2 - x_1)^2 + (y_2 - y_1)^2}$$

where, (x_1, y_1) and (x_2, y_2) are two points, d is the distance between them.

In general, for multi-dimensional data points, it is defined as:

$$d = \| a - b \|$$

d is the distance between point a and b. It is the norm of the vector $(a - b)$, refer to section 3.1.3 for Vector Norm and Distance.

It's implemented in Python:

```
1    def _euclidean(a, b):
2        return np.sqrt(np.sum((a - b)**2, axis=1))
```

It calculates the Euclidean distance between point a and b, both could be multi-dimensional points and doesn't have to be in 2-dimentional. a and b are vectors, the result is a scaler.

The Algorithm of K-Means

There is dataset:

$$x^{(1)}, x^{(2)}, \cdots, x^{(n)}$$

There are five steps involved in the process:

Step 1: Randomly select k data points as initial centroids:

$$\mu_1, \mu_2, \cdots, \mu_k$$

```
3    def initialize(X, K, random_state):
4        np.random.seed(random_state)
5        idx = np.random.choice(X.shape[0], size=K,
6                                replace=False)
7        return X[idx, :]
```

It returns k data points that randomly selected from the dataset X, they are the initial centroids.

Step 2: Calculate the distances between each data points and the k centroids.

For i from 1 to n, then for j from 1 to k:

$$d_j = \| x^{(i)} - \mu_j \|$$

It's implemented as:

```
8    def distance(X, centroids):
9        return np.array([_euclidean(X, centroid)
10                        for centroid in centroids])
```

It calculates the distances for each data point to k centroids, therefor the size of the result is $n \times k$, meaning each data point has k distances corresponding to the k centroids.

Step 3: Assign each data point to the nearest centroid based on the distances found.

For i from 1 to n,

$$c^{(i)} = \arg\min_j(d_j)$$

where $c^{(i)}$ is the cluster of data point i.

It's implemented as:

```
11   def assign(distances):
12       return np.argmin(distances, axis=0)
```

In the previous step, distances are calculated for each data point corresponding to k distances, this step chooses the minimum distance and assign it to the data point, meaning assign the nearest cluster to each data point. The result is in size of $n \times 1$, every data point will be assigned a cluster.

Step 4: Update centroids by taking the average of the data points in each cluster.

For j from 1 to k:

$$\mu_j = \frac{\sum_{i=1}^{n} 1\left\{c^{(i)} = j\right\} x^{(i)}}{\sum_{i=1}^{n} 1\left\{c^{(i)} = j\right\}}$$

where $c^{(i)}$ is the cluster of data point i;

$x^{(i)}$ is the i-th data point;

n is the number of data points;

μ_j is the centroid of cluster j.

It's implemented as:

```
13    def update(X, label, k):
14      centroid_ = []
15      for j in range(k):
16        temp_ = X[label==j].mean(axis=0)
17        centroid_.append(temp_)
18      return np.vstack(centroid_)
```

It simply calculates the average of data points for each cluster and returns the updated centroids.

Step 5: Repeat Step 2 to 4 until convergence, which means the centroids don't change any more, or a given max iteration number.

Below is the full code of KMeans class, the above functions are re-written in Python class functions.

```
1    class KMeans:
2      def __init__(self, X, clusters, random_state=0):
3        self.X = X
4        self.K = clusters
5        self.samples, self.features = X.shape
6        # Step 1: initialize centroids
7        self.centroid = self.initialize(random_state)
8      def _euclidean(self, a, b):
9        return np.sqrt(np.sum((a - b)**2, axis=1))
10     def initialize(self, random_state):
11       np.random.seed(random_state)
12       idx = np.random.choice(self.samples,
13                              size=self.K,
14                              replace=False)
15       return self.X[idx, :]
16     def distance(self, X, centroid):
17       return np.array([self._euclidean(X, centroid)
18                        for centroid in self.centroid])
19     def assign(self, distances):
20       return np.argmin(distances, axis=0)
```

```
21    def update(self, label):
22      centroid_ = []
23      for j in range(self.K):
24        temp_ = self.X[label==j].mean(axis=0)
25        centroid_.append(temp_)
26      return np.vstack(centroid_)
27    def fit(self, epoch):
28      for _ in range(epoch):
29        # Step 2: find distances
30        distances_ = self.distance(self.X,
31                                   self.centroid)
32        # Step 3: assign data points
33        self.label = self.assign(distances_)
34        # Step 4: update centroids
35        self.centroid = self.update(self.label)
36    def predict(self, X):
37      distances_ = self.distance(X, self.centroid)
38      return self.assign(distances_)
```

The K-Means process is shown in Figure 4.26,

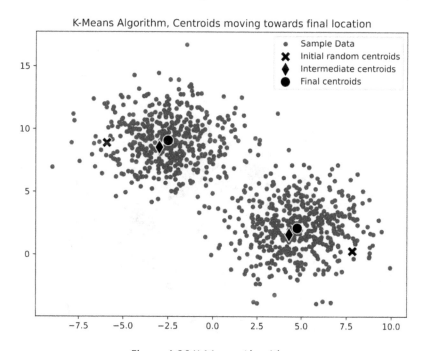

Figure 4.26 K-Means Algorithm
Generated by source code at K_Means_Algorithm_Implementation.ipynb

There are sample data in two clusters, $k = 2$, two initial centroids are selected randomly from the sample data, shown as black x in above figure; run the K-Means step #2 to #4 for several iterations, the centroids gradually move from their initial positions towards the center of each cluster, as ♦ shape in above figure. Finally, they converge at the center of each cluster as black circles.

The final results are shown in Figure 4.27, it comes up with not only the centroids but also the label for each data point.

The centroids appear in the center of each cluster, each centroid has minimum sum of distances from each data point within the cluster. The label of 0 and 1 are assigned to each data point as well, as shown in the Figure 4.27 in different shapes.

In summary, K-Means does not need the label to perform learning process, this is why it's one of the unsupervised algorithms. As the result it will find out the labels for the data points and categorize them.

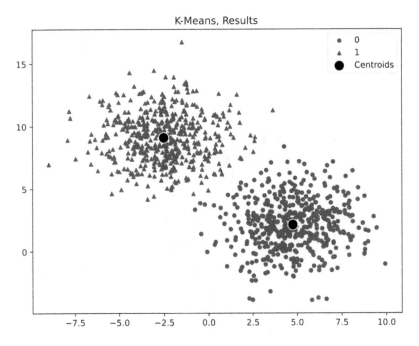

Figure 4.27 K-Means, Results
Generated by source code at K_Means_Algorithm_Implementation.ipynb

Now back to the T-Shirts example in the beginning of this section, the maker will eventually categorize all people in the three groups, L, M and S; and will also find out the centroid for each group, each centroid has minimum distances to all people in the corresponding group, meaning it should be the best fit for all people in the group. K-Means is a good tool for this purpose, then the maker can make the T-Shirts based on the three centroid sizes.

4.4.4 Color Quantization

One of the applications of K-Means is Color Quantization, what is it?

Based on wikipedia:

> *Color quantization or color image quantization is quantization applied to color spaces; it is a process that reduces the number of distinct colors used in an image, usually with the intention that the new image should be as visually similar as possible to the original image.*
>
> From https://en.wikipedia.org/wiki/Color_quantization

The purpose of color quantization is 1) to reduce the number of colors and then reduce the memory and the size required to store the image; and 2) to display the image in some devices that might have limitations on the number of distinct colors.

And the requirement of color quantization is that the visual appearance of the resulting image should be kept as much as possible, and not to lose the quality too much.

How many distinct colors can an image have? In theory an image has blue, green and red channels, each has 8-bits meaning $2^8 = 256$ values, therefore totally 24-bits $2^{24} = 16,777,216$ possible distinct colors. Although in most cases there are not so many distinct colors in an image.

K-Means is one of the effective methods for this purpose, a distinct color in the image consists of blue, green and red values, these three values are considered a data point for K-Means. Suppose an image has n pixels, they are the dataset for the K-Means, the objective is to reduce the distinct colors to k, which is the clusters. K-Means will figure out the similarities, categorize the colors into k clusters, and come up with k centroids. Then replace all colors within each cluster with its centroid, the result image will have only k distinct colors. And these colors have minimum sum of distances to the original colors in the cluster, this ensures the visual appearance of the result image is kept as much as possible.

The following code snippets will count the distinct colors in an image, an image, for example a picture, is loaded into `image` variable, and passed to the below function, the result is the distinct colors in the image.

```
1   def get_distinct_colours(image):
2       unique,counts=np.unique(
3                   image.reshape(-1, image.shape[-1]),
4                   axis=0, return_counts=True)
5       return counts.size
```

The previous section 4.4.1 introduces the K-Means provided by `sklearn.cluster` package, now we will introduce the same function from another package – OpenCV, short for `cv2`, which provides computer vision related functionalities including some machine learning tools, such as K-Means. Since it is specialized in image processing, it will be used here for color quantization.

Here are the codes:

```
11  def color_quantization(image, clusters):
12      X = image.reshape((-1,3))
13      X = np.float32(X)
14      criteria = (cv2.TERM_CRITERIA_EPS +
15                  cv2.TERM_CRITERIA_MAX_ITER,
16                  10, 1.0)
17      ret,label,center=cv2.kmeans(X, clusters, None,
18                              criteria, 10,
19                              cv2.KMEANS_PP_CENTERS)
20      center = np.uint8(center)
21      result = center[label.flatten()]
22      result = result.reshape((image.shape))
23      return result
```

Line 11 is to define the function for color quantization, the parameter `image` is the image to quantize, and `clusters` is the k value.

Line 12 is to reshape the image data, originally it is in (width, height, channel), where the channel is always 3, for blue, green and red. The data needs to be transformed to (width × height, 3). And Line 13 is to transform the data type to `np.float32`. This is required by OpenCV K-Means function.

Line 14, 15 and 16 is to define criteria to terminate the K-Means process, `cv2.TERM_CRITERIA_EPS` is the desired accuracy, which is set to 1.0, meaning K-Means process stops when the centroids move less than this accuracy value; `cv2.TERM_CRITERIA_MAX_ITER` is the maximum iteration number, which is set to 10.

Line 17, 18 and 19 is to call the `cv2.kmeans()` function with necessary parameters. As the results, the centroids are in `center` variable, and labels of data points are in `label`.

Line 20 is to convert `center` to `np.uint8`, because they are the final distinct color values of the result image.

Line 21 is to generate a new image based on `label` values and the colors in `center`. All the similar colors are grouped in one cluster and have the same label, so all of them will use its centroid color.

Line 22 is to reshape the new image back to the size of (width, height, channel).

Original Image (distinct colors = 116)

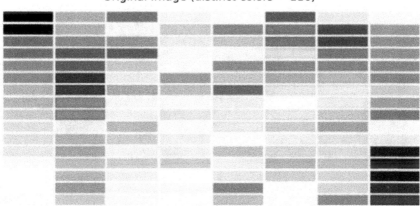

Quantized image (distinct colors = 8)

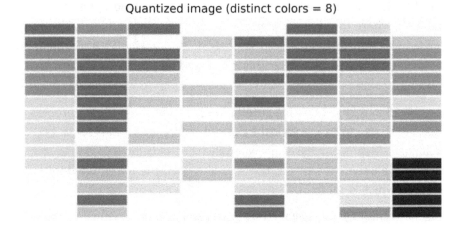

Figure 4.28 A Sample Color Palette
Generated by source code at Color_Quantization.ipynb

Now generate a sample color palette, and apply the above two functions to retrieve distinct colors and quantize the colors, as Figure 4.28

The original image at the top has 116 distinct colors, the lower image is quantized to 8 colors. By comparing the two images, a specific red color replaces all similar red colors – dark red, light red, rose, etc.; and a specific green replaces all greens -- light green, grass green etc.; and so on.

As another example, apply the color quantization on a picture and see the results:

Original Image (distinct colors = 62941)   Quantized image (distinct colors = 32)

Generated by source code at Color_Quantization.ipynb

It's straightforward to read the results and see how the visual appearances are changed after the color quantization.

The full source code is at *Color_Quantization.ipynb* in the Github repository, feel free to try it with other images.

4.5 Principal Component Analysis (PCA)

Principal Component Analysis (PCA) is one of the unsupervised learning methods. It is used for dimensionality reduction in machine learning and statistics. Based on wikipedia:

> *Principal component analysis (PCA) is the process of computing the principal components and using them to perform a change of basis on the data, sometimes using only the first few principal components and ignoring the rest.*

From https://en.wikipedia.org/wiki/Principal_component_analysis

4.5.1 Introduction

To simply put, PCA is famously known as a dimensionality reduction technique. The reason to use it is because for example a dataset with two features: x_1 and x_2, it's very easy to visualize the data points, like Figure 4.11 or Figure 4.23 in previous sections, as they can be drawn on a 2D plot. However, if there is a dataset with more than 3 features, like the one in 4.2.4 – breast cancer dataset, it's not possible to visualize the data because there are 30 features or variables.

PCA can reduce high dimensional data to low dimensions while keeping maximum information from dataset. So the 30 features in breast cancer dataset can be reduced to 2 features with the maximum information from the dataset, then the dataset can be visualized in a 2D plot. PCA is an unsupervised learning method, same as K-Means in section 4.4, the labels are not needed.

PCA is mostly used for data visualization purpose, it's also used to make the learning or fitting process faster by reducing the number of variables. PCA may be used in pre-processing steps, like data scaling, before the data is fed into the main layers of machine learning algorithms; or it may be used by itself for data visualization.

Now generate sample data in 2D and use PCA to transform them to 1D,

```
1    import numpy as np
2    from sklearn import datasets
3    from sklearn import preprocessing
4    centers=[(-2,-2), (0,-1), (2,0), (4,1),(6,2)]
5    X, _ = datasets.make_blobs(n_samples=50,
6                                    centers=centers,
7                                    n_features=2,
8                                    cluster_std=1,
9                                    random_state=101)
10   scaler = preprocessing.StandardScaler()
11   X = scaler.fit_transform(X)
```

Because PCA is unsupervised, we don't need the labels normally in y from line 5, n_features=2 in line 7 means the data has two features, or two variables. And as usual the data X is scaled in line 10 and 11.

Apply PCA to transform the sample data to 1D to see how PCA works.

```
12   from sklearn import decomposition
13   pca = decomposition.PCA(n_components=1)
14   X_pca = pca.fit_transform(X)
15   X_reverse = pca.inverse_transform(X_pca)
```

Line 13 is to apply the PCA and its parameter is set n_components=1, meaning to transform the original 2D data to 1D.

The result in X_pca is 1D data, in order to visualize it in the original 2D space, `inverse_transform()` is used to convert the result back to the original 2D space.

As shown in Figure 4.29, the ★shaped are original sample data points; the ● shaped, which appear in a line, are PCA transformed to 1D and then reverse transformed back to the original 2D space. The dashed lines show how each original data point is mapped to the PCA results.

This looks quite similar to the Linear Regression in Figure 4.5 at page 113, however, they are different. The dashed lines in linear regression are perpendicular to x-axis, they are vertical distances from the data points to the line. The dashed lines for PCA in Figure 4.29 are perpendicular to the result 1D datasets which appear as a line, which illustrates how the sample data points are transformed to the result dataset.

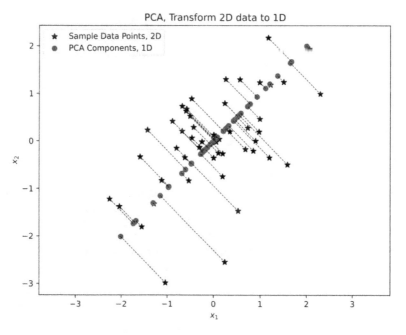

Figure 4.29 PCA, Transform Data from 2D to 1D
Generated by source code at PCA_Introduction.ipynb

After a PCA model is created and fit with sample data, the results can be obtained from the attributes of the model, below table shows the main attributes:

Attributes	Description
n_components_	The number of components.
mean_	The mean value estimated from input dataset.
explained_variance_ratio_	Percentage of variance explained by each of the selected components.
components_	Principal axes in feature space, representing the directions of maximum variance in the data.

Other attributes can be found in the `sklearn` documentations.

Now print out the results of the above PCA model:

```
21    print("Components_:\n", pca.components_)
22    print("PCA Mean:\n", pca.mean_)
23    print("Explained variance ratio:\n",
24                    pca.explained_variance_ratio_ )
```

```
Components_:
 [[-0.7071 -0.7071]]
PCA Mean:
 [-0.  0.]
Explained variance ratio:
 [0.8641]
```

The `pca.components_` are the vectors that decide the direction of the principal axes in the original feature space, in this case the 2D space. Simply put, this decides the direction of the result line which is the ● shaped data in Figure 4.29. It represents the direction of maximum variance in the original data. In this case there are two features in the original data, so `pca.components_` have two elements in the vector; and the PCA result is 1D, so `pca.components_` has only one vector, meaning there is only one principal component in the result. Will explain it more in later sections.

The `pca.mean_` is the mean, or average value of the input sample data. In this case it is zero-mean dataset.

The `explained_variance_ratio_` is the percentage of variance by the components. In this case it's *86.41%*, meaning after the data is transformed there are *86.41%* of the original information is kept in the result dataset.

PCA is based on *orthogonal transformation* which is a mathematical technique to transform the features of a data set onto a new coordinate system. The component which describes the most variance is called the first principal component and is placed at the first coordinate. In this case there is only one principal component because the result data is in 1D.

If the result data is more than 1D, the attribute which describes the second variance is called a second principal component and so on. In short, the complete dataset can be expressed in terms of principal components. Usually, the most of variances are explained by two or three principal components.

Now let's transform the 2D data into 2D space and see how the orthogonal transformation is working. Generate the 2D sample data and apply PCA and set n_components=2 this time,

```
1    centers=[(-2,-2), (0,-1), (2,0), (4,1),(6,2)]
2    X1, _ = datasets.make_blobs(n_samples=200,
3                                n_features=2,
4                                centers=centers,
5                                cluster_std=1,
6                                random_state=101)
7    scaler = preprocessing.StandardScaler()
8    X1 = scaler.fit_transform(X1)
9    pca1 = decomposition.PCA(n_components=2)
10   pca1.fit(X1)
```

```
Components_:
 [[ 0.7071   0.7071]
  [-0.7071   0.7071]]
PCA Mean:
 [-0.   0.]
Explained variance ratio:
 [0.8586 0.1414]
```

This time there two vectors in `pca.components_`, and two values in `pca.explained_variance_ratio_`, because the result dataset is in 2D. The first component is the principal component and it represents *85.86%* of the information from original dataset; the second component is the second principal component, and it represents *14.14%* of the information. Both components represent *100%* of the original information, in another word there is nothing lost in this transformation.

As shown in Figure 4.30, the ★ shaped points are original sample data, the *PCA Component 1* is the principal component that represents *85.86%* of the variance of the dataset; *PCA Component 2* is the second principal component with *14.14%* of the variance.

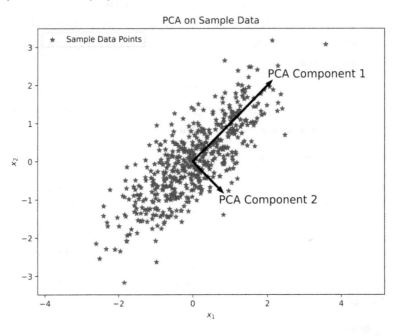

Figure 4.30 PCA on a 2D Dataset
Generated by source code at PCA_Introduction.ipynb

As the result of the transformation, Figure 4.31 shows the 2D space with *PCA Component 1* as *x*-axis and *PCA Component 2* as *y*-axis. This represents the *orthogonal transformation* from original 2D space to a new 2D space.

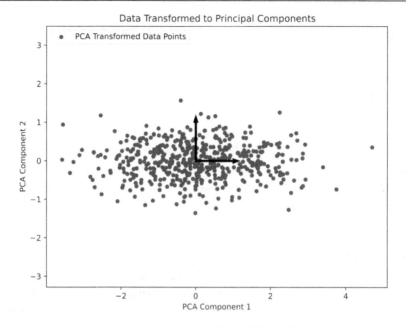

Figure 4.31 PCA Results for 2D to 2D Transformation
Generated by source code at PCA_Introduction.ipynb

So far we have discussed the dataset with one or two features in 1D or 2D spaces because it's easy for visualization.

Now revisit the Breast Cancer Dataset that discussed in section 4.2.4, which has *30* features and two clusters of output: *0* for malignant or *1* for benign. It was not possible to visualize the data because of too many features. Now apply the PCA to reduce the data from 30 features to 2 features, and visualize the data in 2D space.

```
1   from sklearn import decomposition
2   from sklearn import datasets
3   from sklearn import preprocessing
4   data = datasets.load_breast_cancer()
5   scaler = preprocessing.StandardScaler()
6   X2 = scaler.fit_transform(data.data)
7   pca2 = decomposition.PCA(n_components=2)
8   pca2.fit(X2)
9   X_pca2 = pca2.transform(X2)
```

Number of components: 2
Explained variance ratio:

```
[0.4427 0.1897]
Explained variance:
[13.305   5.7014]
Components_:
[[ 0.2189  0.1037  0.2275  0.221   0.1426
 ...
```

By reading the results, the number of components is 2 so it can be visualized in a 2D space, the principal component comes with *44.27%* of the variance of the dataset, and the second principal component has *18.97%* of the variance. Totally *63.24%* of variance is captured by this transformation, meaning some information is lost by this transformation.

Since this is for visualization purpose, some loss of the information doesn't matter. The result is like Figure 4.32, the x and y axes are the two principal components, with this kind of transformation the data points can be plotted in a 2D space for visualization, it was not possible in its original 30 features.

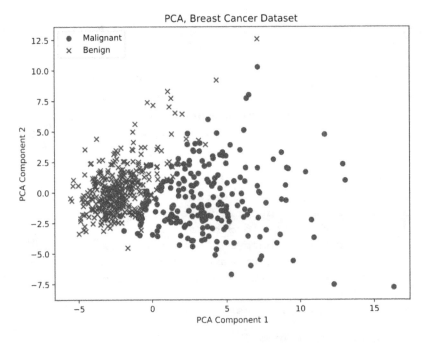

Figure 4.32 PCA on Breast Cancer Dataset
Generated by source code at PCA_Introduction.ipynb

The • shaped data points represent malignant and the × shaped represent benign. Please note, the information of malignant and benign is coming from the label of the original datasets, PCA is not doing the classification and not identifying the labels.

4.5.2 Select the Number of Components

How to select the number of components for PCA? as mentioned above when selected n_components=2, the transformation only captured 63.24% of the information from the original dataset, which was OK for visualization purpose. But if for the purpose of pre-processing of the data it's not a good idea for the information lost at this step, then how to choose the components to capture 90% to 95% of the information?

If call the PCA() function without any parameters, then all components are used to do the transformation,

```
1   pca = decomposition.PCA()
```

Figure 4.33 shows the number of components vs cumulative variance ratio.

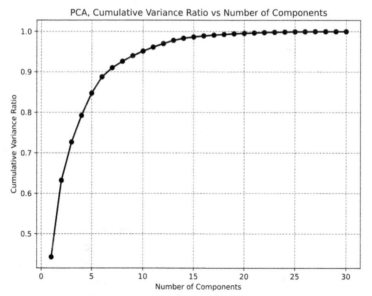

Figure 4.33 PCA Components vs Variance Ratio
Generated by source code at PCA_Introduction.ipynb

Because the dataset has *30* features, totally *30* components are generated. If one component is selected then the variance ratio is *0.4427* or *44.27%*; if two then *0.6324* or *63.24%*, which was the case in last section.

If 7 components are selected more than *90%* is captured; if 10 components are selected it's almost *0.95* or *95%*. And if more than 10 it's gradually approaching to *1* or *100%*.

An alternative way, just specify a percentage in `PCA()` parameter without the number of components, like `n_components=0.9`, the function will automatically pick up a number of components and keep the cumulative variance ratio same or greater than the specified value.

```
1  pca = decomposition.PCA(n_components=0.9)
2  pca.fit(X)
3  print("Number of components:", pca.n_components_)
4  print("Explained variance ratio:\n",
5                      pca4.explained_variance_ratio_ )
```

```
Number of components: 7
Explained variance ratio:
 [0.4427 0.1897 0.0939 0.066  0.055  0.0402 0.0225]
```

As the above results shown, the number of components is 7, and the variance ratio has seven values, they are corresponding to the seven principal components, and the sum up of the seven values is *0.91* or *91%*.

4.5.3 Covariance Matrix

In order to deep dive into PCA algorithm, need to understand what the covariance matrix is.

By wikipedia,

> *A covariance matrix (also known as auto-covariance matrix, dispersion matrix, variance matrix, or variance–covariance matrix) is a square matrix giving the covariance between each pair of elements of a given random vector. Any covariance matrix is symmetric and positive semi-definite and its main diagonal contains variances (i.e., the covariance of each element with itself).*
> From https://en.wikipedia.org/wiki/Covariance_matrix

Simply put, a covariance matrix:
- Is a square matrix.
- Its diagonal elements are the variances of all variables.
- Its off-diagonal elements are the covariances between two variables.
- It is symmetric matrix, meaning the elements in a row position is same as that in the column position.
- It is positive semi-definite.

A symmetric matrix Σ is said to be positive semi-definite if for a non-zero U then $U^T \Sigma U \geq 0$.

Variance

The variance is the measurement of variation of a single variable, for example the blood pressure in a group of people. The variances appear in the diagonal of the covariance matrix.

It's defined as:

$$\sigma(x) = \frac{1}{n} \sum_{i=1}^{n} (x_i - \mu)^2$$

Where:

x is the variable, and x_i is the i-th element of the data.

n is the total number of the data.

μ is the mean of x

Covariance

The covariance is the measurement of variation of two variables and how they change together, for example how the blood pressure and the weight are changing together in a group of people.

The covariance can be positive, negative or zero. A positive covariance indicates that the two variables have a positive relationship, for example the blood pressure is increasing together with the weight; a negative covariance indicates that they have a negative relationship, for example the blood pressure is decreasing when weight is increasing; a zero covariance indicates they don't have any relationship, for example the blood pressure is changing without any relationship to weight.

The covariance is defined as:

$$\sigma(x,y) = \frac{1}{n}\sum_{i=1}^{n}(x_i - \mu_x)(y_i - \mu_y)$$

Where:

x and y are the variables, and x_i, y_i are the i-th element of the data.

n is the total number of the data.

μ_x and μ_y are the means of x and y.

The variance can also be considered as a covariance of itself, because it can be written as:

$$\sigma(x,y) = \frac{1}{n}\sum_{i=1}^{n}(x_i - \mu)(x_i - \mu)$$

How to calculate covariance matrix

There is a dataset with m variables/features and n data points:

$$X = (x_1, x_2, \cdots, x_m)$$

It's a matrix of $n \times m$, where each column is a feature/variable, and there are totally m columns; each row is a data point, and there are totally n rows. Then the covariance matrix is defined as:

$$\Sigma = \begin{bmatrix} \sigma(x_1) & \cdots & \sigma(x_1, x_m) \\ \cdots & \cdots & \cdots \\ \sigma(x_m, x_1) & \cdots & \sigma(x_m) \end{bmatrix}$$

It's a $m \times m$ matrix, the elements in diagonal are the variances:

$$\sigma(x_1), \sigma(x_2), \cdots, \sigma(x_m)$$

and the off-diagonal elements are covariances.

Based on the definition of covariances:

$$\sigma(x_i, x_j) = \sigma(x_j, x_i)$$

so the covariance matrix is symmetric along the diagonal, and therefore:

$$\Sigma = \Sigma^T$$

The covariance matrix can be calculated as:

$$\Sigma = \frac{1}{n}(X - \mu)^T(X - \mu)$$

Where μ is the mean of X by variables, meaning $\mu = (\mu_1, \mu_2, \ldots, \mu_m)$.

And if the data is scaled to zero mean in the pre-processing step, the formula is simply:

$$\Sigma = \frac{1}{n}X^T X$$

X is $n \times m$, then X^T is $m \times n$, the result is $(m \times n)(n \times m) = (m \times m)$

```
1    import numpy as np
2    # Gerenate sample data in 2 features
3    mean = np.array([5, 5])
4    cov = np.array([[3, 2], [2, 6]])
5    np.random.seed(1)
6    X = np.random.multivariate_normal(mean, cov,
                                        size=500)
7    # Calculate covariance matrix
8    X = X - np.mean(X, axis=0)
9    Sigma = np.dot(np.transpose(X), X) / X.shape[0]
10   print(Sigma)
```

```
[[2.68969402 1.74712645]
 [1.74712645 5.93163534]]
```

Python also provides `numpy.cov()` function to calculate covariance matrix, it's easy and straightforward to use it.

```
11   import numpy as np
12   Sigma = np.cov(X, rowvar=False)
13   print(Sigma)
```

```
[[2.69508419 1.75062771]
 [1.75062771 5.94352239]]
```

The results of both methods are basically same.

4.5.4 Eigenvectors and Eigenvalues of Covariance Matrix

As mentioned above the covariance matrix Σ is a square matrix, the non-zero eigenvector v and eigenvalue λ make the below equation true:

$$\Sigma v = \lambda v$$

See section 3.1.12 for details of eigenvector and eigenvalue of a matrix.

The conclusion is given here without mathematical proofs, please reference the materials #19 in References section for details. The eigenvectors of the covariance matrix are orthogonal to each other and each represents a principal axis, meaning they are the directions of the axes with the most variance or most information of the data. And the eigenvalues are actually the coefficients of the eigenvectors which are the magnitudes of the variances of the principal components.

Orthogonal means the vectors are mutually perpendicular to each other.

The eigenvectors and eigenvalues always come in pairs; each eigenvector has an eigenvalue. And the total number of them is equal to the number of dimensions of the covariance matrix. For example, for a $m \times m$ matrix, there are m eigenvectors with m corresponding eigenvalues.

By sorting the eigenvalues in descending order from highest to lowest, the highest eigenvalue and its corresponding eigenvector are the first principal component, which represent the most variance and capture the most information of the data; and the second highest eigenvalue and its corresponding eigenvector are the second principal component, and so on.

The total number of eigenvalues is same as the number of dimensions of covariance matrix, which means the number of principal components is same as the features of the dataset. The objective of PCA is to reduce the features of the dataset, say there are totally m features in the dataset, take first k eigenvalues from the ordered eigenvalue list from the highest one, therefore the features are reduced to k, given $k < m$.

Then the percentage of sum of k eigenvalues over the sum of m eigenvalues is the information captured by this feature reduction. This is the PCA process.

$$\text{Information captured} = \frac{\text{Sum of } k \text{ eigenvalues}}{\text{Sum of total } m \text{ eigenvalues}}$$

How to Compute the Eigenvalues

From the above equation:

$$\Sigma v = \lambda v$$

$$\Sigma v = \lambda I v$$

where I is the identity matrix with same size of Σ, then:

$$\Sigma v - \lambda I v = 0$$

Since eigenvector v is non-zero, it can be resolved by determinant of matrix:

$$\det(\Sigma - \lambda I) = |\Sigma - \lambda I| = 0$$

Then solving the determinant to get λ, see section 3.1.11 for determinant of matrix. Finally, it gives a polynomial equation in λ, the roots of which are the eigenvalues $\lambda_1, \lambda_2, \ldots$ and so on.

How to Compute the Eigenvectors

After the eigenvalues are calculated, based on the equation:

$$\Sigma v = \lambda v$$

The eigenvalues can be solved one by one, i.e.

$$\Sigma v_1 = \lambda v_1$$
$$\Sigma v_2 = \lambda v_2$$

... and so on.

It's complicated and not straightforward to calculate eigenvalues and eigenvectors. Fortunately Python provide `np.linalg.eig()` function to calculate them,

```
1   import numpy as np
2   eigenvalues, eigenvectors = np.linalg.eig(Sigma)
3   print("Eigenvalues\n", eigenvalues)
4   print("Eigenvectors\n", eigenvectors)
```

```
Eigenvalues
 [1.93125282 6.70735376]
Eigenvectors
 [[-0.91655452 -0.39990975]
 [ 0.39990975 -0.91655452]]
```

4.5.5 Algorithm and Implementation of PCA

To sum up, the objective of PCA is simply to reduce the number of features or variables of a dataset, while preserving as much information as possible.

There are six steps to implement PCA.

Notations

m	Number of features
n	Number of data samples
X	Input data, or independent variables, in matrix of $n{\times}m$
$x^{(i)}$	i-th sample data, where $i \in [1, n]$
x_j	j-th feature, where $j \in [1, m]$
k	Number of principal components

Step 1: Data Standardization, or Data Scaling

Standard Scalar is used here to scale the data, it was first described in section 4.1.6.

The mean of the dataset is calculated as:

$$\mu_j = \frac{1}{n} \sum_{i=1}^{n} x_j^{(i)}$$

The standard deviation of the dataset:

$$\sigma_j^2 = \frac{1}{n} \sum_{i=1}^{n} (x_j^{(i)} - \mu_j)^2$$

Then the standard scalar is defined as:

$$x_j^{(i)} = \frac{x_j^{(i)} - \mu_j}{\sigma_j}$$

where:

$$j \in [1, m]$$

It can be implemented as,

```
1    import numpy as np
2    def scale(X):
3        mu = np.mean(X, axis=0)
4        sigma = np.std(X, axis=0)
5        return (X - mu)/sigma
```

The result is in the same size as X, which is a $n \times m$ matrix.

Step 2: Compute the Covariance Matrix

Calculate the covariance matrix of the standardized data. As explained in above section 4.5.3, it can be calculated as,

$$\Sigma = \frac{1}{n} X^T X$$

Alternatively, `numpy.cov()` function can be used to calculate the covariance matrix.

```
6    import numpy as np
7    Sigma = np.dot(np.transpose(X), X) / X.shape[0]
8    # Alternatively:
9    Sigma = np.cov(X, rowvar=False)
```

In line 9 the parameter `rowvar=False` is to specify the features in X are in columns, and the data points are in rows. If the data is organized in opposite way, then set `rowvar=True`, which is the default value.

The result covariance matrix is in size of $m \times m$.

Step 3: Compute the Eigenvectors and Eigenvalues of the Covariance Matrix

The details are described in above section 4.5.4, `np.linalg.eig()` function is used to calculate them.

```
10    import numpy as np
11    eigenvalues,eigenvectors = np.linalg.eig(Sigma)
```

Step 4: Sort Eigenvalues in Descending Order

As described in above section 4.5.4, sorting eigenvalues in descending order makes it possible to pick up the principal components in the order of significance.

```
12    import numpy as np
13    idxs = np.argsort(eigenvalues)[::-1]
14    eigenvalues = eigenvalues[idxs]
15    eigenvectors = eigenvectors[idxs]
```

`numpy.argsort()` function is used here to sort the `eigenvalues`, it returns an array of indices of the sorted values.

Now the `eigenvalues` and `eigenvectors` are sorted in descending order.

Step 5: Select First k Eigenvalues from the Sorted List

Select a subset from the sorted eigenvalues and eigenvectors based on the given number of principal components k, meaning select the first k values from the sorted list.

```
16    eigenvectors = eigenvectors[0:k]
17    eigenvalues = eigenvalues[0:k]
```

The results are the k principal components.

Step 6: Transform the data

The last step is to transform the data to the principal components. First standardize the data as step 1. Then do a dot product between the data and the transpose of the eigenvector.

```
18    import numpy as np
```

```
19   def transform(X):
20     X = scale(X)
21     return np.dot(X, np.transpose(eigenvectors))
```

The result is a transformed dataset in size of $n \times k$.

Based on the algorithm, put all code snippets together, here is the code of PCA class,

```
1    class PCA:
2      def __init__(self, n_components):
3        self.n_components = n_components
4        self.eigenvectors = None
5        self.eigenvalues = None
6        self.mean = None
7        self.ratio = None
8      def scale(self, X):
9        self.mean = np.mean(X, axis=0)
10       return (X - self.mean)/np.std(X, axis=0)
11     def fit(self, X):
12       # Step 1: Data Standardization
13       X = self.scale(X)
14       # Step 2: Compute covariance matrix
15       Sigma = np.dot(np.transpose(X), X) / X.shape[0]
16       # Step 3: Compute eigenvalues, eigenvectors
17       eigenvalues, eigenvectors = np.linalg.eig(Sigma)
18       eigenvectors = np.transpose(eigenvectors)
19       # Step 4: Sort eigenvalues in descending
20       idxs = np.argsort(eigenvalues)[::-1]
21       eigenvalues = eigenvalues[idxs]
22       eigenvectors = eigenvectors[idxs]
23       total_ = np.sum(eigenvalues)
24       # Step 5: Select first n_components eigenvectors
25       self.eigenvectors =
                eigenvectors[0:self.n_components]
26       self.eigenvalues =
                eigenvalues[0:self.n_components]
27       self.ratio = self.eigenvalues / total_
28     # Step 6: Transform the data
29     def transform(self, X):
30       X = self.scale(X)
31       return np.dot(X, np.transpose(self.eigenvectors))
```

The n_components in line 2 is the k value which is the number of principal components as input parameter when initializing the class. The ratio in line 7 is the percentage of each principal component, which is representing how much information each principal component captures from the dataset.

Now apply it to the Breast Cancer Dataset and compare with the results in section 4.5.1, where the PCA from sklearn is applied on the same dataset.

```
1    from sklearn import datasets
2    from sklearn import preprocessing
3    data = datasets.load_breast_cancer()
4    scaler = preprocessing.StandardScaler()
5    X = scaler.fit_transform(data.data)
6    y = data.target
7    pca = PCA(n_components=2)
8    pca.fit(X)
9    X_pca = pca.transform(X1)
10   print("mean:\n", pca.mean)
11   print("ratio:\n", pca.ratio)
12   print("eigenvalues:\n", pca.eigenvalues)
13   print("eigenvectors:\n", pca.eigenvectors)
```

```
ratio:
 [0.4427 0.1897]
eigenvalues:
 [13.2816   5.6914]
eigenvectors:
 [[ 0.2189   0.1037   0.2275   0.221    0.1426
 ...
```

The results are very similar to that in section 4.5.1, and if plot the transformed data, the results are almost same as Figure 4.32. The full source codes are in *PCA_Algorithm_Implementation.ipynb*, please see the results there.

4.6   Support Vector Machine (SVM)

4.6.1   What is Support Vector Machine

Support Vector Machine (SVM) is one of the supervised machine learning algorithms, which means the learning or training is based on the sample data as well as the labels. SVM is widely used for resolving classification problems, although it can be used for both regression and classification tasks. It's a simple and fast algorithm, it produces significant accuracy while consuming less computation power.

The objective of the Support Vector Machine algorithm is to find a *hyperplane* between the sample data that can distinctly classifies the data.

What are Hyperplanes

Hyperplanes are decision boundaries that used to classify the data points. Data points falling on one side of the hyperplane belongs to one class, falling on the other side of the hyperplane belongs to another class.

If the number of features of the dataset is 2, meaning the dataset is *2*-dimensional, then the hyperplane is just simply a line; if the number of features is 3 as a *3*-dimensional dataset, then the hyperplane is a *2*-dimensional plane; for a *n*-dimensional dataset, although it's not straightforward to imagine, the hyperplane is a *(n-1)*-dimensional plane.

See Figure 4.34, there are two classes in a *2*-dimensional dataset, ★and▲ shaped data points. There could be many lines between the two classes of the data points, however, the solid line shown in the middle of Figure 4.34 has the maximum margin to the data points, it's the hyperplane; the two dashed-lines in parallel to the hyperplane are the separating lines which used to separate the two classes of data points, the hyperplane has the maximum margin to the two separating lines.

What are Support Vectors

The data points on the separating lines, one ★ data point and two ▲ data points in Figure 4.34 are called *support vectors,* they are wrapped with a circle. The support vectors have the minimum distance to the hyperplane, meaning they are closest to the hyperplane. The support vectors will influence the position and orientation of the hyperplane.

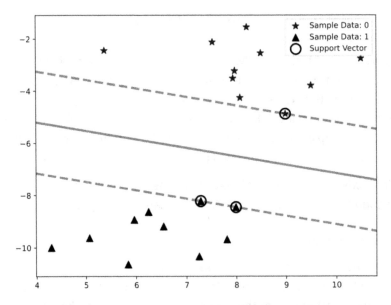

Figure 4.34 Support Vector Machine Introduction
Generated by source code at Support_Vector_Machine_Introduction.ipynb

The goal of Support Vector Machine is to find this hyperplane by calculating the support vectors, and classify the data based on it. If a new data point falls in the upper side of the hyperplane, then it will be classified as ★ data point; and if falls in the lower side of the hyperplane, then classified as ▲ data point.

The above example is simple and straightforward, the data can be separated by a line. In another example, look at the Figure 4.35, the data is distributed as a circle, it's impossible to find a line to separate the data points. In this case a non-linear hyperplane will be used to separate the data, then how to obtain the non-linear hyperplane?

SVM algorithm applies a technique called the *kernel* methods, the data is transformed by a kernel function to make it easier for finding the support vectors and decision boundaries. A linear kernel function will get a linear hyperplane; a non-linear kernel function will get a non-linear one.

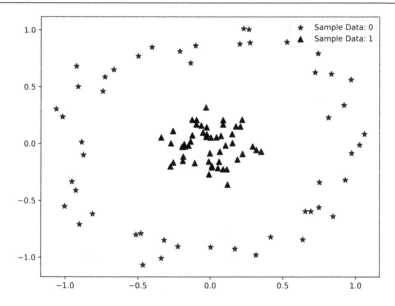

Figure 4.35 Circle Shaped Sample Data
Generated by source code at Support_Vector_Machine_Introduction.ipynb

What are Kernels

The SVM kernel is a function that takes the sample data and transforms it to a required form so that the data can be separated easier. In the case of non-linear kernel functions, usually the data is transformed to the higher dimensional space where the data can be separated.

In the example of Figure 4.35 above, the data is not possible to separate in the 2-dimensional space, a non-linear kernel function can transform the data into 3-dimensional space, from there the data can be separated.

In order to better understand non-linear kernel functions, recall section 3.3.8 of Multivariate Normal Distribution, and Figure 3.29 and Figure 3.30. Below Figure 4.36 is a duplication of Figure 3.29 for convenience of reference. The input data are x and y which are in 2-dimensional space, they are transformed by multivariate gaussian function into a 3-dimensional space, the result is in the vertical p axis. By looking at the 3-D view in Figure 4.36, the center part of x-y plane are transformed to higher p values, that part of data appear at the top of the 3-D view; the outer part of x-y plane are transformed to lower p values, then they appear at the lower part of the 3-D view.

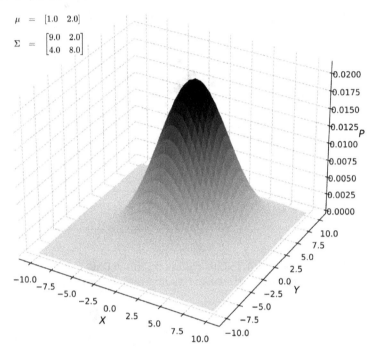

Figure 4.36 Duplicate of Figure 3.29

Now apply the multivariate gaussian function to the circle shaped dataset, the results of transformation are shown as Figure 4.37:

As expected, the ▲ data points which were in the center of the 2D plane are transformed to the top areas of Figure 4.37; while the ★ data points are in the lower part.

Now image a 2-D hyperplane is inserted between the ▲ and ★ data points in the 3-D space of Figure 4.37, they can be successfully separated. Same as the linear case, the hyperplane with the maximum margin, i.e., the maximum distance between data points of both classes is the *Decision Boundary*, and the data points that are closest to the decision boundary are *Support Vectors.*

If transform them back to the original 2-D space, the *Decision Boundary* and the *Support Vectors* are showing in Figure 4.38.

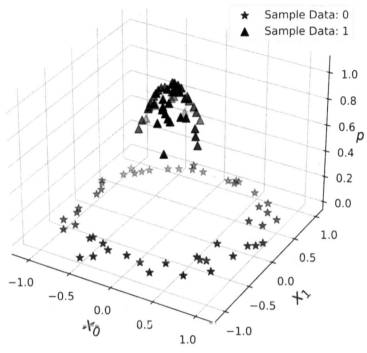

Figure 4.37 SMV - Non-linear Kernel Function

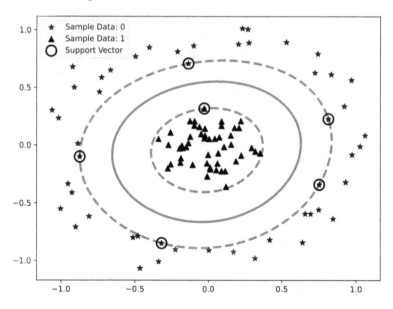

Figure 4.38 SVM - Decision Boundary of Non-linear Kernel
Generated by source code at Support_Vector_Machine_Introduction.ipynb

This time the *decision boundary* is not a line because the Gaussian kernel is a non-linear function. Same as the above linear case, any new data falling on either side of the *Decision Boundary* will be predicted as the corresponding classes. For example, a new data falling on the inner side of the decision boundary will be predicted as ▲; and if outer side then ★.

Implement SVM with `sklearn`

The `sklearn` package provides SVM functions, it's simple and easy to use:

```
1    from sklearn import svm
2    svm = svm.SVC(kernel='linear')
3    svm.fit(X, y)
```

The kernel needs to be specified when initializing the function. In line 2 `kernel='linear'` is specified, meaning linear kernel function will be used. It is explained in the above linear example.

To fit the model both `X` and `y` are sent to the `fit()` function, because this is supervised algorithms, unlike PCA and K-Means, the true label `y` is needed to train the model.

There are some other kernel functions supported by `sklearn` functions.

Gaussian Kernel Radial Basis Function (RBF) is a non-linear kernel function, it's explained in the above non-linear example. Normally this is used for the dataset without any prior knowledge. This is also the default of the function, if nothing specified `kernel='rbf'` is used.

```
1    from sklearn import svm
2    svm = svm.SVC(kernel='rbf', gamma='auto', C=1E6)
3    svm.fit(X, y)
```

Sigmoid Kernel is also a non-linear function, details can be found in section 3.3.2, it transforms the data into the range between 0 and 1.

```
1    from sklearn import svm
2    svm = svm.SVC(kernel='sigmoid')
3    svm.fit(X, y)
```

Polynomial Kernel is also a non-linear function, it is defined as:

$$K(x,y) = (x^T y + c)^d$$

where x and y are input data, d is the degree that specified in parameter.

```
1    from sklearn import svm
2    svm = svm.SVC(kernel='poly', degree=3)
3    svm.fit(X, y)
```

4.6.2 IRIS Dataset Classification

About IRIS Dataset

IRIS is another widely used dataset for machine learning purpose, it includes three Iris flower species -- Iris Versicolour, Iris Setosa and Iris Virginica. This dataset is about the measurements in centimeters of the sepal (length/width) and petal (length/width) of these three species.

To load the IRIS dataset,

```
1    from sklearn import datasets
2    iris = datasets.load_iris()
3    print ("Data structure:", dir(iris))
4    print ("Description:\n", iris.DESCR)
5    print ("Data (first 10):\n",iris.data[0:10])
6    print ("Label:\n", iris.target)
7    print ("Label Name:", iris.target_names)
8    print ("Unique Label:", np.unique(iris.target))
9    print ("Feature:", iris.feature_names)
```

Line 1 and 2 load the Iris dataset from `sklearn` package. There are several attributes come with the dataset that include some detailed information. You can optionally print them out as Line 3 to 9 above. The description of this dataset is in *iris.DESCR* attribute. The data is in *iris.data*; the label is encoded in *iris.target* with value of 0, 1 and 2, which corresponds to the three species. The names of the three species are in the *iris.target_names*. And the names of the features are in *iris.feature_names*.

IRIS isn't a big dataset, it includes the following four features and one label:

1. sepal length in cm (feature)
2. sepal width in cm (feature)

3. petal length in cm (feature)
4. petal width in cm (feature)
5. species (label)

It has totally 150 data points, 50 for each label, it looks something like below table,

Sepal.Length	Sepal.Width	Petal.Length	Petal.Width	Species
5.1	3.5	1.4	0.2	setosa
4.9	3	1.4	0.2	setosa
4.7	3.2	1.3	0.2	setosa
...	...	...	...	setosa
7	3.2	4.7	1.4	versicolor
6.4	3.2	4.5	1.5	versicolor
6.9	3.1	4.9	1.5	versicolor
...	...	...	...	versicolor
6.3	3.3	6	2.5	virginica
5.8	2.7	5.1	1.9	virginica
7.1	3	5.9	2.1	virginica
...	...	...	...	virginica

Figure 4.39 visualizes the Iris dataset, shown sepal and petal length vs width.

After the data is loaded, split it into training and testing sets, the training set is used to train the model and testing set is to evaluate the model.

```
11   from sklearn import model_selection
12   X_train, X_test, y_train, y_test = \
13   model_selection.train_test_split(iris.data,
14                                    iris.target,
15                                    train_size = .75,
16                                    random_state=0)
```

Then apply the SVM model on the train set, and use Gaussian Radial Basis Function (RBF) kernel:

```
17   from sklearn import svm
```

```
18   svm_iris = svm.SVC(kernel='rbf')
19   svm_iris.fit(X_train, y_train)
```

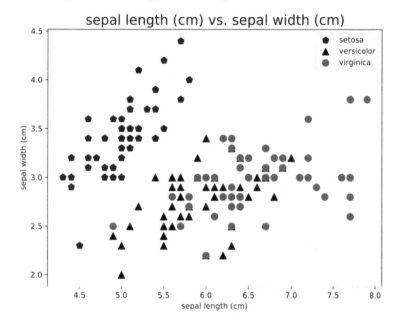

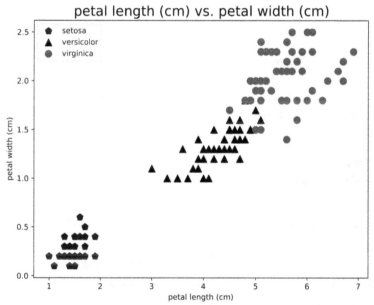

Figure 4.39 Iris Dataset

Generated by source code at Support_Vector_Machine_Introduction.ipynb

Make prediction and evaluate the results, print out the accuracy score, confusion matrix, classification report.

```
21    from sklearn import metrics
22    y_pred = svm_iris.predict(X_test)
23    a_score = accuracy_score(y_test, y_pred)
24    c_matrix = confusion_matrix(y_test, y_pred)
25    c_report = classification_report(y_test, y_pred)
26    print("Accuracy Score:\n", a_score)
27    print("Confusion matrix:\n", c_matrix)
28    print("Classification Report:\n", c_report)
```

```
Accuracy Score:
 0.9736842105263158

Confusion matrix:
 [[13  0  0]
  [ 0 15  1]
  [ 0  0  9]]
```

```
Classification Report:
               precision    recall  f1-score   support
           0        1.00      1.00      1.00        13
           1        1.00      0.94      0.97        16
           2        0.90      1.00      0.95         9
    accuracy                            0.97        38
   macro avg        0.97      0.98      0.97        38
weighted avg        0.98      0.97      0.97        38
```

See section 4.3.3 for the explanation of above results.

The source code is located at *Support_Vector_Machine_Introduction. ipynb*, you might want to play with the code, change the SVM kernels and compare the results for different kernels.

4.6.3 Recognize Handwritten Digits with SVM

This section will use SVM to recognize the hand-written digits dataset, see section 4.3.4 for the dataset, and the result was *0.9667* when used multinomial logistic regression.

Now let's try it with SVM, first load the data and split it to train and test sets:

```
1   from sklearn import datasets
2   from sklearn import model_selection
3   digits = datasets.load_digits()
4   X_train, X_test, y_train, y_test = \
5   model_selection.train_test_split(digits.data,
6                                    digits.target,
7                                    train_size = .75,
8                                    random_state=0)
```

Then apply the SVM model with RBF kernel,

```
9   svm_digits = svm.SVC(kernel='rbf')
10  svm_digits.fit(X_train, y_train)
11  y_pred = svm_digits.predict(X_test)
12  a_score = accuracy_score(y_test, y_pred)
13  c_matrix = confusion_matrix(y_test, y_pred)
14  c_report = classification_report(y_test, y_pred)
15  print("Accuracy Score:\n", a_score)
16  print("Confusion matrix:\n", c_matrix)
17  print("Classification Report:\n", c_report)
```

```
Accuracy Score:
 0.9911111111111112

Confusion matrix:
 [[37  0  0  0  0  0  0  0  0  0]
 [ 0 43  0  0  0  0  0  0  0  0]
 [ 0  0 44  0  0  0  0  0  0  0]
 [ 0  0  0 44  0  0  0  0  1  0]
 [ 0  0  0  0 38  0  0  0  0  0]
 [ 0  0  0  0  0 47  0  0  0  1]
 [ 0  0  0  0  0  0 52  0  0  0]
 [ 0  0  0  0  0  0  0 48  0  0]
 [ 0  1  0  0  0  0  0  0 47  0]
 [ 0  0  0  0  0  1  0  0  0 46]]
```

```
Classification Report:
            precision    recall  f1-score   support
         0       1.00      1.00      1.00        37
         1       0.98      1.00      0.99        43
         2       1.00      1.00      1.00        44
         3       1.00      0.98      0.99        45
```

4	1.00	1.00	1.00	38
5	0.98	0.98	0.98	48
6	1.00	1.00	1.00	52
7	1.00	1.00	1.00	48
8	0.98	0.98	0.98	48
9	0.98	0.98	0.98	47
accuracy			0.99	450
macro avg	0.99	0.99	0.99	450
weighted avg	0.99	0.99	0.99	450

The result looks a little better than the multinomial logistic regression. And again, feel free to play with the source codes and compare the results of different kernels.

4.6.4 Algorithm and Implementation of SVM

The objective of the SVM algorithm is to find a hyperplane that can 1.) distinctly classify the data, and 2.) have the maximum margin to each cluster of the data.

This section is focus on the simple case, linear kernel and binary classes, meaning there are only two classes.

Notations

m	Number of features
n	Number of data samples
X	Input data, or independent variables, in matrix of $n \times m$
y	target value, or dependent output variable, or true label, in matrix of $n \times 1$
$x^{(i)}, y^{(i)}$	i-th sample data and true label
$y_{pred}^{(i)}$	i-th predicted value
x_j	j-th feature, where $j \in [1, m]$
θ	Intercept and coefficient, the size is $m \times 1$.

Linear Kernel

As shown in Figure 4.40, there are two cluster of data: • and ▲ data points.

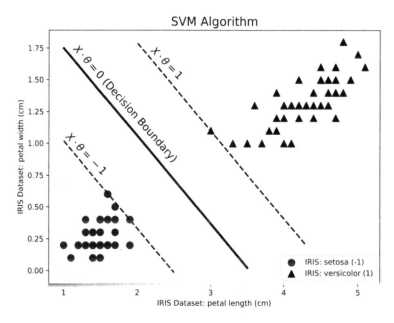

Figure 4.40 SVM Algorithm

Generated by source code at SVM_Algorithm_Implementation.ipynb

SVM is to find the hyperplane, or decision boundary of:

$$X \cdot \theta = 0$$

And the hyperplane has the maximum margin to the two separating hyperplanes:

$$X \cdot \theta = 1$$

and

$$X \cdot \theta = -1$$

where,

$$X = \begin{bmatrix} 1 & x_1 & x_2 & \cdots & x_m \end{bmatrix}$$

and

$$\theta = \begin{bmatrix} \theta_0 \\ \theta_1 \\ \theta_2 \\ \cdots \\ \theta_m \end{bmatrix}$$

Then:

$$X \cdot \theta = \theta_0 + \theta_1 x_1 + \theta_2 x_2 + \cdots + \theta_m x_m$$

In SVM algorithm the clusters are defined as either 1 or -1, unlike the classification problems introduced before which clusters are 0 and 1. Now the data points of cluster 1 are in the upper right side of separating hyperplanes $X \cdot \theta = 1$; the data points of cluster -1 are in the lower left side of $X \cdot \theta = -1$. So, all data points are outside of the two separating hyperplanes.

For any data point of $x^{(i)}$ and $y^{(i)}$, it satisfies the following equations:

$$x^{(i)}\theta \geq 1 \quad \text{if} \quad y^{(i)} = 1$$

$$x^{(i)}\theta \leq -1 \quad \text{if} \quad y^{(i)} = -1$$

The first equation represents the data points in the upper right side, i.e. ▲ data points in Figure 4.40; and the second equation represents ● data points.

The support vectors are those data points on the separating hyperplanes, they satisfy either:

$$x^{(i)}\theta = 1, \text{ or } x^{(i)}\theta = -1$$

Then merge the above two equations together:

$$y^{(i)}(x^{(i)}\theta) \geq 1$$

All data points should satisfy this equation. The goal of SVM algorithm is to find θ that satisfy the equation.

$X\theta$ is implemented as:

```
1   import numpy as np
2   def hypothesis(X, theta):
```

```
 3          return np.dot(X, theta)
```

The distance between the decision boundary and separating hyperplane, i.e. the solid line and the dashed line in Figure 4.40, is:

$$\frac{1}{\| \theta \|}$$

Where $\| \theta \|$ is the norm of θ, and recall from section 3.1.3, the norm of a vector is its magnitude or length, it can be calculated as:

$$\| \theta \|^2 = \theta_0^2 + \theta_1^2 + \cdots + \theta_m^2 = \theta^T \cdot \theta$$

Another goal of SVM algorithm is to maximize this distance, which means to minimize the $\| \theta \|$.

Hinge Loss Function

Hinge loss function is used for computing maximum margin or distance for the classification decision boundary. Even if a data point is classified correctly, it still could cause a penalty if the margin from the decision boundary is not large enough. It's mostly used for support vector machine (SVM).

Hinge loss is defined as:

$$l = \max(0, 1 - y(x \cdot \theta))$$

As discussed above, ideally all data points should satisfy $y(x \cdot \theta) \geqslant 1$, then the hinge loss is 0. By finding θ to minimize the hinge loss function we can correctly classify the data points.

Cost Function with Regularization

The hinge loss function will correctly classify the data by minimizing the loss. The SVM algorithm also needs to maximize the margin, which is to minimize the norm of θ, as discussed above. So a regularization factor needs to be added to the hinge loss.

Therefore, the cost function is:

$$J(\theta) = \frac{\lambda}{2} \sum_{j=1}^{m} \theta_j^2 + \frac{1}{n} \sum_{i=1}^{n} \max\left(0, 1 - y^{(i)}(x^{(i)}\theta)\right)$$

The first part of the cost function is the regularization factor, it is the norm of θ, by minimizing the cost function the norm of θ is also minimized, then the margin of decision boundary is maximized because the margin is 1 over the norm of θ.

The second part of the cost function is the hinge loss, it will correctly classify the data points as much as possible by minimizing the cost function.

λ is regularization parameter which is used to make adjustments between the two parts, its value is something like 0.001 or 0.0001, it is provided to the training or fitting process to adjust the balance between the hinge loss and the regularization factor. Sometimes the SVM algorithm uses C to represent this regularization parameter,

$$C = \frac{1}{\lambda}$$

In this case the value of C is a very large integer, something like 1000, or 10000 and so on. Here in this section, we keep using λ for this purpose.

For the data points that satisfy the below equation,

$$y^{(i)}(x^{(i)}\theta) \geq 1$$

meaning they already in the correct cluster, then the second part of the cost function is zero, therefore the cost function looks like:

$$J(\theta) = \frac{\lambda}{2}\sum_{j=1}^{m}\theta_j^2$$

For these data points, the cost function is only the regularization factor, which will contribute to maximizing the margin of decision boundary.

Otherwise, when $y^{(i)}(x^{(i)}\cdot\theta) < 1$, the hinge loss part of cost function is greater than zero, so both parts exist. To minimize the cost function contributes to both parts -- maximizing the margin as well as classifying the data correctly.

The cost function is implemented as:

```
1    import numpy as np
2    def cost(X, y, theta, lambda_):
```

```
3        sum_ = np.dot(np.transpose(theta), theta).item()
4        cost_ = 0.5 * lambda_ * sum_
5        cost_ += np.mean(np.maximum(0,
                         (1 - y * hypothesis(X, theta))))
6        return cost_
```

Gradient

Same as previous machine learning methods, the gradient descent will also be used to find the minimum value of the cost function.

The gradient is a vector of the same size as θ, each element is a partial derivative of θ_j where $j \in [1, m]$.

The conclusion is given here without mathematical proofs, please reference the materials #20 in References section for details. The gradient vector for SVM cost function is defined as below:

When:

$$y^{(i)}(r^{(i)}\theta) \geq 1$$

the gradient is:

$$\nabla J(\theta) = \begin{bmatrix} \dfrac{\partial}{\partial \theta_0} J(\theta) \\ \dfrac{\partial}{\partial \theta_1} J(\theta) \\ \dots \\ \dfrac{\partial}{\partial \theta_m} J(\theta) \end{bmatrix} = \begin{bmatrix} 0 \\ \lambda\theta_1 \\ \dots \\ \lambda\theta_m \end{bmatrix}$$

Otherwise:

$$\nabla J(\theta) = \begin{bmatrix} \dfrac{\partial}{\partial \theta_0} J(\theta) \\ \dfrac{\partial}{\partial \theta_1} J(\theta) \\ \dots \\ \dfrac{\partial}{\partial \theta_m} J(\theta) \end{bmatrix} = \begin{bmatrix} \displaystyle\sum_{i=1}^{n} y^{(i)} \\ \lambda\theta_1 - \displaystyle\sum_{i=1}^{n} y^{(i)} x_1^{(i)} \\ \dots \\ \lambda\theta_m - \displaystyle\sum_{i=1}^{n} y^{(i)} x_m^{(i)} \end{bmatrix}$$

The gradient descent rule is exactly same as previous machine learning algorithms:

$$\theta = \theta - \alpha \, \nabla J(\theta)$$

where α is the learning rate.

Implementation from Scratch

The full codes to implement SVM:

```
1  import numpy as np
2  class SVM:
3    def __init__(self, X , y):
4      self.y = np.where(y <= 0, -1, 1)
5      self.y = self.y.reshape(-1, 1)
6      self.X = X
7      self.X = np.hstack((np.ones((self.X.shape[0],1)), self.X))
8      self.n, self.m = self.X.shape
9      self.theta = np.zeros((self.m, 1))
10     self.cost_history = []
11     self.epoch_history = []
12   def hypothesis(self, X, theta):
13     return np.dot(X, theta)
14   def cost(self, lambda_):
15     cost_ = 0.5 * lambda_ * np.dot(np.transpose(self.theta),
16                             self.theta).item()
17     cost_ += np.mean(np.maximum(0, (1 - self.y *
18                       self.hypothesis(self.X, self.theta))))
19     return cost_
20   def fit(self, epochs=1000, alpha=0.001, lambda_=0.01):
21     for i in range(epochs):
22       condition = self.y * self.hypothesis(self.X, self.theta)
23       # condition < 1
24       idx = np.where(condition<1)[0]
25       temp = np.dot(np.transpose(self.X[idx,1:]), self.y[idx])
26       self.theta[1:] -= alpha * (lambda_ * self.theta[1:] - temp)
27       self.theta[0]  -= -alpha * np.sum(self.y[idx])
28       # condition >= 1
29       self.theta[1:] -= alpha*(lambda_ *
30                       self.theta[1:])*(self.n-len(idx))
```

```
31          self.epoch_history.append(i)
32          self.cost_history.append(self.cost(lambda_))
33    def predict(self, X):
34       X = np.hstack((np.ones((X.shape[0],1)), X))
35       pred = self.hypothesis(X, self.theta)
36       return np.where(pred <= 0, 0, 1)
```

Line 7 and line 34 are to add intercept to X, meaning add a feature of 1 to X, and there will be a θ_0 added to theta, this is exactly the same as what we did for linear and logistic regression methods.

The labels y of the dataset has two classes 0, and 1, they have to be changed to -1 and 1 for SVM algorithm. Line 4 is for this purpose. And line 36 is to do the opposite after doing the prediction.

Line 10, 11, 31 and 32 are used for collecting the costs during the fitting process in order to plot Figure 4.41.

Line 24 to 30 are the gradient descent process based on the condition of $y^{(i)}(x^{(i)} \cdot \theta') \geq 1$ or not.

Since lambda is a reserved keyword of Python, so lambda_ is used instead in the above codes, it refers to the regularization parameter λ discussed above. And alpha is the learning rate for gradient descent.

Iris dataset is used to test the above SVM class, as described in section 4.6.2, the Iris dataset has 4 features and 3 classes. To make it easy to visualize and explain, we take only two features and two classes.

```
41    import numpy as np
42    from sklearn import datasets
43    iris = datasets.load_iris()
44    X = iris.data
45    y = iris.target
46    idx = np.where(y<2)
47    X = X[idx]
48    y = y[idx]
49    X = X[:,2:4]
```

The Iris dataset has class 0, 1 and 2 in the label, line 46 is to select only 0 and 1 as binary class. Remember the algorithm introduced in this section is for binary-class only.

Line 47 and 48 are to select those x and y corresponding to class 0 and 1. Line 49 is to select features 3 and 4 only, which are petal length and petal width.

Now apply the dataset to SVM class, and print out the classification results,

```
51    from sklearn import metrics
52    svm = SVM(X, y)
53    svm.fit(epochs=1000, alpha=1e-3, lambda_=1e-4)
54    y_pred = svm.predict(X)
55    a_score = metrics.accuracy_score(y, y_pred)
56    c_matrix = metrics.confusion_matrix(y, y_pred)
57    c_report = metrics.classification_report(y, y_pred)
58    print("Accuracy Score:\n", a_score)
59    print("Confusion matrix:\n", c_matrix)
60    print("Classification Report:\n", c_report)
```

```
Accuracy Score:
 1.0

Confusion matrix:
 [[50  0]
 [ 0 50]]

Classification Report:
```

	precision	recall	f1-score	support
0	1.00	1.00	1.00	50
1	1.00	1.00	1.00	50
accuracy			1.00	100
macro avg	1.00	1.00	1.00	100
weighted avg	1.00	1.00	1.00	100

The result looks pretty good, and Figure 4.41 shows the cost history during the fitting process. The cost begins with a higher value and gradually converge to a minimum value.

Figure 4.40 at the beginning of this section is the result from the Iris dataset. The Decision Boundary $X \cdot \theta = 0$ in the middle separates the two classes of data: ● for -1 and ▲ for 1, at the same time keeps the maximum margin to the two separating hyperplanes, $X \cdot \theta = \pm 1$.

The data points on the two separating hyperplanes are support vectors, two ● and one ▲ are support vectors.

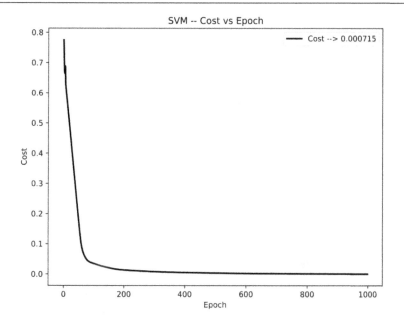

Figure 4.41 SVM -- Cost vs Epoch
Generated by source code at SVM_Algorithm_Implementation.ipynb

How to Plot the Three Hyperplanes in Figure 4.40?

The SVM algorithm has found out the best θ to classify the data and keep the maximum margin, then how to plot the hyperplanes, or lines in this case?

For the Decision Boundary, it satisfies the equation:

$$X \cdot \theta = 0$$

Because there are two features in this case, so:

$$\theta_0 + \theta_1 x_1 + \theta_2 x_2 = 0$$

Figure 4.40 is plotted in x_1-x_2 plane, so the above equation needs to be transformed to x_1-x_2 plane, then:

$$\theta_2 x_2 = -\theta_0 - \theta_1 x_1$$

$$x_2 = -\frac{\theta_0}{\theta_2} - \frac{\theta_1}{\theta_2} x_1$$

This is the decision boundary line in Figure 4.40 on x_1-x_2 plane, the following code is used to plot that line:

```
1    def decision_boundary(theta, x):
2        return -(theta[1]/theta[2])*x
3               -(theta[0]/theta[2])
```

Similarly for the separating hyperplane of $X \cdot \theta = 1$:

$$\theta_0 + \theta_1 x_1 + \theta_2 x_2 = 1$$

$$x_2 = \frac{1 - \theta_0}{\theta_2} - \frac{\theta_1}{\theta_2} x_1$$

and for hyperplane of $X \cdot \theta = -1$:

$$\theta_0 + \theta_1 x_1 + \theta_2 x_2 = -1$$

$$x_2 = -\frac{1 + \theta_0}{\theta_2} - \frac{\theta_1}{\theta_2} x_1$$

The below two functions will plot the two separating hyperplanes:

```
1    def separating_line1(theta, x):
2        return ((1-theta[0])/theta[2])
3               -(theta[1]/theta[2])*x
4    def separating_line2(theta, x):
5        return -((1+theta[0])/theta[2])
6               -(theta[1]/theta[2])*x
```

Reference the source code of *SVM_Algorithm_Implementation.ipynb* to see the details.

Apply to Other Datasets

The Iris dataset is simple and has small amount of data points. Now apply a couple of more dataset to the SVM class to see how it is doing.

Apply Breast Cancer dataset, see section 4.2.4, to the SVM class, the dataset has 30 features, 569 data points and 2 classes:

```
1    from sklearn import datasets
2    from sklearn import preprocessing
3    data = datasets.load_breast_cancer()
4    scaler = preprocessing.StandardScaler()
```

```
 5  X2 = scaler.fit_transform(data.data)
 6  X2_train, X2_test, y2_train, y2_test = \
 7  model_selection.train_test_split(X2,
 8                              data.target,
 9                              train_size = .75,
10                              random_state=0)
```

It's always a good practice to scale the data before applying to any machine learning algorithms. Line 4 is the standard scaler. Line 6 to 10 are to split the dataset into train and test sets.

Run SVM and print out the results,

```
11  from sklearn import metrics
12  svm2 = SVM(X2_train, y2_train)
13  svm2.fit(epochs=1000, alpha=0.001)
14  y2_pred = svm2.predict(X2_test)
15  a2_score = metrics.accuracy_score(y2_test, y2_pred)
16  c2_matrix = metrics.confusion_matrix(y2_test, y2_pred)
17  c2_report = metrics.classification_report(y2_test, y2_pred)
18  print("Accuracy Score:\n", a2_score)
19  print("Confusion matrix:\n", c2_matrix)
20  print("Classification Report:\n", c2_report)
```

```
Accuracy Score:
 0.9790209790209791

Confusion matrix:
 [[51  2]
  [ 1 89]]
```

Classification Report:

	precision	recall	f1-score	support
0	0.98	0.96	0.97	53
1	0.98	0.99	0.98	90
accuracy			0.98	143
macro avg	0.98	0.98	0.98	143
weighted avg	0.98	0.98	0.98	143

Compare this result with the one in section 4.2.4 when applying the sklearn logistic regression method, it's almost same, and actually a little bit better.

Then try the Handwritten Digits dataset, it has been used in section 4.3.4 and section 4.6.3. The dataset has 64 features, 1797 data points and 10 classes for 0, 1, 2 … 9. Remember the algorithm in this section is binary class only, so need to choose only two classes:

```
1  import numpy as np
2  from sklearn import datasets
3  from sklearn import preprocessing
4  digits = datasets.load_digits()
5  X3 = digits.data
6  y3 = digits.target
7  idx = np.where(y3<2)
8  X3 = X3[idx]
9  y3 = y3[idx]
10 X3_train, X3_test, y3_train, y3_test = \
11 model_selection.train_test_split(X3, y3,
12                                      train_size = .75,
13                                      random_state=0)
```

Line 7 is to choose only class 0 and 1; line 8 and 9 are to select X and y accordingly.

Line 10 to 13 are to split dataset to train and test sets.

```
21 from sklearn import metrics
22 svm3 = SVM(X3_train, y3_train)
23 svm3.fit(epochs=1000, alpha=0.001)
24 y3_pred = svm3.predict(X3_test)
25 a3_score = metrics.accuracy_score(y3_test, y3_pred)
26 c3_matrix = metrics.confusion_matrix(y3_test, y3_pred)
27 c3_report = metrics.classification_report(y3_test, y3_pred)
28 print("Accuracy Score:\n", a3_score)
29 print("Confusion matrix:\n", c3_matrix)
30 print("Classification Report:\n", c3_report)
```

```
Accuracy Score:
 1.0

Confusion matrix:
 [[51  0]
  [ 0 39]]

Classification Report:
               precision    recall  f1-score   support
```

0	1.00	1.00	1.00	51
1	1.00	1.00	1.00	39
accuracy			1.00	90
macro avg	1.00	1.00	1.00	90
weighted avg	1.00	1.00	1.00	90

The results look good, all data points in class 0 and 1 are correctly identified.

And again, it's recommended to use Python provided advanced machine learning libraries and packages in the real projects. The above codes are used for better understanding the algorithm only.

4.7 K-Nearest Neighbors

4.7.1 What is K-Nearest Neighbors

The K-Nearest Neighbors (KNN) is a supervised machine learning algorithm, as it relies on labeled input data to learn, and predicts an appropriate output when given new data. KNN is one of the simplest algorithms, and it's also one of the most used algorithms. It is widely used for resolving the classification problems, although it can also resolve regression problems.

KNN is a *lazy* and *non-parametric* algorithm. Lazy means the dataset is not needed when fitting or training the models, instead it's used at the prediction phase. It only stores the dataset in the fitting or training phase, it's lazy because it does almost nothing until last minute when making predictions. This, however, makes prediction slower than fitting or training.

The opposite of lazy is *eager* algorithm, like previous linear and logistic regression, K-Means, SVM etc., the training data is used to fit or train the model.

KNN is *non-parametric* algorithm means it does not make any assumption on the distribution of the dataset. In the case of *parametric* algorithm, like SVM in last section, it has to select appropriate kernel functions based on the distribution of the dataset, but it's not the case for KNN. This is sometimes helpful in the real-word projects where little knowledge about the datasets or the datasets do not follow any mathematical distributions.

Then how does KNN work? Take a look at the sample data in Figure 4.42, there are two classes of data, ▲ for 0 and ● for 1, suppose there is a new data point × in the middle, draw a circle with the new data point as the center and 5 data points included, as the inner dashed circle shown in Figure 4.42.

The 5 data points inside the inner dashed circle are nearest neighbors of the new data point. In this case $k = 5$, meaning the 5 nearest neighbors will decide the class of the new data.

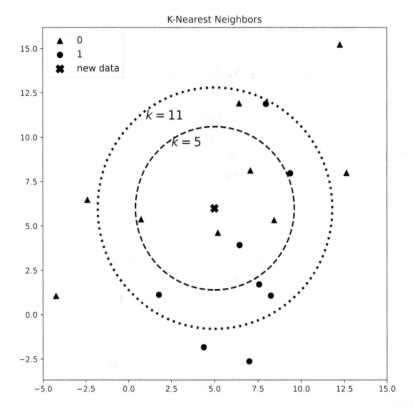

Figure 4.42 K-Nearest Neighbors

Generated by source code at K_Nearest_Neighbors_Introduction.ipynb

Then count how many ▲ and ● in the 5 nearest neighbors from Figure 4.42:

▲ (0): 4

● (1): 1

Since ▲ is more than ● in the 5 nearest neighbors, then the new data point is classified as ▲ (0).

If change k to 11, see the outer dotted circle in Figure 4.42 which includes 11 nearest neighbors. And count the number of each class:

▲ (0): 5

● (1): 6

This time ● is more than ▲, then the new data is classified as ● (1).

Therefore, k is the core factor for KNN, different value might cause different result. If KNN is applied to regression problem, then the new data point is the average of the k nearest neighbors.

In reality, KNN will not draw any circles, it calculates the distances from the new point to each existing point, then sort the distances from near to far, then take k data points with nearest distances and count the number in each class.

sklearn package has neighbors.KNeighborsClassifier for KNN, now apply the dataset of Figure 4.42 to it with $k = 5$,

```
1  from sklearn.neighbors import KNeighborsClassifier
2  k = 5
3  knn = KNeighborsClassifier(n_neighbors=k)
4  knn.fit(X, y)
5  predicted = knn.predict(new_point)
6  print("New data at", new_point[0],
7        "is classified as:", predicted.item())

   New data at [5. 6.] is classified as: 0
```

The result is same as above when counting the data points in the dashed circle in Figure 4.42. Then find out the details of the 5 nearest neighbors:

```
8   neighbors = knn.kneighbors(new_point)
9   print("Distances to the %d neighbors:\n"%k,
10          neighbors[0])
11  print("Data points of %d neighbors:\n"%k,
12          neighbors[1])
```

```
Distances to the 5 neighbors:
 [[1.3930841   2.53372304 2.96550126 3.50262377
   4.31519223]]

Data points of 5 neighbors:
 [[28 18 25 22   5]]
```

The `kneighbors()` function gives the distances from the new point to the *k* nearest neighbors, as well as the indexes of them.

Then try *k* = *11*,

```
1  k = 11
2  knn = KNeighborsClassifier(n_neighbors=k)
3  knn.fit(X, y)
4  predicted = knn.predict(new_point)
5  print("New data at", new_point[0],
6          "is classified as:", predicted.item())
```

```
New data at [5. 6.] is classified as: 1
```

This time the result is 1, as discussed earlier different *k* could cause different result. Later will discuss how to select *k*.

4.7.2 KNN on IRIS and Handwritten Digits Datasets

The IRIS and Handwritten datasets have been applied to several algorithms in previous sections, now apply them to KNN to compare these algorithms.

KNN on Iris Dataset

```
1  iris = datasets.load_iris()
2  X_train, X_test, y_train, y_test = \
3  model_selection.train_test_split(iris.data,
4                                    iris.target,
5                                    train_size = .75,
6                                    random_state=0)
7  k = 7
8  knn = KNeighborsClassifier(n_neighbors=k)
9  knn.fit(X_train, y_train)
10 y_pred = knn.predict(X_test)
```

```
11 a_score = metrics.accuracy_score(y_test, y_pred)
12 c_matrix = metrics.confusion_matrix(y_test, y_pred)
13 c_report = metrics.classification_report(y_test, y_pred)
14 print("Accuracy Score:\n", a_score)
15 print("Confusion matrix:\n", c_matrix)
16 print("Classification Report:\n", c_report)
```

```
Accuracy Score:
 0.9736842105263158

Confusion matrix:
 [[13  0  0]
  [ 0 15  1]
  [ 0  0  9]]
```

Classification Report:

	precision	recall	f1-score	support
0	1.00	1.00	1.00	13
1	1.00	0.94	0.97	16
2	0.90	1.00	0.95	9
accuracy			0.97	38
macro avg	0.97	0.98	0.97	38
weighted avg	0.98	0.97	0.97	38

KNN on Handwritten Digits Datasets

```
1 digits = datasets.load_digits()
2 X2_train, X2_test, y2_train, y2_test = \
3 model_selection.train_test_split(digits.data,
4                                  digits.target,
5                                  train_size = .75,
6                                  random_state=0)
7 k = 1
8 knn2 = KNeighborsClassifier(n_neighbors=k)
9 knn2.fit(X2_train, y2_train)
10 y2_pred = knn2.predict(X2_test)
11 a2_score = metrics.accuracy_score(y2_test, y2_pred)
12 c2_matrix = metrics.confusion_matrix(y2_test, y2_pred)
13 c2_report = metrics.classification_report(y2_test,y2_pred)
14 print("Accuracy Score:\n", a2_score)
15 print("Confusion matrix:\n", c2_matrix)
16 print("Classification Report:\n", c2_report)
```

```
Accuracy Score:
 0.9911111111111112
```

```
Confusion matrix:
[[37  0  0  0  0  0  0  0  0  0]
 [ 0 43  0  0  0  0  0  0  0  0]
 [ 0  0 43  1  0  0  0  0  0  0]
 [ 0  0  0 45  0  0  0  0  0  0]
 [ 0  0  0  0 38  0  0  0  0  0]
 [ 0  0  0  0  0 47  0  0  0  1]
 [ 0  0  0  0  0  0 52  0  0  0]
 [ 0  0  0  0  0  0  0 48  0  0]
 [ 0  0  0  0  0  0  0  0 48  0]
 [ 0  0  0  1  0  1  0  0  0 45]]
```

Classification Report:

	precision	recall	f1-score	support
0	1.00	1.00	1.00	37
1	1.00	1.00	1.00	43
2	1.00	0.98	0.99	44
3	0.96	1.00	0.98	45
4	1.00	1.00	1.00	38
5	0.98	0.98	0.98	48
6	1.00	1.00	1.00	52
7	1.00	1.00	1.00	48
8	1.00	1.00	1.00	48
9	0.98	0.96	0.97	47
accuracy			0.99	450
macro avg	0.99	0.99	0.99	450
weighted avg	0.99	0.99	0.99	450

4.7.3 How to Select k

Recall in section 4.4.2, in order to choose the best number of clusters for K-Means algorithm, Figure 4.25 in Page 175 is generated to show the sum of error vs number of clusters, and a best value is picked up from there.

KNN is similar, plot a figure showing the scores vs k, from there a best k can be selected. Choose k from 1 to a number say 50, create KNN models for each k, and make predictions. The score() function of sklearn's KNeighborsClassifier class will return a score for the prediction, then plot the curve of score vs k.

```
1   scores2 = []
2   max_k = 50
3   for k in range(1, max_k):
4       knn = KNeighborsClassifier(n_neighbors=k)
```

```
5     knn.fit(X2_train,y2_train)
6     score = knn.score(X2_test, y2_test)
7     scores2.append(score)
```

The prediction scores are stored in the `scores2` for the prediction with each k, the curve of score vs k is shown in Figure 4.43:

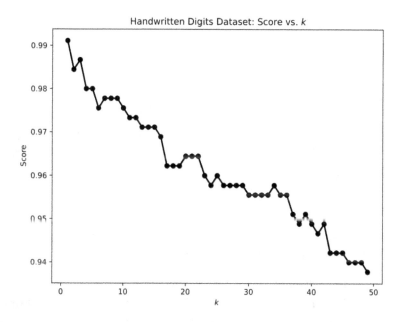

Figure 4.43 KNN: How to Select k

Generated by source code at K_Nearest_Neighbors_Introduction.ipynb

It looks $k = 1$ has the highest score for Handwritten Dataset, then we can use this value to re-generate the KNN model and predict for that dataset.

This is the technique to select best k. Similar plots can be generated for Iris and other datasets, and the best k can be selected from there.

4.7.4 Algorithm and Implementation of KNN

Notations

m	Number of features
n	Number of data samples

X	Input data, or independent variables, in matrix of $n \times m$
y	target value, or dependent output variable, or true label, in matrix of $n \times 1$
$x^{(i)}$, $y^{(i)}$	i-th sample data and true label
x_{new}	New data point to be predicted
y_{new}	Predicted label for x_{new}

Algorithm

There are five steps for KNN:

Step 1: Select a k as the number of nearest neighbors.

Step 2: Calculate the distances from the new data point x_{new} to each data $x^{(i)}$, where i from 1 to n. *Euclidean distance* function is used for calculating the distance, see section 4.4.3 for details. The calculated distance is an array of size n.

```
1   def _euclidean(a, b):
2       return np.sqrt(np.sum((a - b)**2, axis=1))
3   distances = _euclidean(X, x_new)
```

Step 3: Sort the calculated distances in ascending order and get top k items from the sorted distances. These items are the nearest neighbors. At this step the indices of the k nearest neighbors are obtained, the result is an array of size k.

```
4   kneighbors = np.argsort(distances)[:k]
```

Step 4: Get the labels of the k nearest neighbors.

```
5   labels = y[kneighbors]
```

Step 5: Assign the class of new data point y_{new} to the most items from the classes of the k nearest neighbors. For example, the labels or classes of the k nearest neighbors are $[0, 0, 1, 2, 2, 2, 2]$, then assign 2 to y_{new} because 2 is the most items. `scipy.stats.mode()` function will do the job, it picks up the most frequently occurred item from the list.

```
6   pred = scipy.stats.mode(labels)[0]
```

Implementation

Here is the full code of KNN class that implemented from scratch.

```
1    import numpy as np
2    from scipy import stats
3    class KNN:
4      def __init__(self, k):
5        #Step 1: select k
6        self.k = k
7      def _euclidean(self, a, b):
8        return np.sqrt(np.sum((a - b)**2, axis=1))
9      def fit(self, X, y):
10       self.X = X
11       self.y = y
12     def predict(self, X):
13       pred = []
14       for x in X:
15         #Step 2: calculate distances
16         distances = self._euclidean(self.X, x)
17         #Step 3: sort distances
18         kneighbors = np.argsort(distances)[:k]
19         #Step 4: get labels of k nearest neighbors
20         labels = self.y[kneighbors]
21         #Step 5: assign the most labels to new data
22         pred.append( stats.mode(labels)[0] )
23       return np.array(pred).reshape(-1, )
```

Then apply Iris and Handwritten Digit datasets and compare the results with section 4.7.2.

For Iris dataset:

```
1 from sklearn import model_selection
2 from sklearn import datasets
3 from sklearn import metrics
4 iris= datasets.load_iris()
5 X_train, X_test, y_train, y_test = \
6 model_selection.train_test_split(iris.data,
7                                  iris.target,
8                                  train_size = .75,
9                                  random_state=0)
10 k = 7
11 knn = KNN(k)
12 knn.fit(X_train, y_train)
13 y_pred = knn.predict(X_test)
```

```
14 a_score = metrics.accuracy_score(y_test, y_pred)
15 c_matrix = metrics.confusion_matrix(y_test, y_pred)
16 c_report = metrics.classification_report(y_test, y_pred)
17 print("Accuracy Score:\n", a_score)
18 print("Confusion matrix:\n", c_matrix)
19 print("Classification Report:\n", c_report)
```

```
Accuracy Score:
 0.9736842105263158

Confusion matrix:
 [[13  0  0]
  [ 0 15  1]
  [ 0  0  9]]

Classification Report:
              precision    recall  f1-score   support
           0       1.00      1.00      1.00        13
           1       1.00      0.94      0.97        16
           2       0.90      1.00      0.95         9
    accuracy                           0.97        38
   macro avg       0.97      0.98      0.97        38
weighted avg       0.98      0.97      0.97        38
```

For Handwritten dataset:

```
1  digits = datasets.load_digits()
2  X2_train, X2_test, y2_train, y2_test = \
3  model_selection.train_test_split(digits.data,
4                                   digits.target,
5                                   train_size = .75,
6                                   random_state=0)
7  k = 1
8  knn2 = KNN(k)
9  knn2.fit(X2_train, y2_train)
10 y2_pred = knn2.predict(X2_test)
11 a2_score = metrics.accuracy_score(y2_test, y2_pred)
12 c2_matrix = metrics.confusion_matrix(y2_test, y2_pred)
13 c2_report = metrics.classification_report(y2_test, y2_pred)
14 print("Accuracy Score:\n", a2_score)
15 print("Confusion matrix:\n", c2_matrix)
16 print("Classification Report:\n", c2_report)
```

```
Accuracy Score:
 0.9911111111111112
```

MACHINE LEARNING & DEEP LEARNING WITH PYTHON

```
Confusion matrix:
[[37  0  0  0  0  0  0  0  0  0]
 [ 0 43  0  0  0  0  0  0  0  0]
 [ 0  0 43  1  0  0  0  0  0  0]
 [ 0  0  0 45  0  0  0  0  0  0]
 [ 0  0  0  0 38  0  0  0  0  0]
 [ 0  0  0  0  0 47  0  0  0  1]
 [ 0  0  0  0  0  0 52  0  0  0]
 [ 0  0  0  0  0  0  0 48  0  0]
 [ 0  0  0  0  0  0  0  0 48  0]
 [ 0  0  0  1  0  1  0  0  0 45]]
```

Classification Report:

	precision	recall	f1-score	support
0	1.00	1.00	1.00	37
1	1.00	1.00	1.00	43
2	1.00	0.98	0.99	44
3	0.96	1.00	0.98	45
4	1.00	1.00	1.00	38
5	0.98	0.98	0.98	48
6	1.00	1.00	1.00	52
7	1.00	1.00	1.00	40
8	1.00	1.00	1.00	48
9	0.98	0.96	0.97	47
accuracy			0.99	450
macro avg	0.99	0.99	0.99	450
weighted avg	0.99	0.99	0.99	450

The results are almost same as those in section 4.7.2 where `sklearn's`
`KNeighborsClassifier` is used.

4.8 Anomaly Detection

Anomaly detection, also called outlier detection, is a process to identify
and understand the data points that diverge from the dataset's normal
behavior, usually those anomalous data do not belong to the dataset and
generated from the different mechanisms or activities. They might
indicate incidents such as a technical malfunction, unusual network
traffics, fraudulence in online transactions, suspicions credit card
activities, etc.; they might also indicate some potential opportunities, such
as a change in customer's consuming patterns.

In the past the anomaly detection was performed manually, today it's progressively performed automatically with the help of machine learnings. The anomaly detection often applies to unlabelled dataset, which is the unsupervised learning method. The anomaly detection will try to identify data points that are statistically different from the rest in the dataset.

While there are many types of anomaly detection algorithms, this section will focus on the univariate and multivariate Gaussian normal distributions, and the Gaussian mixture model.

4.8.1 Univariate Gaussian Normal Distributions

The univariate Gaussian normal distribution is described in section 3.3.7. It is defined as:

$$p(x; \mu, \sigma^2) = \frac{1}{\sigma\sqrt{2\pi}} e^{-\frac{(\mu - x)^2}{2\sigma^2}}$$

There is a single variable, or a single feature of the dataset:

$$x = [x^{(1)}, x^{(2)}, \dots, x^{(n)}]$$

μ is the mean of the dataset,

$$\mu = \frac{1}{n} \sum_{i=1}^{n} x^{(i)}$$

σ^2 is the variance of the dataset, while σ is the standard deviation,

$$\sigma^2 = \frac{1}{n} \sum_{i=1}^{n} \left(x^{(i)} - \mu\right)^2$$

The univariate Gaussian normal distribution is implemented in Python:

```
1   import numpy as np
2   def normal_distribution(x, mu, sigma):
3       c = 1 / ( sigma * (2 * np.pi)**0.5 )
4       e = ( (x-mu)/sigma )**2
5       return c * np.e**(-0.5 * e)
```

Then generate some normal distributed data with $\mu=1.0$ and $\sigma=1.0$,

```
6    mu = 1.0
7    sigma = 1.0
8    np.random.seed(0)
9    X = np.random.normal(mu, sigma, size=100)
```

The result is plotted as Figure 4.44.

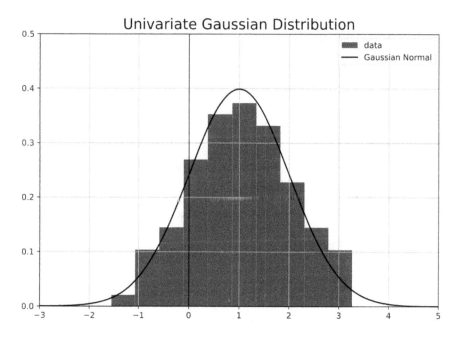

Figure 4.44 Univariate Gaussian Distribution
Generated by source code at Anomaly_Detection.ipynb

The curve is the univariate Gaussian distribution, those data points under the curve are considered normal data, if some data points are deviated from the curve, they are considered anomaly data, or outliers.

`scipy.states.norm` provides the same functionalities:

```
1    from scipy.stats import norm
2    y = norm.pdf(x, mu, sigma)
```

4.8.2 Multivariate Gaussian Normal Distribution

It's very rarely to have only single feature in real world, most often there are multiple features to describe a problem. Therefore, multivariate Gaussian distribution will be often applied for anomaly detection, which is described in detail at section 3.3.8.

To re-cap, it is defined as:

$$p(x; \mu, \Sigma) = \frac{1}{\sqrt{(2\pi)^n \, |\Sigma|}} exp\left(-\frac{1}{2}(x-\mu)^T \Sigma^{-1}(x-\mu)\right)$$

Where x is a matrix of $n \times m$,

$$x = \begin{bmatrix} x_{11} & x_{12} & \cdots & x_{1m} \\ x_{21} & x_{22} & \cdots & x_{2m} \\ \cdots & \cdots & \cdots & \cdots \\ x_{n1} & x_{n2} & \cdots & x_{nm} \end{bmatrix}$$

n is the number of data points, m is the number of features.

μ is the mean for each feature:

$$\mu_j = \frac{1}{n}\sum_{i=1}^{n} x_j^{(i)}$$

and σ^2 is the variance of the dataset:

$$\sigma_j^2 = \frac{1}{n}\sum_{i=1}^{n}(x_j^{(i)} - \mu_j)^2$$

where:

$$j \in [1, m]$$

Σ is the covariance matrix in the size of $m \times m$, see section 4.5.3. The variance σ_j^2 appear in the diagonal of Σ.

Anomaly Detection for 2-Dimensional Dataset

This section will start with 2-dimensional dataset and Gaussian normal distribution and see how the anomaly detection works. Section 3.3.8 has the mathematical derivation and Python implementation of 2-dimensional Gaussian normal distribution, here re-use the codes:

```
1    def normal_distribution_2d(x, y, mu, Sigma):
2        n = 2
3        sigma_det = np.linalg.det(Sigma)
4        c = 1.0 / ((2 * np.pi)**n * sigma_det)**0.5
5        sigma_inv = np.linalg.inv(Sigma)
6        e = ( ( x-mu[0] )**2 * sigma_inv[0,0] +
7              ( y-mu[1] )**2 * sigma_inv[1,1] +
8              ( x-mu[0] ) * ( y-mu[1] ) *
9              (sigma_inv[0,1] + sigma_inv[1,0])
10           )
11       return c * np.e ** (-0.5 * e)
```

Generate normal data in X_nor and y_nor:

```
12   from sklearn.datasets import make_blobs
13   X_nor, y_nor = make_blobs(n_samples=600,
14                             centers=1,
15                             cluster_std=0.4,
16                             random_state=2)
```

And generate anomaly data in X_abn and y_abn, combine them together into X and y:

```
17   np.random.seed(2)
18   X_abn=np.random.normal(np.mean(X_nor, axis=0),
19                          np.std(X_nor, axis=0)*4,
20                          size=[10, 2])
21   y_abn=np.ones(10)
22   X = np.concatenate((X_nor, X_abn))
23   y = np.concatenate((y_nor, y_abn))
```

The labels are in y, normal data has label of 0, anomaly data has label of 1. Since this is unsupervised learning, the labels are not needed for training and prediction. The labels are only used to measure the accuracy of the results.

Since this is a 2-dimensional dataset, it can be visualized as Figure 4.45.

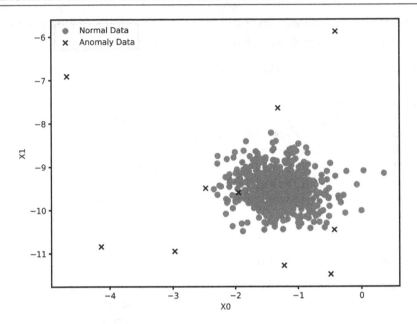

Figure 4.45 Dataset for Anomaly Detection
Generated by source code at Anomaly_Detection.ipynb

Define a function to find out the mean, variance and covariance matrix from the dataset based on the above formula:

```
24   def estimate_gaussian(X):
25       n, m = X.shape
26       mu = 1/n * np.sum(X,axis=0)
27       sigma_ = 1/n * np.sum((X - mu)**2, axis=0)
28       sigma = np.zeros((m, m))
29       np.fill_diagonal(sigma, sigma_)
30       return mu, sigma
```

This function returns the mean and covariance matrix.

Then, calculate the probabilities by 2-D Gaussian normal distribution function:

```
31   mu, sigma = estimate_gaussian(X)
32   p=normal_distribution_2d(X[:,0],X[:,1],mu,sigma)
33   p_nor = p[np.where(y==0)]
34   p_abn = p[np.where(y==1)]
```

Line 31 finds out the mean μ and the covariance matrix Σ, and line 32 calculates the probabilities.

Line 33 and 34 put the probabilities of normal data in `p_nor`, and probabilities of anomaly in `p_abn`.

The data with their probabilities can be visualized in a 3-D view, Figure 4.46.

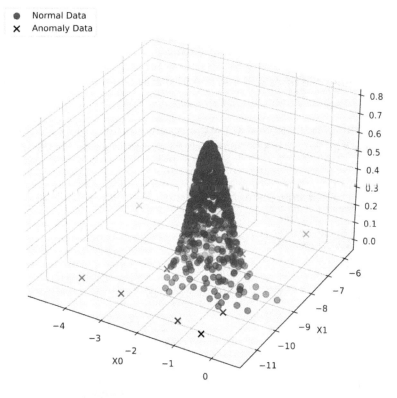

Figure 4.46 Data Applied to Gaussian Normal Distribution
Generated by source code at Anomaly_Detection.ipynb

From the above figure, the majority of normal data • are under the bell-shaped curve, while most of the anomaly data × are deviated from it.

This technique is similar to the Gaussian kernel of Support Vector Machine introduced in section 4.6.1, which was used to find out a decision boundary between different clusters. Here it's used to distinguish the normal data from the anomaly.

A threshold `epsilon` is defined, and the probabilities of the data is checked against the threshold. If the probability of a data point is less than the threshold then the data is considered as anomaly or outliers, and mark it with label of 1, otherwise normal data with label of 0.

```
35    from sklearn.metrics import f1_score
36    epsilon = 0.001
37    predict = (p < epsilon)
38    f1 = f1_score(y, predict, average='micro')
39    print("F1 score = ", f1)
```

```
F1 score =  0.9934426229508196
```

Line 36 defines the threshold and line 37 marks anomaly vs normal data based on the comparison of probabilities and threshold.

Line 38 evaluates the prediction with the measurement of $F1$ score, which is explained in section 4.3.3. The result $F1$ score is 0.99 and is shown in Figure 4.47.

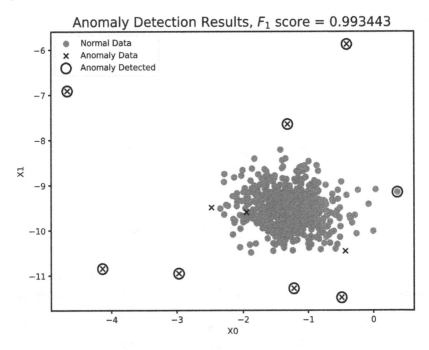

Figure 4.47 Anomaly Detection Results

Generated by source code at Anomaly_Detection.ipynb

There are three anomaly data × not detected which are considered as False Negatives (FN), because they are not deviated from the majority of normal data and located together with normal data, therefore they have the higher probability values and not able to be detected. There is one normal data • detected as anomaly at the right side of Figure 4.47 which is considered as False Positives (FP). That's because it appears to be deviated from the normal and has a lower probability value.

We can define a function to select a best threshold to achieve the best F1 score,

```
40   def select_threshold(yval, pval):
41      bestF1 = 0
42      bestEpsilon = 0
43      s = int(math.log(pval.min(), 10))
44      for exponent in range(s, -1):
45         epsilon = 10**exponent
46         pred = (pval < epsilon)
47         f1 = f1_score(yval, pred, average='micro')
48         if f1 >= bestF1:
49            bestF1 = f1
50            bestEpsilon = epsilon
51      return bestF1, bestEpsilon
52   f1, epsilon = select_threshold(y, p)
53   print("Best F1 score = ", f1)
54   print("Best anomaly threshold = ", epsilon)
```

The idea of above codes is to calculate the $F1$ score for different threshold and pick up the best score. The threshold starts from the minimum probability value in exponents of 10, say 10^{-8}, and calculate the $F1$ score; and then loops through 10^{-7}, 10^{-6}, 10^{-5}, ..., until 10^{-1}, calculate the $F1$ score for each, and finally picks up the best value.

The best score and its corresponding threshold are as below:

```
Best F1 score = 0.9934426229508196
Best anomaly threshold = 0.001
```

The full source code is at *Anomaly_Detection.ipynb*, you might want to play with it and observe how the $F1$ score is changing with different thresholds.

Anomaly Detection for Higher Dimensional Dataset

The above example is a 2-dimensional dataset, for higher dimensional datasets meaning more than 2 features, we will use Python provided functions to detect anomaly data. Python `scipy` package provides `scipy.stats.multivariate_normal` for calculating multivariate Gaussian normal distribution.

Similar as above, first create the dataset with multiple features with `features=8`,

```
1    import numpy as np
2    from sklearn.datasets import make_blobs
3    features = 8
4    X_nor,y_nor = make_blobs(n_samples=600,
5                             n_features=features,
6                             centers=1,
7                             cluster_std=0.4,
8                             random_state=2)
9    np.random.seed(2)
10   X_abn = np.random.normal(
11                   np.mean(X_nor, axis=0),
12                   np.std(X_nor, axis=0) * 2,
13                   size=[10, features])
14   y_abn = np.ones(10)
15   X = np.concatenate((X_nor, X_abn))
16   y = np.concatenate((y_nor, y_abn))
```

Line 4 to 8 generate normal data points with 8 features in `X_nor`, the labels in `y_nor` are all 0; line 9 to 13 generate anomaly data with 8 features in `X_abn`, and line 14 set labels of 1 for them in `y_abn`. Line 15 and 16 combine normal and anomaly data into `X` and `y`.

Then apply the data to the multivariate Gaussian function, and specify a threshold to make predictions,

```
17   mu, sigma = estimate_gaussian(X)
18   p = multivariate_normal.pdf(X, mu, sigma)
19   epsilon = 1e-04
20   predict = (p < epsilon)
21   f1 = f1_score(y, predict, average='micro')
22   print("F1 score", f1)
```

```
F1 score 0.9770491803278688
```

Line 17 is to obtain the mean μ and the covariance matrix Σ of the dataset, and line 18 invokes `scipy`'s function to calculate the probabilities of the dataset based on μ and Σ retrieved from line 17.

Line 19 specifies a threshold `epsilon` and line 20 make the prediction based on the probabilities and the threshold.

Line 21 and 22 calculates the $F1$ score and print out the result.

Finally, similar to above example, `select_threshold()` function can be used to find out the best F1 score with the corresponding threshold,

```
23   f1, epsilon = select_threshold(y, p)
24   print("Best F1 score = ", f1)
25   print("Best anomaly threshold = ", epsilon)
```

```
Best F1 score = 0.9950819672131147
Best anomaly threshold = 1e-06
```

And again, you might want to play with the codes at *Anomaly_Detection.ipynb* and observe how the $F1$ score is changing with different thresholds.

4.8.3 Gaussian Mixture

Gaussian Mixture is an unsupervised learning method for solving classification problems, similar to K-Means in section 4.4. It uses probabilistic model to represent a mixture of multiple Gaussian distributions.

As shown in Figure 4.48, the data is distributed in several clusters, which is considered as multiple Gaussian distributions with different parameters. This method is to identify the clusters by analyzing the probabilities of the data with Gaussian normal distribution formula.

Gaussian mixture is usually used for analysis of the problems like subpopulations within an overall population, for example a specific economy indicator for different countries in the world, the indicator follows Gaussian normal distribution for each country, but different from country to country.

Figure 4.48 is the sample data with three clusters of normal data and some anomaly data scattered around, the three clusters of data follow the Gaussian normal distribution.

Please note, K-Means in section 4.4 can be used to identify the clusters of the data, but not the anomaly data. Here Gaussian mixture can calculate the probabilities of the data, then the anomaly data can be identified by comparing the probabilities with a threshold. Although Gaussian mixture can also predict the clusters, it's not the focus of this section.

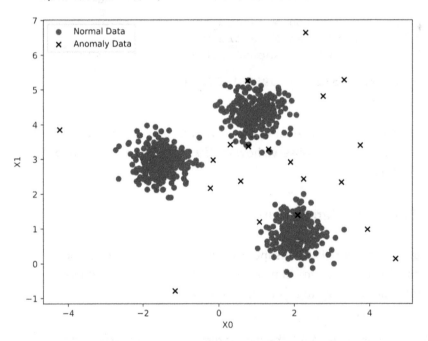

Figure 4.48 Anomaly Detection with Gaussian Mixture
Generated by source code at Anomaly_Detection.ipynb

The below code snippets generate the data in Figure 4.48.

```
1    import numpy as np
2    from sklearn.datasets import make_blobs
3    X_nor, y_nor = make_blobs(n_samples=800,
4                              centers=3,
5                              cluster_std=0.4,
```

```
6                                    random_state=0)
7    y_nor[:] = 0
8    np.random.seed(0)
9    X_abn = np.random.normal(np.mean(X_nor,axis=0),
10                       np.std(X_nor, axis=0) * 1.2,
11                       size=[20, 2])
12   y_abn = np.ones(20)
13   X = np.concatenate((X_nor, X_abn))
14   y = np.concatenate((y_nor, y_abn))
```

Line 3 to 6 generate data in three clusters, line 7 sets the label to 0 for all the three clusters. The labels generated are [0, 1, 2] for the three clusters, but here we only focus on identifying the anomaly data, so set them all to 0 to indicate normal data.

Line 9 to 11 generate 20 anomaly data, and line 12 set the label to 1 for them. Line 13 and 14 merge the normal and anomaly data.

Then apply to Gaussian mixture:

```
15   from sklearn.mixture import GaussianMixture
16   gm = GaussianMixture(n_components=3,
17                          random_state=42)
18   gm.fit(X)
19   p = gm.score_samples(X)
20   threshold = np.percentile(p, 2.5)
21   print("Threshold:", threshold)
```

Line 15 imports the GaussianMixture from sklearn.

Line 16 creates a GaussianMixture model, line 18 fits the model with the data, which includes both normal and anomaly data.

Line 19 is to calculate the log-likelihood of each data point, it's kind of the probabilities but not exactly. It is the natural logarithm of the likelihood of each data, which can be used almost same as probabilities in terms of identifying the anomaly.

Line 20 is to specify a threshold from the log-likelihood of the data, here use percentile to pick up one. Percentile in statistics means to choose a value from a dataset so that the number less than that value is the percentage given. For example, np.percentile(p, 2.5) means to pick a value from p so that the number of values < p has 2.5% in p.

Line 21 print out the threshold value.

```
Threshold: -4.949169107412425
```

It means there are 2.5% values in `p` less than `-4.949`.

Changing this percentile will affect the accuracy to identify the anomaly.

```
22    predict = (p < threshold)
23    X_pred = X[np.where(predict == 1)]
```

The prediction can be made by comparing the log-likelihood `p` with the threshold. Figure 4.49 is the result:

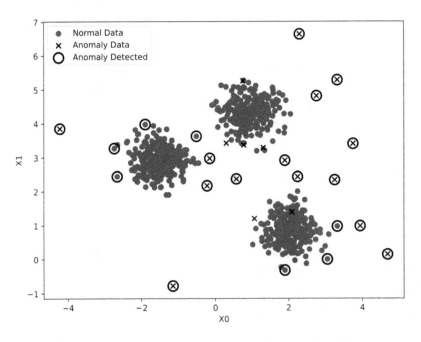

Figure 4.49 Results of Anomaly Detection by Gaussian Mixture
Generated by source code at Anomaly_Detection.ipynb

Since percentile is used to identify them, the number of anomaly data detected is the 2.5% of total data, they are the lowest log-likelihood values in the dataset. Most of anomaly data are identified in Figure 4.49, however there are some false negatives as some × data are not identified because they are inside the clusters of normal data; there are also some false positives as some • data are marked as anomaly because they are located at the edge of the cluster.

Similar to above sections, *F1* score can be calculated based on the predicted values and the true labels,

```
24   from sklearn.metrics import f1_score
25   f1 = f1_score(y, predict, average='micro')
26   print("F1 score", f1)
```

```
F1 score 0.9841463414634146
```

And similarly, create a function to calculate the best F1 score and the best percentage. Loop through the percentage from `0.0, 0.5, 1.0, 1.5` to `10.0`, retrieve the threshold for each percentage and make prediction, then calculate *F1* score and find the maximum one:

```
27   def select_threshold(yval, pval):
28     bestF1 = 0
29     bestPercentage = 0
30     for percentage in range(0, 101, 5):
31       threshold = np.percentile(pval,
32                                 percentage/10)
33       pred = (pval < threshold)
34       f1 = f1_score(yval, pred, average='micro')
35       if f1 >= bestF1:
36         bestF1 = f1
37         bestPercentage = percentage/10
38     return bestF1, bestPercentage
39   f1, percentage = select_threshold(y, p)
40   print("Best F1 score = ", f1)
41   print("Best Percentage = ", percentage)
```

```
Best F1 score = 0.9914634146341463
Best Percentage = 1.5
```

It means if choose percentile of `1.5`, the best result will be achieved at `0.99`.

The full source code is at *Anomaly_Detection.ipynb*.

4.9 Artificial Neural Network (ANN)

4.9.1 What is an Artificial Neural Network (ANN)?

ANN is one of the deep learning algorithms, which tries to learn things in the same or similar way of human. The "neural" tries to mimic the function of neurons of a biological brain. A neuron in human brain looks like Figure 4.50. It has three main parts, *Dendrites, Cell body* and *Axon terminals.*

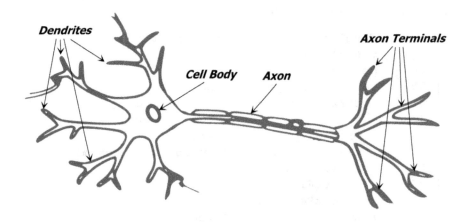

Figure 4.50 Neurons of Human Brain
From https://pixabay.com/vectors/brain-neuron-nerves-cell-science-2022398/

The signals are received by *Dendrites* as inputs by connecting with Axon Terminals of other neurons, and processed in the *Cell body*, and then sent down the *Axon* to the terminals. The *Axon Terminals* are the outputs of the processed signals and connect to the *Dendrites* of other neurons.

There are billions of neurons in human brain becoming neural networks to perform a variety of functions. The artificial neurons mimic the human neurons with simplified mathematical models.

An *artificial neuron* looks like Figure 4.51, the inputs could come from original data or from the output of other neurons. There is an activation function in the center of the neuron where the mathematical calculation is performed on the input data. The results are sent out as output(s), which could be inputs to other artificial neurons. In most of cases the neuron has one output, but it could be more outputs depends on the activation functions.

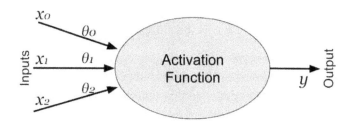

Figure 4.51 Artificial Neuron

The activation functions are mostly from those introduced in section 3.3, such as Identity function, Sigmoid function, Tanh function, ReLU and Leaky ReLU function, Softmax function and so on. In general, for regression problems ReLU or Leaky ReLU are often used, and for classification problems Sigmoid or Softmax are mostly used.

Many *artificial neurons* are joint together to form an *Artificial Neural Network (ANN),* which is used for resolving complicated patterns. Figure 4.52 shows a very simple *Artificial Neural Network*, each artificial neuron is called a node in the network.

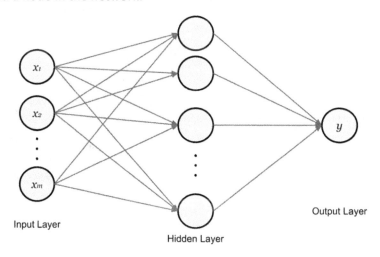

Figure 4.52 Artificial Neural Network (ANN)

There is an *Input Layer* in the left side, which corresponds to the input data, suppose the dataset has m features, there will be m nodes in the input layer, each corresponding to one feature.

There is a *Hidden Layer* in the middle of ANN, which takes the output of *Input Layer* as input and performs the computation.

Right side is an *Output Layer*, it takes the output of Hidden Layer as the input, and generates the result as the output of ANN. In Figure 4.52 there is only one node in the Output Layer, it could have multiple nodes depends on the dimensions of the output data. For example, the handwritten digit dataset has 10 classes in output, then the Output Layer will have 10 nodes, each corresponding to one class. Normally if the dataset has k classes, the Output Layer has k nodes.

An *Artificial Neural Network (ANN)* always has an *Input Layer* and an *Output Layer*, there could be multiple *Hidden Layers* depends on the needs, it's called Multi-Layer Perceptron (MLP) if there are multiple Hidden Layers, as Figure 4.53.

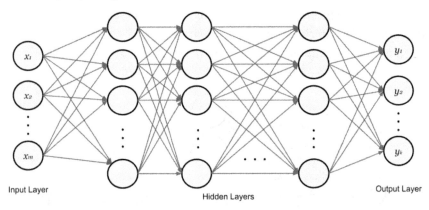

Figure 4.53 Multi-Layer Perceptron (MLP)

There could also be no *Hidden Layer* in which case the *Input Layer* directly connects to the *Output Layer*.

In general, the *Input Layer* should take the raw input data, so the number of nodes of the *Input Layer* should be same as the dimension of input data; the *Output Layer* is the one that make the final predictions, so the number of nodes in the *Output Layer* should be same as the dimension of output data; the number of layers and nodes of *Hidden Layers* depends on the needs, it doesn't mean the more the better, normally it is decided based on the evaluation of the accuracy, a trial and error process is often needed to decide how many hidden layers and how many nodes in each hidden layer. More *Hidden Layers* require more computation costs.

4.9.2 Build an ANN with Tensorflow/Keras

So far, we have used `sklearn` library for previous machine learning algorithms, this section will introduce another open-source and powerful library called *Tensorflow*. Developed by Google, it provides lots of functionalities to perform machine learning, deep learning and other data statistical analysis projects. TensorFlow can run on either CPUs or GPUs, as well as TPUs which are Google's processing units expressly designed to optimize TensorFlow jobs.

Google Colab, as recommended earlier this book in section 2.2, is an ideal environment running Tensorflow projects, as it supports CPUs, GPUs and TPUs which can be configured in the runtime type settings, although the free plan has some limitations.

Another powerful deep learning library is *Keras*, it's also an open-source package for Python and running on the top of Tensorflow, it's can be considered as an interface for Tensorflow.

Keras covers every step of building the ANN models.

Install Tensorflow and Keras Libraries

If Tensorflow and Keras are not installed in the environments, the following command will install them, type the commands in a cell of Google Colab:

```
1   pip install tensorflow
```

Both libraries and their dependencies are installed.

If they are already installed, the following command will update them:

```
2   pip install -U tensorflow
```

The following command will show the information of the libraries:

```
3   pip show tensorflow
```

The output should be something like below:

```
Name: tensorflow
Version: 2.10.0
Summary: TensorFlow is an open source machine learning
framework for everyone.
Home-page: https://www.tensorflow.org/
Author: Google Inc.
Author-email: packages@tensorflow.org
License: Apache 2.0
Location: /usr/local/lib/python3.7/dist-packages
Requires: termcolor, tensorflow-estimator, keras-
preprocessing, astunparse, tensorflow-io-gcs-
filesystem, tensorboard, six, protobuf, flatbuffers,
typing-extensions, h5py, absl-py, google-pasta,
grpcio, libclang, keras, setuptools, gast, opt-einsum,
numpy, packaging, wrapt
Required-by: kapre
```

In order to use them to build an ANN, import the necessary libraries as following:

```
1   from tensorflow import keras
2   from tensorflow.keras import layers
3   from tensorflow.keras.models import Sequential
4   from tensorflow.keras.layers import Dense
```

Sequential Model

`keras` defines models in a sequence of layers. First, create a Sequential model, it tells Keras to create model sequentially, it will make the output of a layer as the input to the next layer:

```
5   model = Sequential()
```

Second, need to make sure the correct number of nodes in input layer is specified. As explained earlier the input layer should have the same nodes as the features of the dataset. In Keras sequential mode there is no explicit input layer, instead the number of input features is specified in the parameter of the hidden layer,

```
6    model.add(Dense(8, input_shape=(4,),
7                        activation='sigmoid'))
```

`model.add()` function is to add a layer to the neural network, `Dense()` is to specify a fully connected layer. The above line 6 and 7 is to add a hidden layer, the first parameter is the number of nodes. The size of input data is specified in `input_shape` parameter, here `input_shape=(4,)` means the input layer has 4 nodes which corresponding to 4 features in the dataset. Keras does not explicitly have an Input layer.

As explained earlier each neuron has an activation function, see Figure 4.51, in line 7 above `activation='sigmoid'` is specified meaning sigmoid function is used for all nodes in this layer, see 3.3.2 for sigmoid function.

More hidden layers can be added in the same way, but don't need to specify `input_shape` any more, because it is fully connected with previous layer which nodes are already specified.

Now add output layer,

```
8    model.add(Dense(3, activation='softmax'))
```

It is the output layer because there are no more layers added thereafter, the nodes specified is 3, meaning there are 3 output variables, and the activation function is `softmax`, see 3.3.9. This layer means typically the output is a classification of 3 classes.

Now we have built an ANN with three layers, an implicit input layer with 4 nodes, one hidden layer with 8 nodes and one output layer with 3 nodes.

A model needs to be compiled after it is built, in order to compile, an optimizer, a loss function and a metrics have to be selected.

Optimizer

An optimizer tells the model what algorithm will be used to train the model, remember we have introduced gradient descent in previous machine learning methods, Tensorflow also support it, and comes with more algorithms. At the time of this writing, Tensorflow has eight optimizer classes and one base class:

Optimizer	Base class for Keras optimizers.
Adadelta	Optimizer that implements the Adadelta algorithm.
Adagrad	Optimizer that implements the Adagrad algorithm.
Adam	Optimizer that implements the Adam algorithm.
Adamax	Optimizer that implements the Adamax algorithm.
Ftrl	Optimizer that implements the FTRL algorithm.
Nadam	Optimizer that implements the NAdam algorithm.
RMSprop	Optimizer that implements the RMSprop algorithm.
SGD	Gradient descent (with momentum) optimizer.

Most of the above optimizers are implementing gradient descent with different algorithms, normally a learning rate should be provided as parameter when using them. Reference https://www.tensorflow.org/api_docs/python/tf/keras/optimizers for details.

Here use `Adam` optimizer with a `learning_rate`:

```
9  Opt_ = keras.optimizers.Adam(learning_rate=0.01)
```

Loss Function

The loss function, also called cost function, is essential to the gradient descent algorithms, the purpose of loss functions is to calculate θ (intercept and coefficient) by finding the minimum value of the loss functions. We have described many loss functions for different machine learning algorithms in previous sections, such as *Mean squared error* for linear regression, *Cross entropy* for logistic regression and *Hinge loss* for SVM, etc.

A loss function needs to be specified for the neural network as well. Keras provides Losses class that covers many types of loss functions, there are three categories of loss functions:

- Probabilistic losses include `BinaryCrossEntropy`, `CategoricalCrossentropy` and so on.
- Regression losses include `MeanSquaredError` and so on.
- Hinge losses include `Hinge`, `CategoricalHinge`, and so on.

Reference https://keras.io/api/losses/ for details.

Here use `CategoricalCrossentropy` as the loss function:

```
10   loss_ = keras.losses.CategoricalCrossentropy()
```

Metrics

Optionally, the neural network needs to specify a metric, which is a function that is used to judge the performance when training the model. The metrics are evaluated and recorded after each epoch on the training dataset, they are available in history object after training process, and optionally they can be displayed in verbose output during the training process.

Keras provides metrics classes in the following categories:

- Accuracy, includes `Accuracy`, `CategoricalAccuracy` classes and so on.
- Probabilistic, includes `BinaryCrossentropy`, `Categorical Crossentropy` classes and so on.
- Regression, includes `MeanSquaredError`, `MeanAbsoluteError` classes and so on.
- Classification, includes `Precision`, `Recall` classes and so on.
- Hinge, includes `Hinge`, `SquaredHinge` classes and so on

Reference https://keras.io/api/metrics/ for details.

Here use `Accuracy` as the metrics:

```
11   metrics_ = keras.metrics.Accuracy()
```

Compile the Model

`compile()` function is used to compile the model, the optimizer, loss function and metrics are specified.

```
9    opt_ = keras.optimizers.Adam(learning_rate=0.01)
10   loss_ = keras.losses.CategoricalCrossentropy()
11   metrics_ = keras.metrics.Accuracy()
12   model.compile(optimizer=opt_,
13                 loss=loss_,
14                 metrics=metrics_)
15   print(model.summary())
```

Line 9 to 11 define the optimizer, loss function and metrics. Line 12 compile the model with these parameters. Line 15 print out the summary of the model, which displays an overview of the model, it looks something like below:

```
Model: <model name>
```

Layer (type)	Output Shape	Param #
Hidden (Dense)	(None, 8)	40
Output (Dense)	(None, 3)	27

```
Total params: 67
Trainable params: 67
Non-trainable params: 0
```

Train the model and make predictions

After the model is built and compiled, it is trained with datasets by calling the `fit()` function,

```
16   model.fit(X_train,y_train,verbose=2,epochs=200)
```

`verbose` specify verbosity mode, if set to 2, it will output the result for each epoch, it evaluates the results on each epoch based on the loss function and metrics specified. The output is something like,

```
Epoch 190/200
4/4 [==============================] - 0s 13ms/step -
loss: 0.0567 - accuracy: 0.0000e+00
```

If set `verbose=0`, it is silent mode, nothing will be displayed during training process.

The `.fit()` function returns a History object, which contains the history of loss and metrics during the training process. The history can be used to visualize the convergence of the losses and metrics.

The `.predict()` function is to make predictions,

```
17   y_pred = model.predict(X_test)
```

The model also provides `evaluate()` function to obtain the final cost and metrics from the model,

```
18    results = model.evaluate(X_test, y_test)
```

`results[0]` has the final cost, and `results[1]` has the metrics, the output is something like:

```
Final loss: 0.104847
Final accuracy: 0.973684
```

Build an ANN model for IRIS Dataset

As explained in section 4.6.2, the IRIS dataset has 4 features, 3 clusters and total 150 data points.

Load the IRIS dataset and split it to train and test sets:

```
1    from sklearn import datasets
2    from sklearn import model_selection
3    iris = datasets.load_iris()
4    X = iris.data
5    y = iris.target
6    X_train, X_test, y_train, y_test = \
7    model_selection.train_test_split(
8                        X,
9                        y,
10                       train_size = .75,
11                       random_state=0)
```

In order to build an ANN model, it's necessary to decide the architecture of the neural network. Since the dataset has 4 features, the input layer must be specified as 4 nodes. The dataset has three clusters, so the output layer must have 3 nodes.

There are no restrictions on the hidden layer, it can be decided based on trial-and-error process considering the accuracy and computation cost. Here choose 8 nodes for hidden layer. The architecture is shown as Figure 4.54.

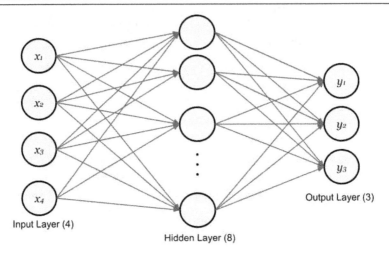

Figure 4.54 ANN model for IRIS Dataset

Below is the code to build the ANN model and compile it,

```
12   from tensorflow import keras
13   from tensorflow.keras import layers
14   from tensorflow.keras.models import Sequential
15   from tensorflow.keras.layers import Dense
16   # Build the ANN model
17   model = Sequential(name="ANN_Iris_Dataset")
18   model.add(Dense(8, input_shape=(4,),
19            activation='sigmoid',
20            name='Hidden'))
21   model.add(Dense(3,
22            activation='softmax',
23            name='Output'))
24   # Define Optimizer, Loss function and Metrics,
25   # and compile the model
26   opt_=keras.optimizers.Adam(learning_rate=0.01)
27   loss_=keras.losses.CategoricalCrossentropy()
28   metrics_=keras.metrics.CategoricalAccuracy()
29   model.compile(optimizer=opt_,
30                 loss=loss_,
31                 metrics=metrics_)
32   print(model.summary())
```

As explained earlier, Keras sequential mode does not explicitly specify input layer, in Line 18 `input_shape=(4,)` specifies the input layer, at the same time it also specifies the hidden layer in the `Dense(8, …)` function, there are 8 nodes in this layer. Line 21 specifies the output layer.

Then line 26, 27 and 28 specify the optimizer, loss function and metrics for the model.

Line 29 compile the model, and line 32 print out the summary of the model, the output is something like below:

```
Model: "ANN_Iris_Dataset"
 Layer (type)      Output Shape              Param #
=====================================================
 Hidden (Dense)    (None, 8)                   40
 Output (Dense)    (None, 3)                   27
=====================================================
Total params: 67
Trainable params: 67
Non-trainable params: 0
```

Before training the model, a pre-processing on the dataset is needed. The labels of the dataset in y_train and y_test look like:

```
[2, 1, 0, 2, 0, 2, 0, 1, 1, 1, 2, …]
```

0, 1 and 2 represent the three clusters. The One-Hot Encoding should be performed before passing the data to the ANN model for training, see section 4.3.2. To recap, One-Hot Encoding will convert 0,1 and 2 to:

```
2 => [0, 0, 1]
1 => [0, 1, 0]
0 => [1, 0, 0]
```

This means each cluster will be represented by three numbers of either 0 or 1. The function `to_categorical(y_test))` can simply achieve this. These three numbers will correspond to the three nodes in output layer of the ANN model, and each node will output either 0 or 1. So in line 22 in above codes `softmax` is used as the activation function for output layer. `softmax` can ensure each output is between 0 and 1.

Below is the code to train and evaluate the model,

```
33   history = model.fit(X_train,
34                        to_categorical(y_train),
35                        verbose0,
```

```
36                          epochs=300)
37   results = model.evaluate(X_test,
38                          to_categorical(y_test))
39   print('Final loss:', results[0])
40   print('Final accuracy:', results[1])
```

```
Final loss:  0.095383
Final accuracy:  0.973684
```

As mentioned earlier, the `history` object returned from `.fit()` function contains the history of loss and accuracy during the training process, it can by used to visualize the results, as shown in Figure 4.55.

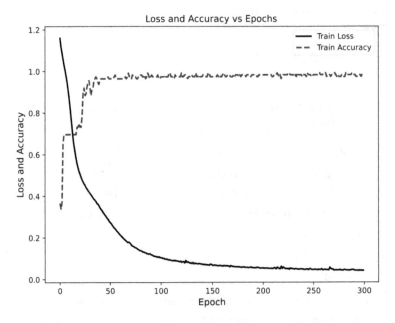

Figure 4.55 Loss and Accuracy vs Epochs
Generated by source code at Artificial_Neural_Network_Introduction.ipynb

The loss starts from 1.4 and converges to around 0.1 as epoch approaches to 300, at the same time the accuracy is approaching to 1.0.

4.9.3 Classification: ANN on MNIST Handwritten Dataset

We have used Hand-written Digits dataset from `sklearn.datasets` before, it's a small dataset. Now we will use MNIST (Modified National Institute of Standards and Technology) dataset, which is also hand-written digits but a larger dataset.

Each image in MNIST has 28 × 28 pixels, there are totally 70,000 images in the dataset, it comes with `keras.datasets` library. Figure 4.56 shows some examples, each digit is a 28 × 28 image, the small number at the left-top corner of each digit is the label of it.

Figure 4.56 MNIST Handwritten Digits Samples
Generated by source code at Artificial_Neural_Network_Introduction.ipynb

Reference https://en.wikipedia.org/wiki/MNIST_database for more details about the dataset.

Load MNIST Dataset

The MNIST dataset comes with **keras** library, it can be loaded by following codes:

```
1  import numpy as np
2  from keras.datasets import mnist
3  np.random.seed(0)
4  (X_train, y_train), (X_test, y_test) =
5                              mnist.load_data()
6  print('X_train: ' + str(X_train.shape))
7  print('y_train: ' + str(y_train.shape))
8  print('X_test:  ' + str(X_test.shape))
9  print('y_test:  ' + str(y_test.shape))
```

```
X_train: (60000, 28, 28)
y_train: (60000,)
X_test:  (10000, 28, 28)
y_test:  (10000,)
```

`mnist.load_data()` function will load the dataset and randomly split it into train and test sets, the train set has 60,000 and test set has 10,000 digit images.

Line 3 sets a random seed, so the dataset is split in the same way every time the code is run, and the results will be kept same.

Pre-processing

In order to feed the datasets into ANN model, the following things must be done.

1. Flatten the data, each data point or digit image has 28×28 pixels, it has to be flattened to 784, meaning the original size of X_train is (60000, 28, 28), it should be converted to (60000, 784).

```
1  # Flatten the images.
2  X_train = X_train.reshape((-1, 784))
3  X_test = X_test.reshape((-1, 784))
```

```
(60000, 784)
(10000, 784)
```

2. Normalize the data, each data value in X_train and X_test is ranging from 0 to 255, which is the color value of each pixel. The data values have to be normalized to [0, 1] as we did previously. StandardScaler() from sklearn library is used here:

```
1    from sklearn import preprocessing
2    scaler = preprocessing.StandardScaler()
3    X_train = scaler.fit_transform(X_train)
4    X_test = scaler.fit_transform(X_test)
```

3. One-hot encoding, the dataset has 10 clusters representing 0 to 9, so the labels in Y_train and Y_test look something like [5, 0, 4, 1, 9, 2, …], they will be converted to,

```
0 => [1. 0. 0. 0. 0. 0. 0. 0. 0. 0.]
1 => [0. 1. 0. 0. 0. 0. 0. 0. 0. 0.]
2 => [0. 0. 1. 0. 0. 0. 0. 0. 0. 0.]
3 => [0. 0. 0. 1. 0. 0. 0. 0. 0. 0.]
4 => [0. 0. 0. 0. 1. 0. 0. 0. 0. 0.]
5 => [0. 0. 0. 0. 0. 1. 0. 0. 0. 0.]
6 => [0. 0. 0. 0. 0. 0. 1. 0. 0. 0.]
7 => [0. 0. 0. 0. 0. 0. 0. 1. 0. 0.]
8 => [0. 0. 0. 0. 0. 0. 0. 0. 1. 0.]
9 => [0. 0. 0. 0. 0. 0. 0. 0. 0. 1.]
```

The below code snippets will do the one-hot encoding:

```
1    from tensorflow.keras.utils import to_categorical
2    to_categorical(y_train)
3    to_categorical(y_test)
```

Build the ANN Model

The MNIST dataset has $28 \times 28 = 784$ pixels, each pixel is a feature of the input data, so there are 784 features in the input layer of the ANN model. And the dataset has 10 clusters, the label has already one-hot encoded, so there are 10 nodes in output layer.

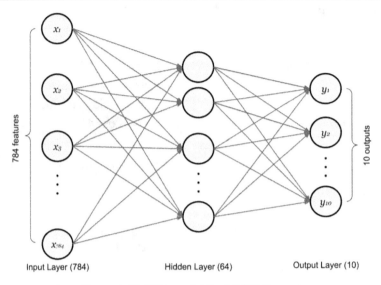

Figure 4.57 ANN model for MNIST Dataset

For now, 64 nodes are specified for the hidden layer, it can be changed later based on accuracy and computation costs. The ANN architecture is shown as Figure 4.57.

The below code snippets build, compile and fit the ANN model.

```
1   from tensorflow.keras.models import Sequential
2   from tensorflow.keras.layers import Dense
3   # Build the model.
4   model = Sequential([
5     Dense(64, activation='sigmoid',
6                 input_shape=(784,)),
7     Dense(10, activation='softmax') ])
8   # Compile the model.
9   model.compile(
10    optimizer='adam',
11    loss='categorical_crossentropy',
12    metrics=['categorical_accuracy'])
13  # Train the model.
14  history = model.fit(
15    X_train,
16    to_categorical(y_train),
17    verbose = 2,
18    epochs = 50 )
```

Line 5 and 6 specifies the input layer of 784, hidden layer of 64, and sigmoid as activation function.

Line 7 specifies output layer of 10, and softmax as activation function.

Line 9 to 12 compile the model with `adam` as optimizer, `categorical_crossentropy` as loss function and `categorical_accuracy` as metrics.

Line 14 to 18 fit the model with train set, the one-hot encoding is applied to `y_train` by `to_categorical()` function in line 16.

Because `verbose = 2` is specified in fitting process, after each epoch there is an output looks something like:

```
Epoch 25/50
1875/1875 - 3s - loss: 0.0060 - categorical_accuracy:
0.9994 - 3s/epoch - 2ms/step
```

After fitting the model, it can be evaluated with `evaluate()` function on the test set:

```
19   results=model.evaluate(X_test,
20                         to_categorical(y_test))
21   print('Final loss:', results[0])
22   print('Final accuracy:', results[1])
```

One-hot encoding is needed here as well, in line 20 `y_test` is one-hot encoded with `to_categorical()` function.

The results returned from `evaluate()` function includes final loss and accuracy in `results[0]` and `results[1]` elements.

The output of above code snippets is:

```
Final loss: 0.228325
Final accuracy: 0.958900
```

Make Prediction and Evaluation

To make a prediction from the ANN model use the `predict()` function, and pass the test dataset, like line 23 below.

```
23   y_pred = model.predict(X_test)
24   y_pred = np.argmax(y_pred, axis=1)
```

Because there are 10 output nodes in the ANN model, the output of `predict()` function looks something like:

```
array([[0, 0, 0, 0, 0, 0, 0, 1, 0, 0],
       [0, 0, 1, 0, 0, 0, 0, 0, 0, 0],
       [0, 1, 0, 0, 0, 0, 0, 0, 0, 0],
       [1, 0, 0, 0, 0, 0, 0, 0, 0, 0],
       [0, 0, 0, 0, 1, 0, 0, 0, 0, 0]],dtype=float32)
```

Each item is represented by 10 values of 0 or 1. In order to get the result of cluster from 0 to 9, the Reverse One-Hot Encode need to be done, which is line 24 above. The `numpy.argmax()` function does the job, it transform the above result to:

```
array([7, 2, 1, 0, 4])
```

This is in the same format of label of dataset in `y_test`.

Then we can use the metrics to evaluate the results as we did in previous sections, such as confusion matrix and classification report:

```
25    from sklearn import metrics
26    a_score=metrics.accuracy_score(y_test,y_pred)
27    c_matrix=metrics.confusion_matrix(y_test,y_pred)
28    c_report=metrics.classification_report(y_test,y_pred)
29    print("Accuracy Score:\n", a_score)
30    print("Confusion matrix:\n", c_matrix)
31    print("Classification Report:\n", c_report)
```

```
Accuracy Score:
 0.9586

Confusion matrix:
[[ 965    0    2    2    0    1    5    3    0    2]
 [   0 1121    7    1    0    1    2    1    2    0]
 [   8    4  983    7    3    1    4   12    9    1]
 [   2    1   16  955    2   13    0    7    7    7]
 [   1    1    4    2  930    2    8    7    7   20]
 [   2    0    2   12    3  850    6    2    8    7]
 [   8    2    2    1    6    8  929    0    2    0]
 [   1    4   12    5    4    1    0  989    2   10]
 [   5    5    9    4    6    9    4   14  914    4]
 [   6    4    0   13   14    4    1   13    4  950]]
```

```
Classification Report:
              precision    recall  f1-score   support
         0       0.97      0.98      0.98       980
         1       0.98      0.99      0.98      1135
         2       0.95      0.95      0.95      1032
         3       0.95      0.95      0.95      1010
         4       0.96      0.95      0.95       982
         5       0.96      0.95      0.95       892
         6       0.97      0.97      0.97       958
         7       0.94      0.96      0.95      1028
         8       0.96      0.94      0.95       974
         9       0.95      0.94      0.95      1009
  accuracy                           0.96     10000
 macro avg       0.96      0.96      0.96     10000
weighted avg     0.96      0.96      0.96     10000
```

In line 14 above when calling the `fit()` function to fit the train set, the return value is saved in **history**, which contains the loss and accuracy value for each epoch on train set. This information can be used to plot the curves of loss and accuracy during the fitting process, as Figure 4.58. The accuracy, which is the curve on the top, is converging at *1.000*, while the loss at the bottom is converging at *0.0019*.

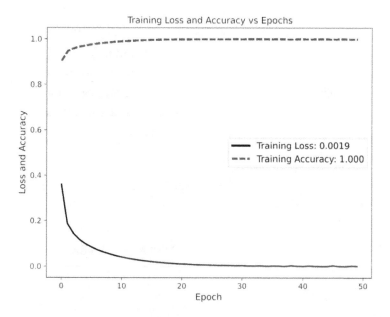

Figure 4.58 Loss and Accuracy of ANN on MNIST dataset
Generated by source code at Artificial_Neural_Network_Introduction.ipynb

Save and Load the Trained ANN Model

It could take some time to fit a model with large dataset, in order not to fit it again and again in the future and save times, the tensorflow/keras libraries provide functions to save and load trained models.

```
1    # Save the model
2    model.save('ann_on_mnist.h5')
```

It's pretty straightforward to save the model with **save()** function. There are two formats to save the models.

HDF5 is standard Hierarchical Data Format (HDF) format to store the large hierarchical data. If h5 is specified in the file name, it will be saved in this format. See https://en.wikipedia.org/wiki/Hierarchical_Data_Format for the details of this format.

If no extension is specified in the file name, the model will be saved in SavedModel format which is a tensorflow native format. See https://www.tensorflow.org/guide/saved_model for details.

The above line 2 will save the model in HDF5 format.

Please note when you are using Google Colab, any saved files will be stored in the temporary workspace that is assigned to your session, when you close the browser or the session is expired, the temporary workspace is gone, you will not be able to retrieve the files. Therefore, make sure the files are downloaded to local machine before closing the browser.

To load a saved model:

```
1    # Load the model
2    from tensorflow.keras.models import load_model
3    savedModel=load_model('ann_on_mnist.h5')
4    savedModel.summary()
```

After the model is loaded successfully, no need to fit it again, it can be used directly to make evaluation and prediction.

4.9.4 Regression: ANN on Diabetes Dataset

Last section we have used the Artificial Neural Networks (ANN) to resolve a classification problem, it can also be used for regression problems. The regression problem deals with the output variables of quantitative values, such as length, height, weight, price, population, etc.

The Diabetes dataset in section 4.1.2 is a typical regression dataset, it has 10 diagnostic measurements as the features, and the objective is to predict the progress of the diabetes disease. It's a regression problem because its output variables are scaler values, something like:

```
[ 78., 152., 311., 178., 332., 135., 220., 346., … ])
```

It's different from the classification problems which are numbers representing different clusters.

Load the Dataset

Now load the dataset from **sklearn** library, and split it to train and test sets:

```
1   from sklearn import datasets
2   from sklearn import model_selection
3   X, y = datasets.load_diabetes(return_X_y = True)
4   X_train, X_test, y_train, y_test = \
5   model_selection.train_test_split(X, y,
6                                    test_size=0.2,
7                                    random_state=1)
```

And check the size of data:

```
8    print("X_train:", X_train.shape)
9    print("y_train:", y_train.shape)
10   print("X_test:", X_test.shape)
11   print("y_test:", y_test.shape)
```

```
X_train: (353, 10)
y_train: (353,)
X_test: (89, 10)
y_test: (89,)
```

X_train and X_test have 10 features, and 353 and 89 data points respectively; y_train and y_test have 353 and 89 output values.

It's a best practice to scale the data before applying to any machine learning models, use StandardScaler() to scale the data:

```
12    from sklearn import preprocessing
13    scaler = preprocessing.StandardScaler()
14    X_train = scaler.fit_transform(X_train)
15    X_test = scaler.fit_transform(X_test)
```

Build the ANN Model

The dataset has 10 features as input and 1 output, so the ANN model will have 10 nodes in the input layer, and one node in the output layer.

Then select two hidden layers with 16 nodes each for now, it can be adjusted based on the results.

The relu is used as activation function for hidden layers, and linear is for output layer. relu is basically same as linear when input value greater than zero, see section 3.3.4 and 3.3.1 for both functions.

The codes to define the ANN model is as below:

```
16    from tensorflow.keras.models import Sequential
17    from tensorflow.keras.layers import Dense
18    model = Sequential([
19      Dense(16, activation='relu',input_shape=(10,)),
20      Dense(16, activation='relu'),
21      Dense(1,  activation='linear') ])
```

The optimizer, loss function and metrics have to be selected to compile the ANN model. Adam is used for optimizer, which is same as previous section when dealing with classification problems. The learning_rate is passed to Adam as parameter which specifies the learning rate for gradient descent.

The MeanSquaredError is used for loss function, since this is regression model, the Mean Squared Error (MSE) is normally used to measure the loss or cost of the algorithm.

The `RootMeanSquaredError` is used for metrics here, it is the square root of the Mean Squared Error. The `MeanSquaredError` can also be used here, if that is the case, the metrics will be same as loss.

The code to compile the ANN model is as below:

```
22   opt_ = keras.optimizers.Adam(learning_rate=0.005)
23   loss_ = keras.losses.MeanSquaredError()
24   metrics_ = keras.metrics.RootMeanSquaredError()
25   model.compile(optimizer=opt_,
26                 loss=loss_,
27                 metrics=metrics_)
```

Train the ANN Model

Then fit the model with train set, tensorflow/keras can do a validation during the training process by specifying a validation_split when calling fit() function, it will split a validation set from the train set, and evaluate the validation set at each epoch, the result is used to fine-tune the model by adjusting its parameters. Consider the validation set is the data used for unit testing during the development.

There is no change for the test set which is still used for final evaluation. Below are the codes to fit the ANN model with validation set of 0.2, or 20%, split from train set, and epochs=100.

```
28   history = model.fit(
29       X_train,
30       y_train,
31       verbose=0,
32       validation_split=0.2,
33       epochs=100 )
```

As explained above, verbose can control the output during the fitting process. verbose=0 will turn off the outputs.

It suggested to turn on the outputs by setting **verbose=2** in the development process, the outputs can be used for monitoring the training process, and model parameters can be adjusted based on these outputs, like the number of hidden layers, the nodes of each hidden layer, the learning rate, the optimizer, the metrics and cost function, and so on.

The `history` returned from `fit()` function can be used to plot the results as Figure 4.59, it shows the history of training loss vs validation loss, both are dropping significantly from a very high number and converging to a specific value.

The most important is the curve of validation loss is very close to the training loss in Figure 4.59, meaning the model trained from the train set performs similar on the validation set. A model is not good if the validation curve is moving far away from the training curve, which means the model performs not well on validation dataset, in this case, need to fine-tune the model by adjusting parameters and try to make both curves go as close as possible.

Please note, it's mentioned earlier the best practice to scale the dataset before applying to any models, however it's noticed in this case the final training loss on scaled data is *2314* which is good, but the final validation loss is *3524*. Compared with Figure 4.59 which is the raw data without scaling, the train loss is *2800* and validation loss is *3054*. The scaled data has a bigger difference between training set and validation set. As the result, in this case it's better to use the non-scaled data on the ANN model. This is an example of fine-tune activities.

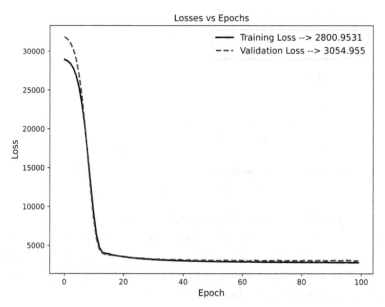

Figure 4.59 ANN on Diabetes Dataset -- Losses vs Epochs
Generated by source code at Artificial_Neural_Network_Introduction.ipynb

A question is why the loss is so big around *3000*? Well, if look at the details of the Diabetes Dataset in section 4.1.2, especially the correlation heatmap at Figure 4.2, most of the features correlate with the target (output) variable in *0.2, 0.4,* or *0.6,* meaning the data points are not perfectly distributed in a linear way, they are scattered far away from a line, therefore the Mean Squared Error (MSE) is big.

If a dataset is distributed in a linear way, meaning not far away from a line, then the correlation values are near *1* or *-1*, meaning strong positive or negative linear relationship with the output variable, therefore the Mean Squared Error (MSE) will be small, and a smaller final loss will be observed.

Evaluate the ANN Model

The ANN model is evaluated with the test set by calling the `evaluate()` function:

```
34   results = model.evaluate( X_test,
35                             y_test )
36   print('Final loss: {:4f}'.format(results[0]))
37   print('Final metrics: {:4f}'.format(results[1]))

Final loss: 3040.157227
Final metrics: 55.137619
```

The loss is the Mean Squared Error and the final value is *3040.15*, which is close to the validation loss of *3054* as shown in Figure 4.59. This means the model performs similar on test set as validation set, and not too far from the train set of *2800*.

The metrics is defined as Root Mean Squared Error and its final value is *55.13*, which is the square root of the loss value.

4.9.5 Algorithm and Implementation of ANN

This section will introduce the algorithms and implement an ANN model from scratch using basic Python libraries like numpy, and apply IRIS dataset on the ANN model.

IRIS dataset is introduced in section 4.6.2, there are 4 features and one output variable which has 3 clusters. Load the IRIS dataset, split it into train and test sets, and one-hot encode the output variable:

```
1    from sklearn import datasets
2    from sklearn.preprocessing import OneHotEncoder
3    from sklearn.model_selection import train_test_split
4    iris = datasets.load_iris()
5    X = iris.data
6    y = iris.target
7    X_train, X_test, y_train, y_test = \
8    train_test_split(X, y, test_size=0.2,
9                            random_state=1)
10   enc = OneHotEncoder(sparse=False)
11   y_train = enc.fit_transform(y_train.reshape(-1, 1))
```

Line 4 to 6 load the dataset into X and y. Line 7 to 9 split it into train and test sets.

Line 10 and 11 do the one-hot encoding on the output label y. As explained earlier, after one-hot encoding the output is transformed as:

```
0 => [1, 0, 0]
1 => [0, 1, 0]
2 => [0, 0, 1]
```

Now the dataset has 4 features as input and 3 outputs. The ANN model we are going to build is like Figure 4.60,

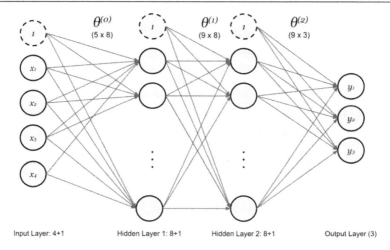

Figure 4.60 ANN Algorithm and Implementation

The Input Layer has 4 nodes which corresponding to the 4 features in the dataset, and there is one more node representing the intercept, or bias. The hypothesis function is:

$$h_\theta(x) = \theta_0 + \theta_1 x_1 + \theta_2 x_2 + \theta_3 x_3 + \theta_4 x_4$$

The extra node is representing the first item in above hypothesis function, it is a constant of 1, meaning $\theta_0 \cdot 1$. To re-cap, why the intercept or bias is important, as explained in the section of linear regression, if there is no intercept or bias, the result line will always pass the origin point meaning if all x's are zero y is always zero, the results might not best fit the dataset. Therefore, the intercept or bias is added here.

Similarly, the Hidden Layer 1 and 2 have 8 + 1 nodes, the extra 1 node is also the intercept or bias which are always 1. It could be 8 nodes, it could be other numbers of nodes, it is specified by a parameter and adjustable.

The Output Layer has 3 nodes corresponding to the 3 outputs – the one-hot encoded outputs.

Create a Class of the ANN Model

Below are the codes to create `ArtificialNeuralNetwork` class,

```
1  import numpy as np
2  class ArtificialNeuralNetwork:
```

```
3    def __init__(self, nodes=[]):
4        np.random.seed(27)
5        self.theta = self.initialize(nodes)
6        self.layers = len(self.theta)
7        self.history = []
```

The class take one parameter nodes which is the structure of the ANN, it is a list of the layers, something like [4, 8, 8, 3].

Line 4 set a random seed so that every time run the code, the result is same.

Line 5 initialize the theta, or weights, of the ANN, will explain later.

Line 6 sets the layers for the calculations later.

Line 7 set history list which is for plotting the results.

Initialize theta, or weights, of the ANN

Next step is to generate and initialize the theta or weights of the ANN. When nodes is passed to the class, the number of the theta is len(nodes) -1. In this case the nodes = [4, 8, 8, 3], there will be 3 theta's. This can also be identified from Figure 4.60, there are three groups of arrows, each corresponding to a theta. The first group of arrows is from Input Layer to Hidden Layer 1, the second is from Hidden Layer 1 to Hidden Layer 2, and the third is from Hidden Layer 2 to Output Layer. And each arrow is corresponding to one elements in theta, meaning each arrow is corresponding to a weight in the ANN model.

The first theta is from Input Layer as input to Hidden Layer 1 as output, its size is (5×8). See Figure 4.60, the Input Layer has 5 nodes, the outputs go to Hidden Layer 1 which has 8 nodes.

The second theta is from Hidden Layer 1 as input to Hidden Layer 2 as output, similarly an intercept is added to the input, so its size is (9×8). Notice the Hidden Layer 1 was the output previously, but now it's the input, see Figure 4.60 again, when it acted as output it has 8 nodes, now it acts as input, an intercept is added, then the number of nodes is 9.

The third `theta` is from Hidden Layer 2 as input to Output Layer as output, its size is `(9×3)`.

The below codes implement the initialization of `theta`, all items are random numbers from *-1* to *1*. And the `theta`'s are created in a list.

```
8    def initialize(self, nodes):
9        theta = []
10       for i in range(1, len(nodes)):
11           w = np.random.uniform(-1,1,(nodes[i-1]+1,
12                                        nodes[i]))
13           theta.append(w)
14       return theta
```

After the `ArtificialNeuralNetwork` class is instantiated with `nodes = [4, 8, 8, 3]`, the result of `theta` looks like:

```
Number of theta: 3
theta 0: (5, 8)
theta 1: (9, 8)
theta 2: (9, 3)
```

Of cause different `nodes` structure will generate different `theta`. And each element inside `theta` is a random value from *-1* to *1*.

Activation Function and Cost Function

As explained earlier, each node in ANN has an activation function, for simplification purposes, sigmoid activation function is used for all nodes in this example, it's defined as:

$$f(x) = \frac{1}{(1 + e^{-x})}$$

See section 3.3.2 for details of sigmoid function.

Same as previous machine learning methods, the gradient descent will be used for training in this ANN model, for this purpose, the derivative of sigmoid function will be used, it's defined as:

$$f'(x) = f(x)(1 - f(x))$$
$$= \frac{e^{-x}}{(1 + e^{-x})^2}$$

See section 3.2.4 for gradient descent.

And a cost function needs to be defined to evaluate the cost during training, Cross Entropy cost function is used here for this classification problem. See section 4.3.5 for the cost function.

Below codes define the sigmoid, sigmoid_derivative and cost functions:

```
15    def sigmoid(self, z):
16        return 1 / (1 + np.exp(-z))
17    def sigmoid_derivative(self, z):
18        return np.multiply(z, 1-z)
19    def cost(self, h, y):
20        return (-np.mean(np.sum(np.log(h)*(y),axis=1)))
21    def add_intercept(self, x):
22        return np.hstack((np.ones((x.shape[0],1)), x))
```

The add_intercept() in line 21 and 22 is a helper function, it adds intercept, or bias, to a dataset, as below:

$$\begin{bmatrix} x_{00} & x_{01} & \cdots & x_{0m} \\ x_{10} & x_{11} & \cdots & x_{1m} \\ \cdots & \cdots & \cdots & \cdots \\ x_{n0} & x_{n1} & \cdots & x_{nm} \end{bmatrix} \implies \begin{bmatrix} 1 & x_{00} & x_{01} & \cdots & x_{0m} \\ 1 & x_{10} & x_{11} & \cdots & x_{1m} \\ 1 & \cdots & \cdots & \cdots & \cdots \\ 1 & x_{n0} & x_{n1} & \cdots & x_{nm} \end{bmatrix}$$

Forward Propagation

Forward propagation is the calculation layer by layer from the Input Layer to the Output Layer.

For the first layer of calculation from Input Layer to Hidden Layer 1, theta for this layer is in the size of (5×8).

$$\theta^{(0)} = \begin{bmatrix} \theta_{00} & \theta_{01} & \cdots & \theta_{07} \\ \theta_{10} & \theta_{11} & \cdots & \theta_{17} \\ \cdots & \cdots & \cdots & \cdots \\ \theta_{40} & \theta_{41} & \cdots & \theta_{47} \end{bmatrix}$$

The output of this first layer of calculation is denoted as $O^{(1)}$.

$$X \cdot \theta^{(0)} = \begin{bmatrix} 1 & x_1 & x_2 & \cdots & x_4 \end{bmatrix} \cdot \begin{bmatrix} \theta_{00} & \theta_{01} & \cdots & \theta_{07} \\ \theta_{10} & \theta_{11} & \cdots & \theta_{17} \\ \cdots & \cdots & \cdots & \cdots \\ \theta_{40} & \theta_{41} & \cdots & \theta_{47} \end{bmatrix}$$

$$O^{(1)} = f(X \cdot \theta^{(0)})$$

The $O^{(1)}$ is in size of (1×8). Please note this is for one data point of X, if it has n data points, X is (n×5), $\theta^{(0)}$ is (5×8), then $O^{(1)}$ is (n×8). Then apply the activation function to every item of $O^{(1)}$, $f()$ is sigmoid function.

In the second layer of calculation from Hidden Layer 1 to Hidden Layer 2, the $O^{(1)}$ becomes input now, the intercept of 1 is added to it, and it's in the size of (1×9) for one data point, and (n×9) for n data points. The theta for this layer is denoted as $\theta^{(1)}$, in the size of (9×8), then:

$$\theta^{(1)} = \begin{bmatrix} \theta_{00} & \theta_{01} & \cdots & \theta_{07} \\ \theta_{10} & \theta_{11} & \cdots & \theta_{17} \\ \cdots & \cdots & \cdots & \cdots \\ \theta_{80} & \theta_{81} & \cdots & \theta_{87} \end{bmatrix}$$

$$O^{(1)} \cdot \theta^{(1)} = \begin{bmatrix} 1 & O_1 & O_2 & \cdots & O_8 \end{bmatrix} \cdot \begin{bmatrix} \theta_{00} & \theta_{01} & \cdots & \theta_{07} \\ \theta_{10} & \theta_{11} & \cdots & \theta_{17} \\ \cdots & \cdots & \cdots & \cdots \\ \theta_{80} & \theta_{81} & \cdots & \theta_{87} \end{bmatrix}$$

$$O^{(2)} = f(O^{(1)} \cdot \theta^{(1)})$$

The size of $O^{(2)}$ is also in size of (1×8), or (n×8) for n data points. Then apply the activation function to every items.

Then it comes to the third layer of calculation which is the last one to get output results. The intercept of 1 is added to $O^{(2)}$, its size is (n×9). $\theta^{(2)}$ for this layer is (9×3). Then

$$\theta^{(2)} = \begin{bmatrix} \theta_{00} & \theta_{01} & \theta_{02} \\ \theta_{10} & \theta_{11} & \theta_{12} \\ \cdots & \cdots & \cdots \\ \theta_{80} & \theta_{81} & \theta_{82} \end{bmatrix}$$

$$O^{(2)} \cdot \theta^{(2)} = [1 \quad O_1 \quad O_2 \quad \cdots \quad O_8] \cdot \begin{bmatrix} \theta_{00} & \theta_{01} & \theta_{02} \\ \theta_{10} & \theta_{11} & \theta_{12} \\ \cdots & \cdots & \cdots \\ \theta_{80} & \theta_{81} & \theta_{82} \end{bmatrix}$$

$$O^{(3)} = f(O^{(2)} \cdot \theta^{(2)})$$

The size of $O^{(3)}$ is (n×3), after applying the activation function, this is the final output of this ANN model. Of cause different ANN models will have different number of layers, and different number of nodes in each layer, the specific sizes are different from the above descriptions, but the idea is same.

To make a prediction from a trained ANN model is to perform the forward propagation from input all the way down to the output. Below are the codes to implement it:

```
23    def forward_propagation(self, X):
24        outputs = [X]
25        x_ = X
26        for j in range(self.layers):
27            x_ = self.add_intercept(x_)
28            output = self.sigmoid(np.dot(x_,
29                                  self.theta[j]))
30            outputs.append(output)
31            x_ = output
32        return outputs
```

Line 24 defines a list to store the outputs. Line 25 take the input X as the working variable x_, the intercept is added to it in line 27.

In the for loop of line 26 to 31 the calculation is performed layer by layer, the output is added to the outputs list. Then take the output as the working variable x_, and add intercept in line 27, then move to next loop to perform next layer's calculation.

The sizes of outputs for this example are as below, 120 is the number of data points.

(120, 8)

(120, 8)

(120, 3)

Back Propagation

Back propagation is an essential part to perform gradient descent in the training processes. It calculates the errors between the true labels and the final output of forward propagation, applies the gradients, updates the `theta` or the weights, and then propagates the calculation from the output layer back to input layer.

Since the `theta` is randomly initialized at the beginning, the first outputs of forward propagation might be far away from the true labels. After many iterations or epochs of forward and back propagation processes, the results should be updated gradually and converge to the final outcomes.

The purpose of back propagation is to update the `theta` based on the errors of outputs.

The codes of back propagation are as below,

```
33   def back_propagation(self, y, outputs, alpha):
34       error = np.matrix(y - outputs[-1])
35       for j in range(self.layers, 0, -1):
36           curr_out = outputs[j]
37           prev_out = self.add_intercept(outputs[j-1])
38           delta = np.multiply(error,
39                       self.sigmoid_derivative(curr_out))
40           self.theta[j-1] += alpha*np.dot(prev_out.T, delta)
41           adj_theta = np.delete(self.theta[j-1], [0], axis=0)
42           error = np.dot(delta, adj_theta.T)
43       return self.theta
```

The calculation begins from the final output in the Output Layer. In line 34 the `error` is the difference of true label `y` and the final output from forward propagation.

The for loop from line 35 to 42 is from the last layer (Output Layer) to the first layer (Input Layer), the calculation is in backwards direction.

For the last layer, from Output Layer to Hidden Layer 2:

$$\varepsilon^{(3)} = y - O^{(3)}$$
$$\delta^{(3)} = \varepsilon^{(3)} f'(O^{(3)})$$
$$\theta^{(2)} = \alpha(O^{(2)} \cdot \delta^{(3)})$$

Where $\varepsilon^{(3)}$ is the error or difference between true label and final output of forward propagation; α is the learning rate; $f'()$ is the derivative of activation function, in this case the derivative of sigmoid function.

The calculation at this layer will update the $\theta^{(2)}$, which is the last `theta` between Output Layer and Hidden Layer 2, see Figure 4.60.

For the layer from Hidden Layer 2 to Hidden Layer 1:

$$\varepsilon^{(2)} = \delta^{(3)} \cdot \theta^{(2)}$$
$$\delta^{(2)} = \varepsilon^{(2)} f'(O^{(2)})$$
$$\theta^{(1)} = \alpha(O^{(1)} \cdot \delta^{(2)})$$

Where $\varepsilon^{(2)}$ is the error of current layer which is calculated by dot production of $\delta^{(3)}$ and $\theta^{(2)}$.

And for the layer from Hidden Layer 1 to Input Layer:

$$\varepsilon^{(1)} = \delta^{(2)} \cdot \theta^{(1)}$$
$$\delta^{(1)} = \varepsilon^{(1)} f'(O^{(1)})$$
$$\theta^{(0)} = \alpha(O^{(0)} \cdot \delta^{(1)})$$

Where $O^{(0)}$ is the raw input data.

Training Process

The training is an iterative process of forward and back propagations. The former calculates the output of each layer, the latter calculates the errors and update the weights for each layer.

```
44    def fit(self, X, y, epochs=100, alpha=0.01, verbose=1 ):
45      for epoch in range(1, epochs+1):
46        outputs = self.forward_propagation(X)
47        self.theta = self.back_propagation(y, outputs, alpha)
48        if(epoch % 10 == 0):
49          accuracy_ = self.accuracy(X_train, y_train)
50          cost_ = self.cost( outputs[-1], y_train )
51          self.history.append([accuracy_, cost_])
52          if verbose != 0:
53            print("Epoch {}".format(epoch), end = ': ')
54            print("Accuracy: %.6f"%accuracy_, end = ', ')
55            print("Cost: %.6f"%cost_)
```

```
56        return np.array(self.history)
```

Line 44 defines `fit()` function, `X` is the data, `y` is the label, `epochs` is the number of iterations, `alpha` is learning rate, `verbose` controls the outputs during fitting process.

For each epoch call forward propagation in line 46 to get outputs, and call back propagation in line 47 passing the outputs and learning rate.

From line 48 to 55, for every 10 epochs calculate the accuracy and cost, store them in the `history` list. And if `verbose!=0` print them out.

The `fit()` function returns the `history`.

Prediction and Evaluation

Prediction is simply to call the forward propagation, and format the final results as output.

The evaluation is to make a prediction first, then count the percent of correct predictions as the accuracy.

```
57    def predict(self, X):
58        outputs = self.forward_propagation(X)
59        f_output = outputs[-1]
60        return (f_output == f_output.max(axis=1,
61                        keepdims=True)).astype(float)
62    def accuracy(self, X, y):
63        y_ = self.predict(X)
64        acc = np.sum(np.equal(y, y_), axis=1)
65        return np.sum(acc == y.shape[1])/y.shape[0]
```

Apply IRIS Dataset

```
1    input_layer = len(X_train[0])
2    output_layer = len(y_train[0])
3    hidden_layer_1 = 8
4    hidden_layer_2 = 8
5    layers = [input_layer,
6                hidden_layer_1,
7                hidden_layer_2,
8                output_layer]
9    epochs = 2000
```

```
10    ann = ArtificialNeuralNetwork(nodes=layers)
11    history = ann.fit(X_train, y_train,
12                      epochs=epochs,
13                      alpha=0.01,
14                      verbose=0 )
```

Since the IRIS Dataset is already loaded and pre-processed at the beginning of this section, now build and train the ANN model:

The training process is shown in Figure 4.61.

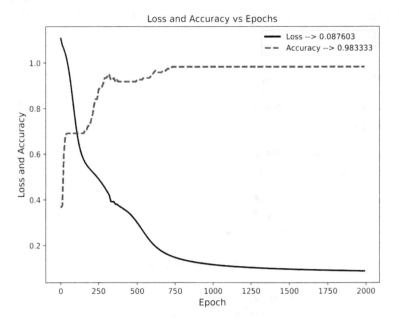

Figure 4.61 Loss and Accuracy vs Epochs

Generated by source code at ANN_Algorithm_Implementation.ipynb

Make evaluations from test set, remember to one-hot encode the label of test set:

```
15    y_ = enc.fit_transform(np.array(y_test)
16                           .reshape(-1, 1))
17    acc = ann.accuracy( X_test, y_ )
18    print("Accuracy:", acc)
```

Accuracy: 1.0

And sklearn metrics can also be used to evaluate the results:

```
1   from sklearn import metrics
2   y_pred = ann.predict(X_test)
3   y_pred = np.argmax(y_pred, axis=1)
4   y_pred = np.squeeze(np.asarray(y_pred))
5   a_score = metrics.accuracy_score(y_test, y_pred)
6   c_matrix = metrics.confusion_matrix(y_test, y_pred)
7   c_report = metrics.classification_report(y_test, y_pred)
8   print("Accuracy Score:\n", a_score)
9   print("Confusion matrix:\n", c_matrix)
10  print("Classification Report:\n", c_report)
```

```
Accuracy Score:
 1.0

Confusion matrix:
 [[11  0  0]
  [ 0 13  0]
  [ 0  0  6]]
```

Classification Report:

	precision	recall	f1-score	support
0	1.00	1.00	1.00	11
1	1.00	1.00	1.00	13
2	1.00	1.00	1.00	6
accuracy			1.00	30
macro avg	1.00	1.00	1.00	30
weighted avg	1.00	1.00	1.00	30

4.9.6 Overfitting and Underfitting

When evaluating the performance and accuracy of a machine learning or a deep learning model like neural network, sometimes the model performs good on the train set but not test set, sometimes the model does not even perform well on train set. The most likely cause of the poor performance is either *overfitting* or *underfitting* of the data.

In order to understand them, let's first explain two important terms, *bias* and *variance*.

Bias is the difference between the mean value of predicted by the model and the mean value of the true target. It's considered as the error rate of the training data, a high bias means a high error rate, and the predicted values are off target. See the right side of Figure 4.62, the predicted values are not in the center of the target.

A low bias means a low error rate, and the predicted values are in target. As shown in the left side of Figure 4.62, the data are in the center of target.

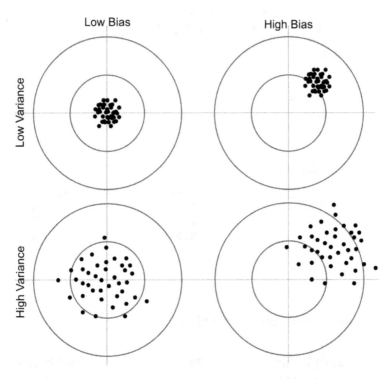

Figure 4.62 Bias vs Variance

The variance is the amount of variability in the predicted values in response to the changes in the training data. A low variance means the data are centralized around a certain point, as shown in the upper part of Figure 4.62. A high variance means the data are scattered away from a certain point, as lower part of Figure 4.62.

Underfitting happens when the model is not able to capture and learn the patterns and trends of the training data, as the result the model is high bias and low variance, it will not perform well on both train set and test set and will be resulting a lower accuracy.

The most likely causes of underfitting are insufficient training data, or over simplified model. For example, the left of Figure 4.63 is underfitting, it is using a linear model to fit the non-linear distributed data,

$$h_\theta(x) = \theta_0 + \theta_1 x$$

The model is too simple for the data.

Figure 4.63 Under-fit, Over-fit and Appropirate-fit

Overfitting is the opposite of underfitting, the model is too sensitive to the training data, it might learn the noises of the training data, as the result it performs well on training data but not testing data. It's low bias and high variance.

The most likely cause of overfitting is the over complicated model and big size of training data, as shown in the middle of Figure 4.63, which is likely to be:

$$h_\theta(x) = \theta_0 + \theta_1 x + \theta_2 x^2 + \theta_3 x^3 + \theta_4 x^4 + \theta_5 x^5 + \cdots$$

It fits exactly to almost all data points in training data, therefore it will not perform well on the testing data.

The *appropriate-fitting* takes the balance of overfitting and underfitting, it captures and learns the patterns from training data, but not over sensitive to the training data, as the result it performs well on both training and testing data. As shown in the right side of Figure 4.63, which is something like:

$$h_\theta(x) = \theta_0 + \theta_1 x + \theta_2 x^2$$

The techniques to reduce overfitting include:

- Reduce the complexity of the model.
- Increase the size of training data.
- Use Dropout for neural networks which is provided by Keras/tensorflow. See material #23 in References.
- Early stopping, monitor the loss during fitting process and stop fitting as soon as the loss begins to increase.

Now we use the ANN model on MNIST dataset which is same as section 4.9.3 to see how the underfitting and overfitting look like.

To make it underfitting, take a portion of the training data, and build a simplified ANN model:

```
1   X_train1 = X_train[0:10000]
2   y_train1 = y_train[0:10000]
3
4   model1 = Sequential([
5     Dense(16, activation='sigmoid',input_shape=(784,)),
6     Dense(10, activation='softmax') ] )
7
8   model1.compile(
9     optimizer='adam',
10    loss='categorical_crossentropy',
11    metrics=['categorical_accuracy'])
12
13  history1 = model1.fit(
14    X_train1, to_categorical(y_train1),
15    validation_data =(X_test, to_categorical(y_test)),
16    verbose=2,
17    epochs=50,
18    batch_size=64 )
```

The X_train and y_train has 60000 data points, here use only 10000 to train the model. And the ANN model is quite simple, there is only one hidden layer with 16 nodes.

The fit() function can take a sub-dataset for validation, now use X_test and y_test for validation purpose. The retune value of fit() function contains the history of loss and accuracy values for both train and validation results, they are used to plot the result in Figure 4.64. The solid line at the bottom is the loss for training data, the dashed line at the bottom is the loss for testing data.

And the solid line at the top is accuracy for training data, the dashed line at the top is the accuracy for testing data.

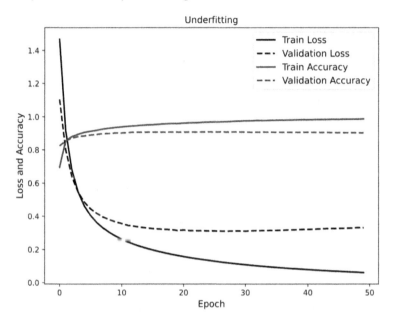

Figure 4.64 Underfitting of ANN on MNIST Dataset
Generated by source code at Overfitting_Underfitting.ipynb

Now look at the overfitting,

```
1    model = Sequential([
2      Dense(128, activation='sigmoid',input_shape=(784,)),
3      Dense(128, activation='sigmoid'),
4      Dense(128, activation='sigmoid'),
5      Dense(64, activation='sigmoid'),
6      Dense(10, activation='softmax') ])
7
8    model.compile(
9      optimizer='adam',
10     loss='categorical_crossentropy',
11     metrics=['categorical_accuracy'] )
12
13   history = model.fit(
14     X_train, to_categorical(y_train),
```

```
15       validation_data=(X_test, to_categorical(y_test)),
16       verbose=2,
17       epochs=50,
18       batch_size=64 )
```

The model is over complicated as line 1 to 6, there are 4 hidden layers
with 128, 128, 128 and 64 nodes for each. The result is shown in Figure
4.65:

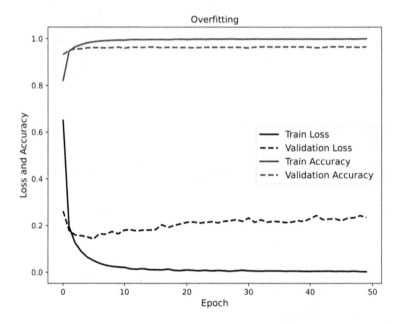

Figure 4.65 Overfitting of ANN on MNIST Dataset
Generated by source code at Overfitting_Underfitting.ipynb

And then the appropriate fitting,

```
1    model2 = Sequential([
2      Dense(64, activation='sigmoid',input_shape=(784,)),
3      Dropout(0.35),
4      Dense(10, activation='softmax') ] )
5
6    model2.compile(
7      optimizer='adam',
8      loss='categorical_crossentropy',
9      metrics=['categorical_accuracy'] )
10
```

```
11   history2 = model2.fit(
12     X_train, to_categorical(y_train),
13     validation_data=(X_test, to_categorical(y_test)),
14     verbose=2,
15     epochs=50,
16     batch_size=64 )
```

The ANN model is defined in line 1 to 4, one hidden layer of 64 nodes, and add a `Dropout(0.35)` to reduce the overfitting, the result is shown as Figure 4.66:

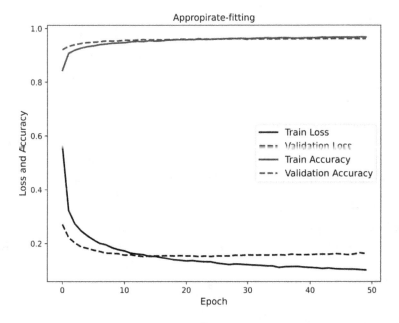

Figure 4.66 Appropriate fitting on MNIST Dataset
Generated by source code at Overfitting_Underfitting.ipynb

Compare the above three figures, overfitting and underfitting have separated accuracy lines between training and testing data, and the accuracy on testing is lower than that of training. And the loss lines are moving far away gradually as epoch increases, the loss for testing is increasing gradually, meaning the more training epochs the bigger loss on testing data, although the loss on training data is flat. And in Figure 4.64 for underfitting, the loss on training data is decreasing meaning it does not converge at the epoch of 50.

The appropriate fitting takes a good balance between the two, as Figure 4.66, the two accuracy lines almost same as epoch increases, and the loss for testing is flat and not increasing as epoch increases. It performs well on both training data and testing data.

4.10 Convolutional Neural Network (CNN)

4.10.1 Introduction

In the previous section of artificial neural network (ANN), the MNIST dataset has images of 28 × 28 pixels, which means there are 784 pixels for each image, in order to feed the data into ANN, the input layer has 784 nodes to take the input data.

Consider a high-resolution 4K picture which has 3840 × 2160 pixels, it means 8 million pixels, and each pixel has three color channels, it's not realistic to build a neural network to correspond so many input data for each picture, let alone tens of thousands of pictures to process.

A convolutional neural network (CNN) is a type of deep learning method to process computer vision tasks such as images and pictures. CNN is designed to automatically identify objects and patterns in the images, for example the eyes, faces, etc. They can also be quite effective for classifying non-image data such as audio and signal data.

What is Convolution

Convolution is a mathematical operation on two functions, f and g, to produce a third function $(f * g)$ that represents how the shape of one is modified by the other. It's defined as:

$$(f * g)(t) = \int_{-\infty}^{\infty} f(\tau)g(t - \tau)d\tau$$

We are not going to deep-dive into the mathematical details here, the basic idea is to consider one function as the original image, and the other function as a feature, the convolution operation is to identify or extract the feature from the original image.

For example, there is a 1D array:

$$f = \begin{bmatrix} 1 & 3 & 2 \end{bmatrix}$$

And there is another 1D array:

$$g = \begin{bmatrix} 3 & 4 & 1 & 0 & 2 & 5 \end{bmatrix}$$

The convolution of $f * g$ is defined as the integral of one array sweeping over the second and multiplied at each position of overlapping. The rule of convolution is as below, the first item of the result is calculated as:

$$2 \times 1 + 3 \times 4 + 1 \times 3 = 17$$

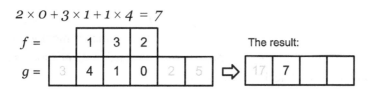

Then f is shifted towards right for one item and calculate the sum for the second item of the result:

$$2 \times 0 + 3 \times 1 + 1 \times 4 = 7$$

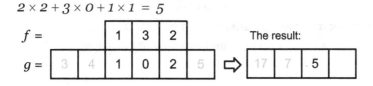

And then f is shifted again towards right, and calculate the rest items,

$$2 \times 2 + 3 \times 0 + 1 \times 1 = 5$$

$$2 \times 5 + 3 \times 2 + 1 \times 0 = 16$$

The convolution can be understood more clearly using the animations from wikipedia at https://en.wikipedia.org/wiki/Convolution.

Python `numpy.convolve()` function can do the convolution for 1D array,

```
1    import numpy as np
2    f = np.array([2, 3, 1])
3    g = np.array([3, 4, 1, 0, 2, 5])
4    conv = np.convolve(f, g, mode = 'valid')
5    print(conv)
```

The result is:

```
[17  7  5 16]
```

The Convolution Neural Network (CNN) is made up of three layers, the convolution layer, the pooling layer and a fully connected layer. These layers are introduced in the following sections

4.10.2 Convolution Layer

The above example is to process 1-dimensional array which is mostly used for signal processing. Because the images are 2-dimensional, let's look at how the convolution works for a 2D array.

Say, there is an image which is a 2D matrix as below left one, there is a 3×3 matrix which is the feature, also called kernel, as below in the middle one. The rule of convolution is the feature/kernel will sweep over the image from top-left corner towards right in horizontal direction, and then towards down in vertical direction, and multiply at each position of the overlapping.

The first item of the convolution result is calculated as:

$$1 \times 1 + 1 \times 3 + 1 \times 1 + 1 \times 1 + 0 \times 1 + 1 \times 1 + 1 \times 2 + 0 \times 1 + 1 \times 9 = 18$$

and it is shown as below:

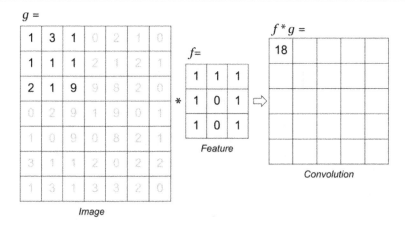

Then the feature matrix is shifted towards right, and the second item is calculated as:

$$1\times3 + 1\times1 + 1\times0 + 1\times1 + 0\times1 + 1\times2 + 1\times1 + 0\times9 + 1\times9 = 17$$

and it is shown as below:

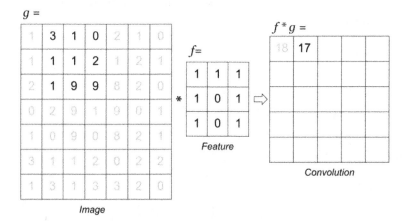

The feature, or kernel, matrix is continuously shifting towards right, and then towards down, and calculate the result items one by one. Finally, it reaches the bottom-right corner of the original image,

$$1\times8 + 1\times2 + 1\times1 + 1\times0 + 0\times2 + 1\times2 + 1\times3 + 0\times2 + 1\times0 = 16$$

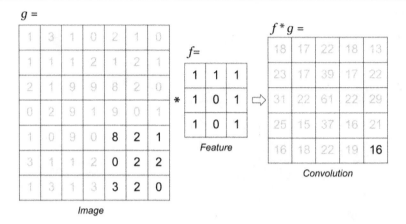

Image

The purpose of convolution is to identify a specific object from the original image. The feature, or kernel, in above example is the shape of Π, it's sweeping over the whole image and identify the shape. As Figure 4.67, the Π shape appears in the middle of the original image, and the value of *61* in the convolution result also appears in the middle, the value is significantly larger than all other values, meaning the shape is identified in the middle of the original image.

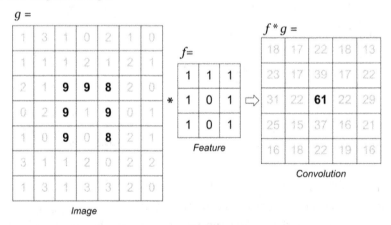

Image

Figure 4.67 Convolution for 2D Matrix

If the shape appears in different part of the original image, the largest value will appear in the corresponding position of the convolution result. Consider the original image is a dog, and the feature or kernel is its nose, then the convolution operation is able to identify the nose. It doesn't matter where the nose is in the original image, it will always identify its location.

Padding and Stride

In the above example, suppose the original image size is $i_h \times i_w$, and the feature/kernel size is $k_h \times k_w$, then the size of convolution output is:

$$(i_h - k_h + 1) \times (i_w - k_w + 1)$$

In above example, the image size is 7×7, the kernel size is 3×3, the size of output is:

$$(7 - 3 + 1) \times (7 - 3 + 1) = 5 \times 5$$

Padding and stride are techniques of convolution to control the size of outputs. The convolution might lose some information if the features appear in the boundary or corners of the image, although it depends on the kernel size, larger kernel might lose more information.

Padding is used to resolve this kind of problems, add some rows to the top and bottom of the image; and add some columns to the left and right as well. In general, add p_h rows to the image, half on top and half on bottom; and add p_w columns half on left and half on right, all padding rows and columns have value of 0. As shown in Figure 4.68.

Then the convolution is performed on the padded matrix, the size of output will be:

$$(i_h + p_h - k_h + 1) \times (i_w + p_w - k_w + 1)$$

In most of cases, choose $p_h = k_h - 1$ and $p_w = k_w - 1$, and kernel size is odd number, like 3, 5, 7, 9 and so on. Then the same number of paddings will be added to top and bottom, and same for left and right. In the above example, kernel size is 3×3, the padding size is 2×2 meaning one on top, one on bottom, one on left and one on right, as shown in Figure 4.68.

$g =$

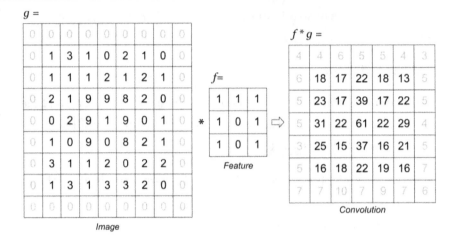

Figure 4.68 Padding for Convolution

As the result, the convolution output is in the size of 7×7, which is same as the original image size.

Stride is another technique of convolution. When the feature/kernel slides over the input image in the above example, it starts from the upper-left corner and moves to right by one element at a time by default, and after it reaches the very right, it moves down by one element by default. The stride is the number of elements the feature/kernel traverses on each move, in this case the stride is 1 by default.

$g =$

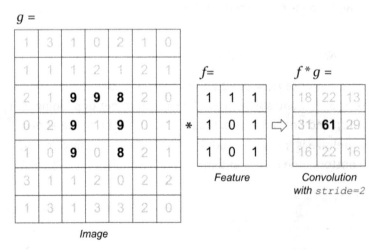

Figure 4.69 Convolution with Stride=2

Sometimes the feature/kernel will traverse more than one element, for example, two or three elements on each move, then the stride is 2 or 3. Figure 4.69 shows the convolution with stride=2.

In general, if the stride is s_w in horizontal direction, and s_h in vertical direction, then the convolution output size is:

$$\frac{(i_h + p_h - k_h + s_h)}{s_h} \times \frac{(i_w + p_w - k_w + s_w)}{s_w}$$

In most of cases, the padding is selected as $p_h = k_h - 1$ and $p_w = k_w - 1$, then the output size is:

$$\frac{(i_h + s_h - 1)}{s_h} \times \frac{(i_w + s_w - 1)}{s_w}$$

The purpose of stride is to reduce the size of the original image for computational efficiency, while keep the features of the original image. In Figure 4.69 the Π shape can also be captured in the convolution result, the value of 61 is still in the middle of the result, that is significantly larger than other values. Most often it is used when the feature/kernel is large because it captures a large area of the original image.

Python Implementation of Convolution

In Python the convolution is implemented by below code snippets:

```
1    import numpy as np
2    def convolution2d(image, kernel,
3                         stride=[1,1], padding=[0,0]):
4        p_h, p_w = padding
5        s_h, s_w = stride
6        image = np.pad(image,
7                        [(p_h, p_h), (p_w, p_w)],
8                        mode='constant',
9                        constant_values=0)
10       k_h, k_w = kernel.shape
11       i_h, i_w = image.shape
12       output_h = (i_h - k_h) // s_h + 1
13       output_w = (i_w - k_w) // s_w + 1
14       output = np.zeros((output_h, output_w))
15       for y in range(0, output_h):
16           for x in range(0, output_w):
```

```
17          c = image[y*s_h : y*s_h+k_h,
18                     x*s_w : x*s_w+k_w]
19          c = np.multiply(c, kernel)
20          output[y][x] = np.sum(c)
21      return output
```

The above example of no padding can be calculated:

```
22   image = np.array([[1, 3, 1, 0, 2, 1 ,0],
23                     [1, 1, 1, 2, 1, 2 ,1],
24                     [2, 1, 9, 9, 8, 2 ,0],
25                     [0, 2, 9, 1, 9, 0 ,1],
26                     [1, 0, 9, 0, 8, 2 ,1],
27                     [3, 1, 1, 2, 0, 2 ,2],
28                     [1, 3, 1, 3, 3, 2 ,0]])
29   kernel = np.array([[1, 1, 1],
30                      [1, 0, 1],
31                      [1, 0, 1]])
32   conv2d = convolution2d(image, kernel)
33   print(conv2d)
```

```
[[18. 17. 22. 18. 13.]
 [23. 17. 39. 17. 22.]
 [31. 22. 61. 22. 29.]
 [25. 15. 37. 16. 21.]
 [16. 18. 22. 19. 16.]]
```

The above example of padding=2 can be calculated:

```
34   conv2d = convolution2d(image, kernel,
35                          padding=[1,1])
36   print(conv2d)
```

```
[[ 4.  4.  6.  5.  5.  4.  3.]
 [ 6. 18. 17. 22. 18. 13.  5.]
 [ 5. 23. 17. 39. 17. 22.  5.]
 [ 5. 31. 22. 61. 22. 29.  4.]
 [ 3. 25. 15. 37. 16. 21.  5.]
 [ 5. 16. 18. 22. 19. 16.  7.]
 [ 7.  7. 10.  7.  9.  7.  6.]]
```

The above example of stride=2 and no padding can be calculated:

```
37   conv2d = convolution2d(image, kernel,
38                          stride=[2,2] )
```

```
 39   print(conv2d)
```

```
[[18. 22. 13.]
 [31. 61. 29.]
 [16. 22. 16.]]
```

Convolution for an Image

Then how the convolution works on a picture? Consider a picture of a dog, when human look at the picture we do not look at each pixel one by one from top-left towards bottom-right, instead we look at the features or objects in the picture, like eyes, nose, mouth, ears, head, body and tails, then we are able to identify the dog in the picture. And in most of cases we ignore the background or colors in order to identify the dog.

As Figure 4.70, it's not colorful and without backgrounds, but there is enough information to identify the features of a dog, because all the important features are in the picture, like ears, eyes, noses, etc.

First to identify the eyes of the dog, there is a feature/kernel for the eye, the convolution operation is applied to the feature, in the convolution results there will be two eyes identified in the corresponding location.

Figure 4.70 A Picture of Dog
Image by Clker-Free-Vector-Images from Pixabay at
https://pixabay.com/vectors/puppy-dog-labrador-retriever-33402/

The convolution result is called feature map in the CNN model, because it contains the features detected and the location of them.

In Figure 4.71, the feature of eyes is swept over the image and the eyes of the dog are identified, the two • marks in the feature map (the convolution result) appear as the largest value.

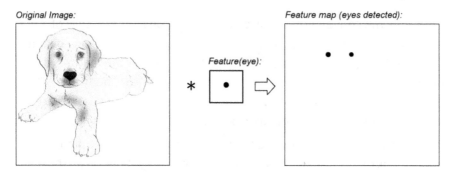

Figure 4.71 Convolution to Identify the Eyes

Second to identify the nose of the dog, this time the feature/kernel is for the nose. As Figure 4.72, the nose is also detected in the results:

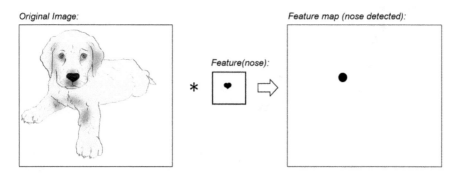

Figure 4.72 Convolution to Identify the Nose

And then similarly, it will apply other features/kernels to identify ears, mouse, heads, and maybe legs, etc.

There are multiple features/kernels in this layer, for example, eyes, noses, ears, mouth, legs, etc. Therefore, multiple feature maps are generated correspondingly. These feature maps are grouped as channels, and they are the output of this convolution layer.

A color picture has three color channels for BGR, meaning B for blue, G for green and R for red. The convolution is performed on each color channel, and then the results are summed up by channels, and become the output of the convolution.

As the result, this convolution layer will output n channels of feature maps in 2D matrices. Each feature map might have the same size of the original image or might reduce the size to some extent depends on the stride as introduced earlier. The important thing is this convolution layer is not to reduce the size but identify the features.

The features/kernels will be part of learning process of the convolutional neural network, meaning it will be learning by itself during the training.

4.10.3 Pooling Layer

The purpose of pooling layer is to reduce the size while keeping the features. It is normally applied after the convolution layer. There are different types of pooling methods, the most widely used are max pooling and average pooling.

Same as convolution, the operation begins from the upper-left corner:

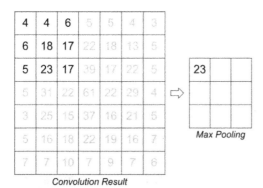

Convolution Result

Max Pooling

This is a 3 × 3 kernel and in the case of max pooling, take the maximum value from the 3 × 3 area covered by the kernel in the upper-left, which is 23, this is the first value in the max pooling result.

In the case of average pooling, take the average value of the area covered by the kernel and take it as the first value of the result.

Then slide the kernel to the next position, and find the maximum, or average of the covered area of matrix. Different from convolution, it will not overlap the already covered elements.

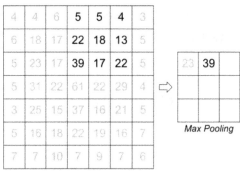

Convolution Result

Max Pooling

Finally, the kernel will traverse the entire input matrix and get the result:

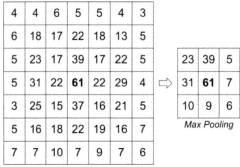

Convolution Result

Max Pooling

The result of the pooling layer significantly reduces the size of input, while keeps the features. In the above max pooling result, the value in the middle is 61, which is the same as that identified by convolution layer. Say this is identified as the nose of the dog, it is still in the max pooling result.

Same as convolution, the Padding and Stride still apply to the pooling layer in the same way.

Here is the python implementation of max pooling:

```
1   import numpy as np
2   def maxpooling2d(image, kernel=[3,3],
3                    stride=[0,0], padding=[0,0]):
4     p_h, p_w = padding
5     s_h, s_w = stride
6     k_h, k_w = kernel
7     image = np.pad(image,
8                    [(p_h, p_h), (p_w, p_w)],
9                    mode='constant',
10                   constant_values=0)
11    i_h, i_w = image.shape
12    output_h = -(-i_h // (k_h + s_h))
13    output_w = -(-i_w // (k_w + s_w))
14    output = np.zeros((output_h, output_w))
15    for y in range(0, output_h):
16      for x in range(0, output_w):
17        y_, x_ = y*(s_h+k_h), x*(s_w+k_w)
18        c = image[y_: y_+k_h, x_ : x_+k_w]
19        output[y][x] = np.amax(c)
20    return output
```

Then run the `convolution2d()` followed by `maxpooling2d()`,

```
21  conv2d = convolution2d(image, kernel,
22                         padding=[1,1])
23  maxp2d = maxpooling2d(conv2d, kernel=[3,3])
24  print(maxp2d)
```

The max pooling result is:

```
[[23. 39.  5.]
 [31. 61.  7.]
 [10.  9.  6.]]
```

The purpose of this layer is to reduce the size of data, or down-sampling. It takes the n channels of feature maps from the convolution layer, and performs pooling operations on every channel, then outputs n channels of pooling results, each as 2D matrix.

4.10.4 Fully Connected Layer

The fully connected layer is same as artificial neural networks (ANNs) introduced in section 4.9, as shown in Figure 4.73.

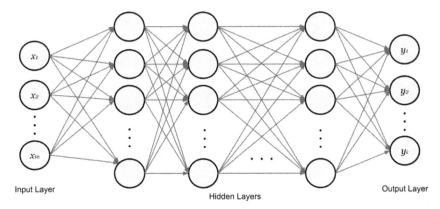

Figure 4.73 Fully Connected Layer

The output of pooling layer consists of n channels of 2D matrices, they are flattened into an 1D array and then connected to the input of fully connected layer. This is considered as input to artificial neural network (ANN), and then the classification calculation is performed in this layer.

Although there are several hidden layers shown in Figure 4.73, it depends on the needs, it could be only one hidden layer, or even no hidden layers. Some adjustments and fine-tunes are normally needed at this layer to make sure it's not overfitting and underfitting.

4.10.5 CNN Architecture

As mentioned above, a CNN is made of convolution layer, pooling layer and fully connected layer. Now put them together, the architecture of the CNN is shown as Figure 4.74. There are two layers of convolution/pooling.

The original picture becomes the input of the CNN model. A number of features are applied to the picture in the first convolution layer, it generates n1 feature maps. And then goes to the pooling layer, max pooling is performed on the feature maps and generate n1 channels of pooling output.

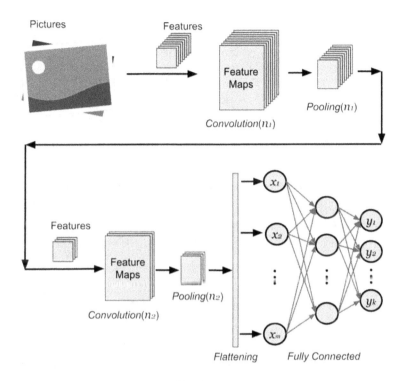

Figure 4.74 CNN Architecture

Consider the first convolution/pooling layer is to identify some features like edges, eyes, nose, mouth, ears, paws etc. The output of this layer becomes the input of second convolution/pooling layer.

In the second convolution layer, again, a number of features are applied to the input data, and this layer generates n_2 channels of feature maps, the pooling operations will be performed on these feature maps.

Consider the second convolution/pooling layer is to identify next level of features like head, body, legs of the dog, this is higher level of features because head includes eyes, nose, mouth and ears, and legs include paws.

Sometimes, depends on the needs more layers of convolution/pooling might be added. After two or multiple layers of convolution/pooling, the amount of data is significantly reduced, and the features are extracted in the output.

The next operation is flattening, because the output of pooling layer consists of n_2 channels of 2D matrix, they will be flattened to a 1D array in order to feed into the fully connected layer.

Finally, the data goes to the fully connected neural network for classification calculation, it's exactly same as the ANN in previous section.

The good thing is you don't worry about how to build the features/kernels, they will be learning by themselves during the training process where thousands or even tens of thousands of images are used for training. The back propagation process will be able to update the features/kernels in the convolution layer and make them best fit to the dataset during the training process. You only need to specify the size and the number of features/kernels, and then the CNN will take care of the rest.

4.10.6 Build a CNN Model with Tensorflow/Keras

As described in section 4.9.2, tensorflow and keras are libraries for deep learning, they will be used to build the CNN models. If the libraries are not installed, follow section 4.9.2 to install them.

The CIFAR-10 Dataset

This section will use CIFAR-10 dataset as example, it's a collection of images that widely used for machine learning or computer vision purposes. It contains 60,000 color images in ten different clusters, each has 32 × 32 pixels. And each cluster has 6,000 random images.

Although this dataset is not real world pictures and is in very low resolution (32 × 32), it's ideal for learning purpose, because it does not cost high computation resources, users can quickly try different algorithms without long time (many hours) of training process.

The dataset comes with keras library and divided randomly into train set of 50,000 and test set of 10,000. The ten clusters are evenly and randomly divided into both train and test sets, meaning each cluster has 5,000 in training set and 1,000 in test set. The ten clusters are airplane, automobile, bird, cat, deer, dog, frog, horse, ship and truck.

See details of CIFAR-10 dataset at:
https://www.cs.toronto.edu/~kriz/cifar.html

Now load the CIFAR-10 dataset,

```
1   import keras
2   from keras.datasets import cifar10
3   (X_train, y_train), (X_test, y_test) =
4                            cifar10.load_data()
5   print("X_train", X_train.shape)
6   print("y_train", y_train.shape)
7   print("X_test", X_test.shape)
8   print("y_test", y_test.shape)
```

```
X_train (50000, 32, 32, 3)
y_train (50000, 1)
X_test (10000, 32, 32, 3)
y_test (10000, 1)
```

There are 50000 in train set and 10000 in test set, each is (32,32,3), because they are color images, each has BGR color channels.

The cluster labels are in y_train and y_test, they look something like:

```
[6, 9, 2, 3, 4, 5, 0, 3 ... ]
```

Each cluster is represented by a number from 0 to 9.

The source codes at *CNN_on_CIFAR10.ipynb* show 100 random sample images with their labels from the dataset, reference it to see how the images look like.

Build a CNN Model

Same as the ANN model in previous section, first create a Sequential model which tells Keras to create model sequentially.

The sequential mode will make the output of each layer as the input to the next layer.

```
1   from keras.models import Sequential
```

```
2    from keras.layers import Dense, Dropout, Flatten
3    from keras.layers import Conv2D, MaxPooling2D
4    cnn_model = Sequential()
```

Then the convolution and max pooling layers are added to the model:

```
5     cnn_model.add(Conv2D(128,
6                          kernel_size=(3, 3),
7                          input_shape = (32, 32, 3),
8                          strides = (1, 1),
9                          padding = "same",
10                         activation = 'relu'))
11    cnn_model.add(MaxPooling2D(pool_size = (2, 2)))
```

Convolution layer is added by `Conv2D()` function to the model, the first parameter is the number of features, it's a best practice that the number should be the power of 2, like 4, 8, 16, 32, 64, 128, etc., although this is not required. Here set 128 as the number of features.

The second parameter of `Conv2D()` is kernel size of the features, it's commonly to use odd number, like 1×1, 3×3, 5×5 or 7×7, and so on. The third parameter is the size of input image, the fourth and fifth parameters are the stride and padding, the last parameter is the activation function, ReLU function is used here, see section 3.3.4, it will convert all negative values to 0, and linear for positive values.

As mentioned earlier, only the number and size of the features need to be specified, the contents will be learned by themselves during the training process.

Optionally, the stride and padding can be specified in the parameters. As explained earlier, `strides = (1, 1)` specifies strides for horizontal and vertical are 1 and 1, meaning the kernel moves one by one in both directions. `padding="same"` specifies the paddings will be added accordingly to make the output same size as input. The padding can also be specified as `"valid"`, means no padding. Therefore `strides = (1, 1)` and `padding= "same"` will make the output the same size as the input.

The input are color images, so each image has RGB three color channels, as explained earlier, the convolution will be performed on each color channel, and then the result values of the three channels will be summed up to generate the convolution results.

The pooling layer is added by `MaxPooling2D()` function, it performs the max pooling operation on the convolution outputs, the pool size is 2×2.

Then two more convolution/pooling layers are added following the first one:

```
12   cnn_model.add(Conv2D(64,
13                        kernel_size=(3, 3),
14                        strides = (1, 1),
15                        padding = "same",
16                        activation = 'relu'))
17   cnn_model.add(MaxPooling2D(pool_size = (2, 2)))
18   cnn_model.add(Dropout(0.25))
19
20   cnn_model.add(Conv2D(32,
21                        kernel_size=(3, 3),
22                        strides = (1, 1),
23                        padding = "same",
24                        activation = 'relu'))
25   cnn_model.add(MaxPooling2D(pool_size = (2, 2)))
26   cnn_model.add(Dropout(0.25))
```

The second layer has 64 feature/kernels, and third layer has 32. The kernel size, activation function and pool size do not change.

In line 18 and 26 `Dropout()` is added to the model, the purpose is to reduce overfitting. Basically, the dropout layer will randomly ignore some neuron nodes during the training, meaning these ignored nodes are temporarily not calculated in both forward propagation and back propagation.

See section 4.9.6 for overfitting vs underfitting.

And also see material #23 in References section to learn how the dropout will reduce overfitting, this book is not going to deep-dive into this details.

The parameter of `Dropout()` is the percentage of neuron nodes to drop temporarily. Here 0.25 is specified, meaning 25% of nodes will be dropped during the training.

Now there are three layers of convolution/pooling in the CNN model, first layer has 128 features, second has 64 and third 32. Next is to flatten the output into a 1D array in order to feed into the fully connected neural network.

```
27   cnn_model.add(Flatten())
```

The last one is the fully connected layer, it's basically same as an artificial neural network, its input is the output of flatten layer.

```
28   cnn_model.add(Dense(units = 256,
29                       activation = 'relu'))
30   cnn_model.add(Dropout(0.5))
31   cnn_model.add(Dense(units = 128,
32                       activation = 'relu'))
33   cnn_model.add(Dropout(0.5))
34   cnn_model.add(Dense(units = 10,
35                       activation = 'softmax'))
```

There are no needs to specify input size because it's connected to the previous flatten layer, which output automatically becomes input for this layer. The first hidden layer has 256 nodes, second 128 nodes, the activation functions are also ReLU.

And Dropout() is also added in between to reduce overfitting.

The output layer has 10 nodes corresponding to the ten clusters of the dataset, so the activation function is softmax, see section 3.3.9.

Finally compile the model, with adam as optimizer, accuracy as metrics and categorical_crossentropy as loss, see section 4.9.2 for details.

```
36   cnn_model.compile(
37                     optimizer='adam',
38                     loss='categorical_crossentropy',
39                     metrics=['accuracy'])
```

This CNN model is much more complex than the previous ANN model, the structure can be displayed by summary() function:

```
40   cnn_model.summary()
```

The structure of the CNN model is shown as:

```
Model: "sequential"
```

```
Layer (type)                    Output Shape          Param #
=================================================================
conv2d (Conv2D)                 (None, 32, 32, 128)        3584
max_pooling2d (MaxPooling2D)    (None, 16, 16, 128)           0
conv2d_1 (Conv2D)               (None, 16, 16, 64)         73792
max_pooling2d_1 (MaxPooling2D)  (None, 8, 8, 64)              0
dropout (Dropout)               (None, 8, 8, 64)              0
conv2d_2 (Conv2D)               (None, 8, 8, 32)          18464
max_pooling2d_2 (MaxPooling2D)  (None, 4, 4, 32)              0
dropout_1 (Dropout)             (None, 4, 4, 32)              0
flatten (Flatten)               (None, 512)                   0
dense (Dense)                   (None, 256)              131328
dropout_2 (Dropout)             (None, 256)                   0
dense_1 (Dense)                 (None, 128)               32896
dropout_3 (Dropout)             (None, 128)                   0
dense_2 (Dense)                 (None, 10)                 1290
=================================================================
Total params: 261,354
Trainable params: 261,354
Non-trainable params: 0
```

Each layer is shown in one line in the summary above. The first line is the convolution layer with the name of `conv2d` and type of `Conv2D`, where the name is unique in the model. The output size of this layer is `(32,32, 128)`, because the number of kernels is specified as 128, and each image size is 32 by 32.

The next is max pooling layer, the kernel size was specified as `(2, 2)`, so the output of this layer becomes `(16, 16, 128)`, which is reduced from the previous layer.

And the same things happen in the next two convolution and max-pooling layers. The dropout layers do not change the size from inputs to outputs.

The flatten layer converts the previous output of `(4, 4, 32)` into 1D array of size `(512)`, and it becomes the input of the fully connected neural network layer.

The fully connected neural network has two hidden layers of 256 and 128, then the final output is 10, which corresponds to the ten clusters of the dataset.

Before starting the training, it's necessary to normalize the input data, as we did before, `StandardScaler()` from `sklearn` library will be used:

```
41    from sklearn import preprocessing
42    scaler = preprocessing.StandardScaler()
43    X_train = scaler.fit_transform(
44                 X_train.reshape(-1, X_train.shape[-1]))
45                 .reshape(X_train.shape)
46    X_test = scaler.transform(
47                 X_test.reshape(-1, X_test.shape[-1]))
48                 .reshape(X_test.shape)
```

The standard scaler only take a 2D matrix as parameter, here X_train is (50000, 32, 32, 3), line 44 is to transform/reshape it to 2D matrix, perform the standard scaler, and then line 45 is to reshape it back to the original size. The same operation is done for X_test as well in line 47 and 48.

Then the training process:

```
49    history = cnn_model.fit(
50                 X_train,
51                 to_categorical(y_train),
52                 batch_size = 128,
53                 epochs = 100,
54                 verbose = 1,
55                 validation_data=(X_test,
56                             to_categorical(y_test))
57           )
```

The one-hot encoding is performed on y_train and y_test at line 51 and 56, by to_categorical() function, it was described in previous sections.

This training process could take some time due to the amount of data and the complexity of the model. Depends on the hardware resources, e.g. CPUs vs GUPs, it could take from minutes to hours. In my case, it took about 10 minutes in Google Colab with GPU runtime.

If the training is run on local machine, and if the hardware is not powerful enough, you might get errors in fit() process, in this case try to reduce the batch_size. If not help, then try to use a subset of sample data, say, X_train[0:5000], y_train[0:5000]. However, it only eliminates the error but not do a good job for training. To perform the training of deep learning projects a powerful machine is needed.

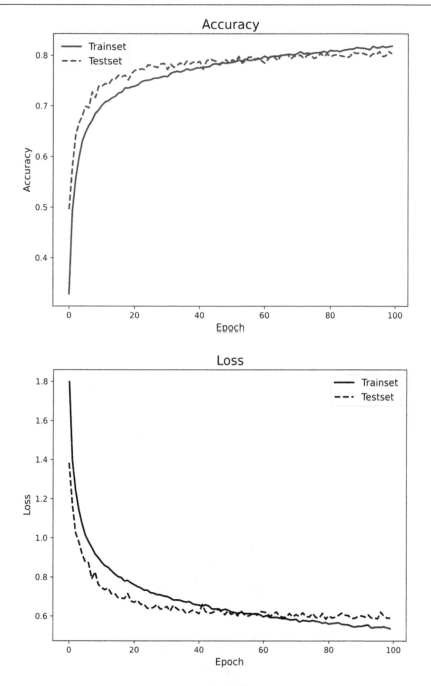

Figure 4.75 CNN on CIFAR10 Dataset
Generated by source code at CNN_on_CIFAR10.ipynb

The test set is used for validation in the training process, the results of train and test sets are shown in Figure 4.75. Both test and train sets go almost together in accuracy and loss, meaning this model is not overfitting nor underfitting.

The full source code is available at CNN_on_CIFAR10.ipynb.

In most cases the model of this complexity will not get a good result at first try, it's usually necessary to adjust parameters and try back and forth until reaching a better result. The factors to adjust in the fine-tune process include number of layers, number of features in conv2d layer, kernel sizes, number of hidden layers in fully connected layer, number of nodes of each layer, etc. In my case I have tried many times to achieve the results of Figure 4.75.

Once the model is trained, it can be saved to a file, and can be loaded later to avoid the long training process next time.

```
58  from tensorflow.keras.models import load_model
59  # Save the model
60  cnn_model.save('cnn_on_cifar-10.h5')
61  # Load the model
62  cnn_model = load_model('cnn_on_cifar-10.h5')
63  cnn_model.summary()
```

The model can be evaluated by its evaluate() function,

```
64  score = cnn_model.evaluate(X_test,
65                      to_categorical(y_test))
66  print('Test loss:', score[0])
67  print('Test accuracy:', score[1])
```

```
Test loss: 0.6104579567909241
Test accuracy: 0.794700026512146
```

It can also be evaluated by the metrics provided by sklearn, as we did in previous sections.

```
68  from sklearn import metrics
69  y_pred = cnn_model.predict(X_test)
70  y_pred = np.argmax(y_pred, axis=1)
71  a_score = metrics.accuracy_score(y_test, y_pred)
72  c_matrix = metrics.confusion_matrix(y_test, y_pred)
```

```
73   c_report=metrics.classification_report(y_test,y_pred)
74   print("Accuracy Score:\n", a_score)
75   print("Confusion matrix:\n", c_matrix)
76   print("Classification Report:\n", c_report)
```

Accuracy Score:
 0.7947

Confusion matrix:
```
[[825  18  32   3  14   2   5   5  73  23]
 [ 11 917   2   3   2   0   5   0  16  44]
 [ 62   0 700  21  86  22  71  23   9   6]
 [ 37   9  71 580  57  96  82  39  16  13]
 [ 18   3  41  21 830   8  34  38   7   0]
 [ 16   3  53 191  50 584  27  63   5   8]
 [  6   6  33  35  24   3 881   5   6   1]
 [ 17   0  42  21  39  20   6 848   2   5]
 [ 38  15   7   5   4   0   4   2 909  16]
 [ 20  59   7   7   0   2   3  11  18 873]]
```

Classification Report:

	precision	recall	f1-score	support
0	0.79	0.82	0.80	1000
1	0.89	0.92	0.90	1000
2	0.71	0.70	0.70	1000
3	0.65	0.58	0.61	1000
4	0.75	0.83	0.79	1000
5	0.79	0.58	0.67	1000
6	0.79	0.88	0.83	1000
7	0.82	0.85	0.83	1000
8	0.86	0.91	0.88	1000
9	0.88	0.87	0.88	1000
accuracy			0.79	10000
macro avg	0.79	0.79	0.79	10000
weighted avg	0.79	0.79	0.79	10000

4.10.7 Popular CNN Architectures

LeNet was introduced in 1990's by Yann LeCun, it starts the era of Convolutional Neural Networks (CNN), see the original paper called *"Gradient-Based Learning Applied to Document Recognition"* at material #24 in References section. Although the limitation of computation capabilities made the algorithm difficult to implement until recent years.

There are several popular CNN architectures, such as:

- LeNet-5
- AlexNet
- VGG16
- Inception V1
- ResNet-50

This section will introduce LeNet-5 only, which is considered as a popular and classic CNN architecture. It is used for recognizing the handwritten and machine-printed characters and is designed for the input of 32×32 grayscale images.

The LeNet-5 architecture is shown in page 7 (Fig. 2) of the original paper at http://yann.lecun.com/exdb/publis/pdf/lecun-01a.pdf, which is not included in this book.

The architecture is straightforward and simple, it consists of two layers of convolutional and pooling, the pooling is average pooling which is different from the max pooling in the previous example in 4.10.6. Then the fully connected layer includes two hidden layers, and the final output layer is a softmax classifier of ten outputs.

The MNIST dataset is handwritten digits in grayscale, each image size is 28×28, it is used in the LeNet-5 model. Load MNIST dataset and normalize the data with standard scaler:

```
1   import numpy as np
2   from keras.datasets import mnist
3   from sklearn import preprocessing
4   # Load MNIST dataset
5   np.random.seed(0)
6   (X_train, y_train), (X_test, y_test) =
7                           mnist.load_data()
8   print("X_train", X_train.shape)
9   print("y_train", y_train.shape)
10  print("X_test", X_test.shape)
11  print("y_test", y_test.shape)
12  # Normalize the data
13  scaler = preprocessing.StandardScaler()
14  X_train = scaler.fit_transform(
15                          X_train.reshape((-1, 784)))
```

```
16  X_test = scaler.fit_transform(
17                     X_test.reshape((-1, 784)))
18  X_train = X_train.reshape(X_train.shape[0],28,28,1)
19  X_test = X_test.reshape(X_test.shape[0],28,28,1)
20  input_shape = X_train.shape[1:]
```

Then build the LeNet-5 model:

```
21  import tensorflow as tf
22  import keras
23  import keras.layers as layers
24  from keras.models import Sequential
25  lenet5 = keras.Sequential()
26  lenet5.add(layers.Conv2D(filters=6,
27                     kernel_size=(3, 3),
28                     activation='relu',
29                     input_shape=input_shape))
30  lenet5.add(layers.AveragePooling2D())
31  lenet5.add(layers.Conv2D(filters=16,
32                     kernel_size=(3, 3),
33                     activation='relu'))
34  lenet5.add(layers.AveragePooling2D())
35  lenet5.add(layers.Flatten())
36  lenet5.add(layers.Dense(units=120,activation='relu'))
37  lenet5.add(layers.Dense(units=84,activation='relu'))
38  lenet5.add(layers.Dense(units=10,activation='softmax'))
39  lenet5.compile(optimizer='adam',
40                 loss='categorical_crossentropy',
41                 metrics=['accuracy'])
42  lenet5.summary()
```

The structure of LeNet-5 model is displayed as following:

```
Model: "sequential"
```

Layer (type)	Output Shape	Param #
conv2d (Conv2D)	(None, 26, 26, 6)	60
avg_pooling2d (AvgPooling2D)	(None, 13, 13, 6)	0
conv2d_1 (Conv2D)	(None, 11, 11, 16)	880
avg_pooling2d_1 (AvgPooling2D)	(None, 5, 5, 16)	0
flatten (Flatten)	(None, 400)	0
dense (Dense)	(None, 120)	48120
dense_1 (Dense)	(None, 84)	10164
dense_2 (Dense)	(None, 10)	850

```
Total params: 60,074
Trainable params: 60,074
Non-trainable params: 0
```

The first Conv2D layer has 6 features with size of `(3,3)`, the activation function is ReLU, the input shape is `(28, 28, 1)`. Note, the dataset loaded from `mnist.load_data()` has the size of `(28, 28)`, it has to be reshaped to `(28, 28, 1)` in order to feed into `Conv2D()` function. The output size is `(26, 26, 6)`, which is different from the original data size because no padding specified in the function.

The pooling layer is using average pooling, the default pool size is `(2, 2)`, no padding and no stride. Then the output size is `(13, 13, 6)`.

The second Conv2d layer has 16 features with size of `(3,3)`, and the same ReLU function. The output size is `(11, 11, 16)`. The pooling layer is the same as the previous layer, its output size is `(5, 5, 16)`.

Then the flatten layer converts the output of `(5, 5, 16)` into 1D array of 400, then feed them into the fully connected layers.

The fully connected layers have two hidden layers, first 120 nodes and second 84 nodes. The final layer has 10 outputs corresponding to the ten clusters of the dataset.

Train the LeNet-5 model:

```
43    batch_size = 128
44    epochs = 100
45    # Train the LeNet-5 model
46    history =
47    lenet5.fit(X_train, to_categorical(y_train),
48                batch_size = batch_size,
49                epochs = epochs,
50                verbose = 2,
51                validation_data=(X_test,
52                            to_categorical(y_test)) )
```

The training process could take some time because the amount of data, select GPU as computation resources if possible.

If the training is run on local machine without powerful hardware, you might get errors in `fit()` process, in this case try to reduce the `batch_size`. If not help, then try to use a subset of sample data, say, `X_train[0:5000], y_train[0:5000]`. However, it might eliminate the error but not do a good job for training, because only a subset of data is used to train the model. Deep learning requires powerful hardware due to the complexity of the model and the amount of data, if the local machine do not have enough computational resources, consider using a cloud environment, see section 2.2.

Evaluate the model after the training:

```
53   score = lenet5.evaluate(X_test,
54                          to_categorical(y_test))
55   print('Test loss:', score[0])
56   print('Test accuracy:', score[1])
```

```
Test loss: 0.08838732540607452
Test accuracy: 0.9911999702453613
```

The accuracy achieves 99.1%, which is pretty good. The confusion matrix and classification report are shown as below:

```
57  from sklearn import metrics
58  y_pred = lenet5.predict(X_test)
59  y_pred = np.argmax(y_pred, axis=1)
60  a_score = metrics.accuracy_score(y_test, y_pred)
61  c_matrix = metrics.confusion_matrix(y_test, y_pred)
62  c_report = metrics.classification_report(y_test,
        y_pred)
63  print("Accuracy Score:\n", a_score)
64  print("Confusion matrix:\n", c_matrix)
65  print("Classification Report:\n", c_report)
```

```
Accuracy Score:
 0.9912

Confusion matrix:
[[ 974    0    0    0    0    0    3    1    2    0]
 [   0 1132    1    1    0    0    1    0    0    0]
 [   0    1 1024    1    0    0    1    3    2    0]
 [   0    0    2 1004    0    2    0    0    1    1]
 [   0    0    1    0  974    0    3    0    0    4]
 [   2    0    0    5    0  883    1    0    0    1]
```

327

```
[   2   3   0   0   2   3 946   0   2    0]
[   0   1   4   1   0   0   0 1019   1    2]
[   2   0   1   2   0   3   0   1 961    4]
[   0   0   0   0   7   3   0   2   2  995]]
```

```
Classification Report:
              precision    recall  f1-score   support
           0       0.99      0.99      0.99       980
           1       1.00      1.00      1.00      1135
           2       0.99      0.99      0.99      1032
           3       0.99      0.99      0.99      1010
           4       0.99      0.99      0.99       982
           5       0.99      0.99      0.99       892
           6       0.99      0.99      0.99       958
           7       0.99      0.99      0.99      1028
           8       0.99      0.99      0.99       974
           9       0.99      0.99      0.99      1009
    accuracy                           0.99     10000
   macro avg       0.99      0.99      0.99     10000
weighted avg       0.99      0.99      0.99     10000
```

The LeNet-5 is straightforward, simple and efficient to recognize the handwritten digits, and it's good to get started with convolutional neural networks (CNNs). The full source code is in *CNN_LeNet_5.ipynb*.

Other popular CNN architectures like AlexNet, VGG16, Inception V1 and ResNet-50 are more complex than LeNet-5 and they are not included in this book. Please reference materials #25 to #28 in the References section for details.

4.11 Recommendation System

4.11.1 Introduction

A recommendation system, also called recommender system, is a machine learning algorithm to provide recommendations to the clients or consumers with the most relevant merchandises. For example, when purchase a smart phone from e-commerce websites like Amazon.com or eBay.com, the system will provide recommendations with the most relevant items like the headsets, phone cases, and chargers; when watch a romance movie from Netflix, it will provide recommendations with other romance movies, etc.

The algorithm is to find out information based on relevancy, and the most relevant information will be recommended to the users.

The recommendation system consists of two categories: *Content-based filtering* and *Collaborative filtering*.

Content-based filtering is the algorithm to make recommendations based on the contents, or attributes of the products. The algorithm will learn the user's preferences from the previous activities and find out the relevant items based on the contents or attributes of these items. For example, a user watched Star Wars series of movies, the algorithm might think this user is a fan of fantasy and adventure, it will find out other fantasy and adventure movies and recommend to the user.

The contents or attributes of movies include the directors, casts and genres of the movies. The algorithm will make recommendations based on this information.

The drawback of the content-based filtering is the necessitates of great efforts to identify the attributes of the products which might require the knowledge in the domain and most likely manual work. Although the movies come with these attributes when they are produced, consider millions of products in Amazon.com, it needs lots of work to identify the attributes of all products, and it might also need expertise on the products.

The Collaborative filtering, on the other hand, makes recommendations based on the users' interaction with the products. Millions of users interact with millions of products by leaving ratings, specifically a user purchases a product and leaves a rating indicating if s/he likes or dislikes the item. This rating data is fed into the collaborative filtering algorithm as input, and recommendations are made based on the rating data.

There is no need to identify the contents or attributes of each item, however it needs to collect the user ratings, and that's all to make recommendations.

Furthermore, collaborative filtering is divided into two sub-categories: *memory-based* and *model-based* methods.

Memory-based method is simple and straightforward because it doesn't use any models. The recommendations are made based on the "memory" of historical data.

Model-based method, on the other hand, uses a machine learning model to train the data and make recommendations, for example a deep learning neural network.

4.11.2 Content-based Filtering

Content-based filtering uses the information of contents or attributes of the products to make recommendations. Let's look at several movies as example, the movies' data comes with genres as attributes, like action, adventure and so on. Figure 4.76 shows six movies and their genres.

#	Movie Title	Action	Adventure	Crime	Drama	Romance	War
0	Star Wars (1977)	1	1	0	0	1	1
1	Legends of the Fall (1994)	0	0	0	1	1	1
2	Natural Born Killers (1994)	1	0	0	0	0	0
3	Return of the Jedi (1983)	1	1	0	0	1	1
4	Starship Troopers (1997)	1	1	0	0	0	1
5	Pulp Fiction (1994)	0	0	1	1	0	0

Figure 4.76 Movie Genres

Star Wars (1977) has genres of action, adventure, romance and war; while *Legends of the Fall (1994)* has drama, romance and war, etc.

Say a user watched *Star Wars (1977)*, how the content-based filtering algorithm will recommend movies? It will find the similar or relevant movies to *Star Wars (1977)*, there are different ways to find out the similarity. Cosine similarity is a simple and straightforward method for this purpose, see section 3.1.14.

Each row or each movie in Figure 4.76 is considered as a vector, the cosine similarity is calculated between *Star Wars (1977)* and other movies.

```
1    import numpy as np
```

```
2    from numpy.linalg import norm
3    star_wars    = np.array([1, 1, 0, 0, 1, 1])
4    legends_fall = np.array([0, 0, 0, 1, 1, 1])
5    cos_sim = np.dot(star_wars, legends_fall) / \
6                (norm(star_wars)*norm(legends_fall))
7    print("Cosine Similarity is:", cos_sim)
```

```
Cosine Similarity is: 0.577
```

The above code snippets calculate the cosine similarity between *Star Wars
(1977)* and *Legends of the Fall (1994)*, line 3 and 4 take the genres as
vectors; line 5 and 6 calculate the cosine similarity of the two vectors. The
result is 0.577, because both movies are same in some genres and
different in some others, see Figure 4.76.

Similarly, the cosine similarity values between *Star Wars (1977)* and other
movies can also be calculated. Then the largest value is the most relevant
item to recommend.

Alternatively, instead of calculating it one by one, we can calculate the
pairwise values with cosine_similarity() function, then everything is
calculated in one shot:

```
1    from sklearn.metrics.pairwise
2            import cosine_similarity
3    movies = np.array(
4        [ [1, 1, 0, 0, 1, 1],
5          [0, 0, 0, 1, 1, 1],
6          [1, 0, 0, 0, 0, 0],
7          [1, 1, 0, 0, 1, 1],
8          [1, 1, 0, 0, 0, 1],
9          [0, 0, 1, 1, 0, 0] ])
10   cos_sim = cosine_similarity(movies)
11   cos_sim_df = pd.DataFrame(cos_sim)
12   cos_sim_df
```

The result looks like:

	0	1	2	3	4	5
0	1.000	0.577	0.500	1.000	0.866	0.000
1	0.577	1.000	0.000	0.577	0.333	0.408
2	0.500	0.000	1.000	0.500	0.577	0.000
3	1.000	0.577	0.500	1.000	0.866	0.000
4	0.866	0.333	0.577	0.866	1.000	0.000
5	0.000	0.408	0.000	0.000	0.000	1.000

The genres in Figure 4.76 are organized in a matrix called `movies` in line 3 to 9, and `cosine_similarity()` is invoked in line 10.

The result is a symmetry matrix, its diagonal elements are all 1.0, because the diagonals are cosine similarity between themselves, for example the element in (1, 1), meaning row 1 column 1, is the cosine similarity between movie #1 and itself.

The result is symmetry matrix because the element in (i, j) is same as that in (j, i), for example the value in (4, 1) is same as that in (1, 4) which is 0.333, because the cosine similarity between movie #1 and #4 is same as that between movie #4 and #1.

Based on this result matrix, if want to find relevant movies to *Star Wars (1977)* which is movie #0, just simply take row 0, or column 0 since they are same.

	0	1	2	3	4	5
0	1.000	0.577	0.500	1.000	0.866	0.000

Remove the diagonal element because it's the similarity value to itself. Then sort the remaining values in descending order:

	3	4	1	2	5
0	1.000	0.866	0.577	0.500	0.000

This is the recommendations to the user who watched movie #0. The movie #3 has 1.0 similarity meaning exactly same type of movie #0, and #4 has 0.866 and so on.

Now cross-check the above result with Figure 4.76, movie #3 is *Return of the Jedi (1983)*, its genres are exactly same as movie #1, therefore it shows 1.0 similarity in the result. The movie #4, *Starship Troopers (1997)*, has only 1 different genre from movie #0, then 0.866. And movie #5 has totally different genres from movie #0, then 0.0 similarity.

This is the idea of content-based filtering. Let's look at how to implement it in Python with a real dataset.

MovieLens Dataset

MovieLens at https://grouplens.org/datasets/movielens/ has published a number of movies related datasets for machine learning purpose, this section will use the 100K Dataset, it includes 100K ratings from 943 users on 1682 movies.

Import libraries and load the dataset:

```
1    import pandas as pd
2    import numpy as np
3    from zipfile import ZipFile
4    from pathlib import Path
5    import matplotlib.pyplot as plt
6    from tensorflow import keras
7    from sklearn.metrics.pairwise import cosine_similarity
8    movielens = 'ml-100k'
9    url = 'http://files.grouplens.org/datasets/movielens/
10   ml-100k.zip'
11   movielens_file = keras.utils.get_file(
12       fname = movielens + '.zip',
13       origin = url,
14       cache_dir='./' )
15   datasets_path = Path(movielens_file).parents[0]
16   movielens_dir = datasets_path / movielens
17   # Extract the data file.
18   if not movielens_dir.exists():
19       with ZipFile(movielens_file, "r") as zip:
20           zip.extractall(path=datasets_path)
```

The above code will download the dataset from the URL at http://files.grouplens.org/datasets/movielens/ml-100k.zip, unzip and save it in the current directory.

There are a number of files in the dataset, u.item is the file with movie data, we will use this information for content-based filtering.

```
21   movie_col = ['movieid', 'title', 'releasedate',
22                'videoreleasedate', 'IMDbURL',
23                'unknown', 'Action', 'Adventure',
24                'Animation', 'Children', 'Comedy',
25                'Crime', 'Documentary', 'Drama',
26                'Fantasy', 'Film-Noir', 'Horror',
27                'Musical', 'Mystery', 'Romance',
28                'Sci-Fi', 'Thriller', 'War',
29                'Western']
30   movies = pd.read_csv( movielens_dir/"u.item",
31                         sep='|',
```

```
32                              header=None,
33                              names=movie_col,
34                              encoding='latin-1')
35    movies
```

The movies data looks something like Figure 4.76, there are totally 1682 movies in rows, and 19 genres in columns.

Content-based Filtering

We will manipulate the data to perform the content-based recommendations.

Create a matrix of genres by removing the unrelated columns:

```
36    genre_matrix = movies.drop(['movieid',
37                  'title',
38                  'releasedate',
39                  'videoreleasedate',
40                  'IMDbURL'], \axis=1)
41    genre_matrix
```

The `genre_matrix` looks something like:

	Action	Comedy	Crime	Drama	Fantasy	Sci-Fi	War	...
1	0	1	0	0	0	0	0	...
2	1	0	0	0	0	0	0	...
3	0	0	0	0	0	0	0	...
4	1	1	0	1	0	0	0	...
5	0	0	1	1	0	0	0	...
6	0	0	0	1	0	0	0	...

Each row represents a movie identified by the movie ID; each column represents a genre identified by the column name.

Then calculate the cosine similarity of `genre_matrix`:

```
42    movie_similarity = cosine_similarity(genre_matrix)
43    movie_similarity_df = pd.DataFrame(movie_similarity,
44                          columns=movies.movieid,
45                          index=movies.movieid)
46    movie_similarity_df
```

The result looks like:

Id	1	2	3	5	6	. . .
1	1.00000	0.00000	0.00000	0.33333	0.00000	...

2	0.00000	1.00000	0.57735	0.33333	0.33333	...
3	0.00000	0.57735	1.00000	0.00000	0.57735	...
4	0.33333	0.33333	0.00000	1.00000	0.33333	...
5	0.00000	0.33333	0.57735	0.33333	1.00000	...
...	...	...	...	...	...	...

It's a symmetry matrix with all diagonals of 1.0, it's also a square matrix, the number of row and columns are same, which equals to the total number of movies in the dataset. The IDs in both row and column represent the movie ID.

Make Recommendations

When a user purchases a movie to watch or puts the movie into the shopping cart, the system will recommend a number of relevant movies to the user. For example, the user selects movie ID 50, and the system will recommend 10 relevant movies,

```
47   RECOMM_MOVIE = 50
48   RECOMM_COUNT = 10
49   movies[movies['movieid'] == RECOMM_MOVIE]
```

The details of the selected movie are:

```
ID  title             ReleaseDate   IMDbURL
50  Star Wars (1977)  01-Jan-1977   http://us.imdb.com/M/ti...
```

Finally make the recommendations:

```
50   recommendations = movie_similarity_df.copy()
51   recommendations.rename(columns =
52                    {RECOMM_MOVIE:'similarity'},
53                    inplace = True)
54   recommendations.drop(index=RECOMM_MOVIE,
55                    inplace=True)
56   recommendations = recommendations['similarity'] \
57        .sort_values(ascending=False) \
58        .reset_index() \
59        .merge(movies, how="left", on="movieid") \
60        .head(RECOMM_COUNT)
61   recommendations[['movieid','title','similarity']]
```

Line 50 makes a copy of the cosine similarity matrix; and line 51 to 53 rename the column of the selected movie to `similarity`. And line 54 and 55 remove the row of the diagonal element of the selected movie.

Line 56 chooses the column named `similarity`, and ignores all other columns. Line 57 sort the column in descending order, then the most relevant items are listed at the top.

Line 59 merges the `movies` data by `movieid` to retrieve the detailed information like title, release date, IMDb URL etc. And line 60 gets the top `RECOMM_COUNT` items.

The recommendation results are show as below:

```
    ID    title                                  similarity
0   181   Return of the Jedi (1983)              1.00000
1   172   Empire Strikes Back, The (1980)        0.91287
2   498   African Queen, The (1951)              0.89443
3   271   Starship Troopers (1997)               0.89443
4   373   Judge Dredd (1995)                     0.77460
5   897   Time Tracers (1995)                    0.77460
6   1239  Cutthroat Island (1995)                0.77460
7   241   Last of the Mohicans, The (1992)       0.77460
8   230   Star Trek IV: The Voyage Home …        0.77460
9   229   Star Trek III: The Search for …        0.77460
```

Conclusion

Content-based filtering algorithm utilizes only the item information to make recommendations, it doesn't need information from other users, like ratings, etc. However, the prerequisite is the detailed contents and attributes are collected and associated with the items or products, which might require expertise in the domain.

4.11.3 Collaborative Filtering, Memory-based

Collaborative filtering uses similarities between users and items simultaneously to provide recommendations. It considers all users, all items and all user-item ratings, the idea is similar users will like similar items, therefore the recommendations are made to a user based on the interests and preferences of other similar users.

Below is a user-item matrix, the users give ratings to the movies from 1 to 5. There are two users Tom and Bob listed in the rows, and there are five movies shown in the column.

	Toy Story	*GoldenEye*	*Star Wars*	*Supercop*	*Twister*
Tom	5	4		5	1
Bob	5	5	2		

Because Tom and Bob both give high rating on *Toy Story* and *GoldenEye*, they are considered as similar users. Tom also gives high rating on *Supercop*, so Bob most likely wants to watch it as well, so the movie will be recommended to Bob. This is the basic idea of collaborative filtering.

MovieLens Dataset

This section will use the same MovieLens dataset again, but load a different file `ml-latest-small.zip`, which is a little different from the one in previous section, it includes 100,836 ratings from 610 users on 9742 movies.

Import libraries and load the dataset:

```
1    import pandas as pd
2    import numpy as np
3    from zipfile import ZipFile
4    from pathlib import Path
5    import matplotlib.pyplot as plt
6    from tensorflow import keras
7    from sklearn.metrics.pairwise
8        import cosine_similarity
9    movielens = 'ml-latest-small'
10   url = 'http://files.grouplens.org/datasets/movielens/
11                           ml-latest-small.zip'
12   movielens_file = keras.utils.get_file(
13       fname = movielens + '.zip',
14       origin = url,
15       cache_dir='./')
16   datasets_path = Path(movielens_file).parents[0]
17   movielens_dir = datasets_path / movielens
18   # Extract the data file.
19   if not movielens_dir.exists():
20       with ZipFile(movielens_file, "r") as zip:
21           zip.extractall(path=datasets_path)
22   # Load movies and ratings data
23   ratings = pd.read_csv(movielens_dir/"ratings.csv")
```

```
| 24    movies = pd.read_csv(movielens_dir/"movies.csv")
```

The zip file is downloaded from the URL and saved in the current directory, unzip the file and load `ratings.csv` file to `ratings`, and `movies.csv` file to `movies`.

`ratings` look like:

userId	movieId	rating	timestamp
1	1	4.0	964982703
1	3	4.0	964981247
1	6	4.0	964982224
1	47	5.0	964983815
1	50	5.0	964982931
...	...	...	...

100836 rows × 4 columns

And `movies` look like:

ID	title	genres
1	Toy Story (1995)	Adventure|Animation|...
2	Jumanji (1995)	Adventure|Children|...
3	Grumpier Old Men (1995)	Comedy|Romance
4	Waiting to Exhale (1995)	Comedy|Drama|...
5	Father of the Bride Part...	Comedy
...	...	...

9742 rows × 3 columns

Find out the number of unique users and unique movies:

```
| 25    n_users = ratings['userId'].nunique()
| 26    n_movies = ratings['movieId'].nunique()
| 27    n_users, n_movies
```

(610, 9724)

Collaborative Filtering

In order to manipulate the data effectively, data validation is performed as below:

* a movie is valid at least 30 users have rated it.
* a user is valid at least 20 ratings have been given by the user.

```
| 28    ratings = ratings[ratings.groupby("movieId")
```

```
29                              ["movieId"].transform("size") > 30]
30    ratings = ratings[ratings.groupby("userId")
31                              ["userId"].transform("size") > 20]
```

Create the user-movie matrix, the users are listed in rows and movies are in columns,

```
32    user_movie = ratings.pivot_table(index="userId",
33                                      columns="movieId",
34                                      values="rating" )
35    user_movie = user_movie.subtract(
36                              user_movie.mean(axis=1),
37                              axis = 0 )
38    user_movie = user_movie.fillna(0)
39    user_movie
```

The results are:

```
movieId  1       2       3       4       5       6       ...
userId
1        -0.366  0.000   -0.366  0.000   0.000   -0.366  ...
2        0.000   0.000   0.000   0.000   0.000   0.000   ...
3        0.000   0.000   0.000   0.000   0.000   0.000   ...
4        0.000   0.000   0.000   0.000   0.000   0.000   ...
5        0.363   0.000   0.000   0.000   0.000   0.000   ...
...      ...     ...     ...     ...     ...     ...     ...
```

Line 32 to 34 convert `ratings` to the `user_movie` matrix, the users are in rows and identified by `userId`, the movies are in columns and identified by `movieId`. This is a sparse matrix which means it's comprised of mostly zero values, because not every user rates every movie, instead a user might rate only a few movies.

Line 35 to 37 normalizes the matrix. First obtain the mean (or average) value by users, say a user rates 30 movies, then calculate the mean (or average) rating of these 30 movies, this is done in line 36. Then subtract this mean rating from every user's rating. For example, the mean rating for the first user (`userId=1`) is `4.366`, the rating for the first movie (`movieId=1`) is `4.0`, then the normalized value is `-0.366`, this is the value in top-left corner of above results.

The next step is to find the similar users, cosine similarity is again used for this purpose, same as previous section. Reference section 3.1.14 for details of cosine similarity. Each row of `user_movie` matrix has the ratings for a user; therefore each row can be considered as a vector for a user, cosine similarity can be calculated by the vectors.

```
40    user_similarity = cosine_similarity(user_movie)
41    user_similarity_df = pd.DataFrame(user_similarity,
42                            columns=user_movie.index.values,
43                            index=user_movie.index.values)
44    user_similarity_df
```

The results are:

	1	2	3	4	5	6	...
1	1.000	0.001	0.001	0.048	0.022	-0.045	...
2	0.001	1.000	0.000	-0.017	0.022	-0.021	...
3	0.001	0.000	1.000	-0.011	-0.032	0.005	...
4	0.048	-0.017	-0.011	1.000	-0.030	0.014	...
5	0.022	0.022	-0.032	-0.030	1.000	0.009	...
6	-0.045	-0.021	0.005	0.014	0.009	1.000	...
...	...	...	...	...	...	...	...

The cosine similarity result is a symmetry matrix, all the diagonal elements are 1.000. It's also a square matrix, the number of row and columns are same and equals to the number of users.

Make Recommendations

With the similarity matrix in place, the recommendations can be made for a user. Say we want to recommend 10 movies for userId=6.

```
45    RECOMM_USER = 6
46    RECOMM_COUNT = 10
```

Then find similar users to RECOMM_USER,

```
47    user_similarity_df.drop(index=RECOMM_USER,
48                            inplace=True)
49    similar_users=user_similarity_df[RECOMM_USER] \
50                        .sort_values(ascending=False) \
51                        .head(10)
52    similar_users
```

Line 47 and 48 remove the diagonal elements for the selected user. Line 49 selects the column of the selected user RECOMM_USER; line 50 sort the column in descending order, because the largest value indicates most similar user. And then take the top 10 users:

```
        userId   similarity
   0     181      0.263749
   1     126      0.223044
   2     584      0.218799
   3     411      0.195856
   4     179      0.192669
   5     470      0.18911
   6     136      0.180533
   7     94       0.172542
   8     379      0.168927
   9     486      0.154106
```

These users are most similar to RECOMM_USER=6. Next, find out the movies watched by the selected user, if the user has ratings on the movies, then the movies are considered watched by the user.

```
53   user_watched = ratings[ratings['userId'] == 6 \
54         .sort_values(by='rating', ascending=False) \
55         .merge(movies, on='movieId', how='inner')
```

And find out the movies rated by the similar users,

```
56   similar_users_watched =
57   ratings[ratings['userId'].isin(similar_users.index)]
58         .groupby(['movieId'])['rating'].mean() \
59         .sort_values(by='rating', ascending=False)
```

There could be multiple users rating on the same movie, the result is grouped by movieId and with mean (or average) rating in line 58, and then the ratings are sorted descending order.

Finally, make recommendations by removing the movies already watched by RECOMM_USER from similar_users_watched,

```
60   recommendations =
61   similar_users_watched[similar_users_watched['movieId']
62         .isin(user_watched['movieId']) == False] \
63         .merge(movies[['movieId', 'title']],
64                     on='movieId', how='inner') \
65         .head(RECOMM_COUNT)
66   recommendations
```

Take the top RECOMM_COUNT movies from the results to obtain the final recommendation:

```
  movieId rating  title
0   5060    5.0    M*A*S*H (a.k.a. MASH) (1970)
1   2502    5.0    Office Space (1999)
2   1197    5.0    Princess Bride, The (1987)
3   1196    5.0    Star Wars: Episode V - The Empire ...
4   2542    5.0    Lock, Stock & Two Smoking Barrels (1998)
5   1136    5.0    Monty Python and the Holy Grail (1975)
6   2580    5.0    Go (1999)
7   1097    5.0    E.T. the Extra-Terrestrial (1982)
8   2599    5.0    Election (1999)
9   1092    5.0    Basic Instinct (1992)
```

Conclusion

Collaborative filtering algorithm utilizes users' rating information to make recommendations. It finds out the similar users based on the ratings information using one of the similarity methods, like cosine similarity. Then the algorithm finds out the items rated by the similar users and make recommendations. This algorithm does not need the attributes of the items, e.g., the genres of movies, therefore not require the expertise in the domain.

The memory-based collaborative filtering is simply performed by manipulating the data without using any models.

4.11.4 Collaborative Filtering, Model-based

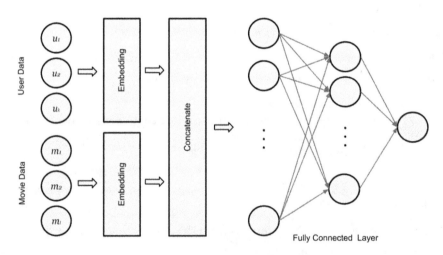

Figure 4.77 Collaborative Filtering with Deep Neural Network

The model-based collaborative filtering uses a machine learning model to train the users' rating data and makes recommendations. In this section a deep neural network model will be built for this purpose.

The architecture of the model is shown in Figure 4.77, and will be implemented with Keras.

The idea of the model is to learn from the users' rating data by providing the userId and movieId as input and the ratings as output. Because each user only makes ratings on a small fraction of movies, say only 50 or 60 out of thousands of movies, when convert the ratings data into the user-movie matrix meaning the users in rows and movies in columns, it's a sparse matrix with lots of zeros.

The purpose of this model is to learn from the available rating data and predict the ratings that users would give to the movies they have not watched, and finally make recommendations based on the predictions. In another word, the zeros in user-movie matrix can be filled with the predicted ratings from this model.

The inputs of the model are userId and movieId, the output is the rating.

Below are the descriptions of the layers of the model:

Embedding Layer

The unique number of users and movies are quite large, they could be thousands or tens of thousands, or maybe millions, depending on the dataset. Normally they are identified by userId or movieId ranging from 0 to a quite large number. This type of data is categorical as we have discussed in earlier sections, before the categorical data is fed into the machine learning models, they have to be pre-processed, a widely used technique is one-hot encoding if the unique number of data is not big, see section 4.3.2.

However, the one-hot encoding generates a sparse matrix, the majority of elements are zeros, only the diagonals are ones, and the size of matrix is same as the unique number of the data. If the unique number is huge, the one-hot generates a huge sparse matrix, it's not efficient for the neural networks, because it needs a huge number of nodes to correspond to the input matrix, then requires lots of computation resources and normally needs huge amount of data to train the model.

This problem can be resolved by embedding, which can map the high-dimensional data into a lower-dimensional space. So the huge sparse input matrix can be translated to a dense matrix, and the size could be shrunk to a much smaller value. A dense matrix means most of elements are non-zero.

The embedding will learn by itself as part of the neural networks, all we need is to add the embedding layers in the neural network and specify the size of input and output dimensions. The output size is a parameter that could impact the overfitting of the model, it should be adjusted together with other model parameters in the fine-tune process.

The collaborative filtering uses both user and movie as input data, in the architecture of Figure 4.77, there are two embedding layers, one for user data and another for movie data.

Concatenate Layer

Concatenate layer just simply combines two embedding outputs together and generates a single output.

Fully Connected Layer

The concatenated data is fed into the fully connected layer, which is an artificial neural network, whose input nodes are defined based on the output of the concatenate layer. The hidden layers are adjustable during the fine-tune process by monitoring the overfitting and underfitting.

Implement with Python and Keras

Loading data is exactly same as what we did in section 4.11.2, it's not repeated here, the full codes are available in the source codes at Github.

This section is focusing on the building deep neural network model. In previous sections like 4.9 and 4.10, `keras.models.Sequential()` was used to build the sequential models, that function is good for linear architectures meaning one layer is followed by the other. But this model in Figure 4.77 is kind of different, two input branches are merged together and then move forward. This type of non-linear multi-inputs structure can be effectively handled by *Keras Functional API*, which is a more flexible to build the model. More details can be found at https://keras.io/guides/functional_api/.

Here are the codes, following the conventions of *Keras Functional API*:

```
1    import pandas as pd
2    import numpy as np
3    from tensorflow import keras
4    from tensorflow.keras.layers import Dense, Input,
5              Embedding, Flatten, Concatenate, Dropout
6    from tensorflow.keras.models import Model
7    n_users = ratings['userid'].nunique()
8    n_movies = ratings['movieid'].nunique()
9    movie_inp = Input(shape=[1])
10   movie_emb = Embedding(n_movies+1, 64)(movie_inp)
11   movie_vec = Flatten()(movie_emb)
12   user_inp = Input(shape=[1])
13   user_emb = Embedding(n_users+1, 64)(user_inp)
14   user_vec = Flatten()(user_emb)
15   conc = Concatenate()([movie_vec, user_vec])
16   fc1 = Dense(64, activation="relu")(conc)
17   dp1 = Dropout(0.25)(fc1)
18   fc2 = Dense(32, activation="relu")(dp1)
19   dp2 = Dropout(0.1)(fc2)
20   out = Dense(1)(dp2)
```

Line 7 and 8 get the unique numbers of movies and users. Line 9 to 11 build the embedding layer for movie data, which includes an `Input()` to take input data in line 9, an `Embedding()` to translate the input data from higher dimensional to lower dimensional vectors in line 10, and a `Flatten()` to transform the data to one dimensional output in line 11. Each function takes the previous output as input following the conventions of *Keras Functional API*. `Embedding()` has two parameters, the first one is the size of input, which is the unique number of movies plus 1. The reason of plus 1 is to add the intercept or bias as we normally did in previous sections. The second parameter is to specify the output size of embedding. The embedding in line 10 will translate whatever number of movies into vectors of size 64.

Line 12 to 14 are exactly same as above but dealing with user data. Line 15 is the concatenate layer, the embedded user and movie vectors are concatenated in this layer. The size of both user and movie vectors are 64, after concatenation the output is a vector of 128 (=64+64), it becomes the input of the fully connected layer.

Line 16 to 20 define the fully connected layer, line 16 is the hidden layer of 64 nodes with ReLU activation function; line 18 is the second hidden layer of 32 nodes with ReLU also; there are two dropout layers for reducing overfitting purpose; and finally, the output layer of one node.

Build the model, compile it and show the summary:

```
21    model = Model([user_inp, movie_inp], out)
22    model.compile("adam", "mean_squared_error")
23    model.summary()
```

Line 21 builds the model using [user_inp, movie_inp] as input, and out as output. Line 22 compiles the model with adam as optimizer and mean_squared_error as loss.

The diagram of the model's architecture is shown in Figure 4.78.

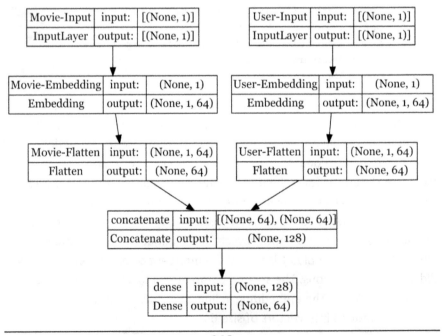

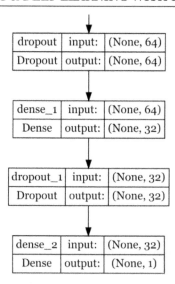

Figure 4.78 Architecture Diagram of the Deep Neural Network
Generated by Recommendation_Collaborative_Filtering_Neural_Network.ipynb

Then train the model, normally the data is split into train and test set, the train set is for training, and test set for validation. In this example however, instead of splitting train and test, we use the full dataset for training and prediction to explain the idea of model-based collaborative filtering.

```
24    history = \
25    model.fit(x = [ratings["userid"],ratings["movieid"]],
26              y = ratings.rating,
27              batch_size=256,
28              epochs=200,
29              verbose=1 )
```

ratings is the data loaded from MovieLens dataset, see previous section or the full source code for how to load it. The model is trained with userid and movieid columns as input and rating column as the label. The training result is shown as Figure 4.79,

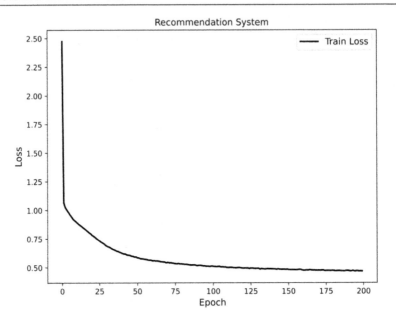

Figure 4.79 Model-based Collaborative Filtering

Source code at Recommendation_Collaborative_Filtering_Neural_Network.ipynb

After the model is trained, how the prediction works? Select a user, make predictions and compare the predictions with the actual ratings. Let's take a user of `userid=660`:

```
30    ur = ratings[ratings['userid'] == 660]
31    ur['prediction'] = model.predict([ur.userid,
32                                       ur.movieid])
33    ur.sort_values(by='rating', ascending=False) \
34       .head(10)
```

Line 30 selects the rows only for user ID of 660 which contain the movies and ratings the user rated. Line 31 and 32 make predictions from the model with the `userid` and `movieid`. Line 33 sorts the data by `rating` in descending order, and line 34 display the top 10 records. The result shows the user's actual rating and the model's prediction side by side:

userid	movieid	rating	prediction
660	173	5	4.246075
660	151	5	3.970993
660	168	5	3.866111

660	50	4	4.224977
660	316	4	4.194629
660	22	4	3.602246
660	272	4	3.988786
660	603	4	4.197037
660	179	4	3.565965
660	172	4	4.152786

The first line of the result means user ID 660 gives movie ID 173 a rating of 5, while the model predicts the rating as 4.246.

From the above results, the actual and predicted ratings are almost close, although there are still some discrepancies. The dataset used in this example is a small one, the MovieLens provides bigger datasets such as ml-25m which includes 25 million rating data. By training with the bigger datasets hopefully the predictions would be much closer to the actual ratings, although it might take more computation resources and more time to train, feel free to try it as the homework.

Make Recommendations

The recommendations can be made to a specific user with the trained model by the following steps,

1. Get all movies from `ratings` data, except those rated by the specific user.
2. Remove the duplicated movies
3. Predict ratings by the specific user for each movie in the list, using the trained model.
4. Sort the list by prediction and take top movies as the recommendation.

```
35   RECOMM_USER = 660
36   RECOMM_COUNT = 10
37   recomm = ratings[ratings['movieid']\
38       .isin(ur['movieid'])==False][['movieid']]\
39       .drop_duplicates()
40   recomm.insert(0, 'userid', RECOMM_USER)
41   recomm['prediction'] = \
42       model.predict([recomm.userid, recomm.movieid])
```

```
43    recomm.sort_values(by='prediction',ascending=False)\
44         .drop('userid', axis=1) \
45         .merge(movies[['movieid', 'title']],
46              on='movieid', how='inner') \
47         .head(RECOMM_COUNT)
```

Line 35 specifies a user to make recommendations, line 36 specifies the count of recommendations.

Line 37 selects `movieid` column from `ratings`, line 38 selects the `movieid` that not rated by the user, or not in `ur` retrieved in line 30.

Line 39 removes the duplicated `movieid` in the list, and line 40 inserts a `userid` column with value of RECOMM_USER.

Line 41 and 42 make predictions from the model by providing `userid` and `movieid` as inputs. The predictions are the ratings that the user would make on the un-rated movies, the top values are the recommendations for the user.

Line 43 to 47 are to sort the prediction values, merge the `movieid` with title and show the top RECOMM_COUNT records as final recommendations:

```
      movieid   prediction    title
0     408       4.48223       Close Shave, A (1995)
1     169       4.33005       Wrong Trousers, The (1993)
2     178       4.32040       12 Angry Men (1957)
3     152       4.28310       Sleeper (1973)
4     258       4.23919       Contact (1997)
5     198       4.21342       Nikita (La Femme Nikita) (1990)
6     589       4.19249       Wild Bunch, The (1969)
7     519       4.16766       Treasure of the Sierra Madre, …
8     45        4.14794       Eat Drink Man Woman (1994)
9     165       4.12767       Jean de Florette (1986)
```

The above result means all the new movies that are not rated by the user. And if the user would rate on the movies the values in `prediction` column would be the ratings, based on the trained model.

Conclusion

Model-based collaborative filtering algorithm utilizes the machine learning models, in this section a deep neural network model, to learn from the users' rating data, and makes predictions for any users rating on any items or movies. And the recommendations are made based on the predictions, those highest predicted items are recommended to the users.

4.12 Generative Adversarial Network

4.12.1 Introduction

A Generative adversarial network (GAN) is a deep learning algorithm designed to generate synthetic data samples from nothing to imitate the training dataset. The generated synthetic data samples are similar enough to the original dataset. In another word, GAN is designed to learn to mimic the original data. It was introduced by Ian Goodfellow and other researchers at the University of Montreal in 2014, the paper is at https://arxiv.org/abs/1406.2661 and also in material #29 in References.

GAN is an unsupervised learning method, it consists of two neural networks: a *generator* and a *discriminator*. The *generator* creates new synthetic data samples, while the *discriminator* decides if a data sample is real (meaning from the training dataset), or fake (meaning generated by the generator).

Both generator and discriminator are working together but in an adversarial manner in the training process. The generator is working hard and trying to generate data samples in order to make the discriminator thinking they are real data; while the discriminator is trying its best to correctly distinguish the real and fake data samples. The goal of training a GAN is to find a balance at which the generator is able to generate synthetic data samples with qualities good enough so that they are indistinguishable from real training dataset.

It can be understood as a student (generator) and a teacher (discriminator), the student draws a picture, the teacher reviews the picture and compares it with a real picture and tells the student the picture is not good and how to improve it; the student re-draws the picture based on the teacher's comments, the teacher reviews it again. After tens of thousands or even millions of iterations, the student is able to draw the picture that is good enough to mimic the real picture.

The GAN model can be described as Figure 4.80:

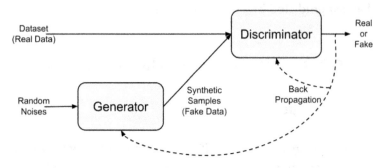

Figure 4.80 How GAN Works

Generative adversarial networks (GANs) can be used in many areas, including but not limited to:

- Image generation: produce synthetic images to imitate the real images in a training dataset, such as hand-written digits, faces, landscapes, etc.
- Audio generation: produce synthetic audio samples, such as music or speech.
- Text generation: produce synthetic text that is similar to a training dataset of real text, such as news articles, poetry and so on.
- Drug discovery: generate synthetic molecules with specific properties, which can be useful for tasks like identifying potential new drugs.

Here are the steps to build a generative adversarial network (GAN):

1. A GAN requires a dataset to learn from, the dataset should be large enough to contain a diverse set of examples. The data samples from dataset are considered as real data, they are labelled as one.
2. Create a generator network, which is a neural network that takes a random noise vector as input and produces a synthetic data sample as output. The architecture of the generator should be well considered and decided, including the number of layers, the types of layers and the nodes of each layer. If the data samples are images, convolutional layers might be considered. The outputs of the generator are fake data samples and will be labelled as zero.

3. Create a discriminator network, which is also a neural network that takes a data sample as input and produces a single scalar value representing the probability that the sample is real or fake. Again, the architecture of the discriminator should be well designed in order to be able to effectively identify the real and fake samples.

4. Create a GAN network that connects the generator and discriminator so that the generator creates synthetic samples that are fed into the discriminator, which decides if they are real or fake. The generator's weights are updated in the back propagation based on the errors between the discriminator's output of the synthetic samples and the real labels; while the discriminator's weights are also updated in the back propagation based on the errors between its predictions and the true labels of the samples (real or fake).

5. Train the GAN by training the generator and discriminator in alternation. First train the discriminator using a batch of real and fake samples; then train the generator using a batch of noise vectors as input. Training should continue until the generator is able to produce synthetic samples that are indistinguishable from real ones and the discriminator is unable to differentiate between real and fake samples.

6. After the GAN model is trained, the generator is able to mimic the original dataset, it can be used to produce synthetic samples from the noise vectors as input. The generated samples are similar to the original dataset, but completely new data that is not found in the original dataset.

4.12.2 Deep Convolutional GAN on MNIST Dataset

This section introduces one of the extensions of GAN – Deep Convolutional GAN, or DCGAN, on the MNIST handwriting digits datasets. It was first introduced by Alec Radford & Luke Metz in 2016, see paper at https://arxiv.org/abs/1511.06434.

Generator Model

The architecture of generator is shown in Figure **4.81**:

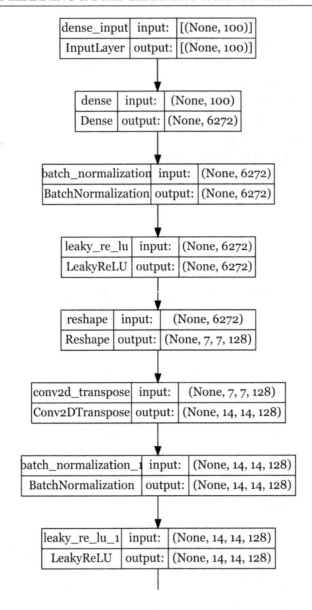

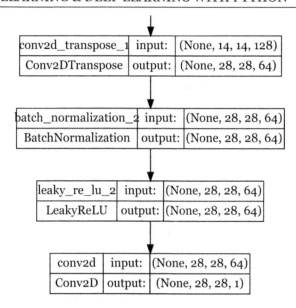

Figure 4.81 Generator Architecture

The input layer takes input of random noise of size 100.

The dense layer outputs 6272 nodes, which is 7×7×128. Why this number? As introduced in CNN (Convolutional neural network), the image size is 7×7 and 128 kernels, this makes the number of 6272.

Next layer is Batch Normalization which transforms the data to mean of 0 and standard deviation of 1. Then apply Leaky ReLU activation function. And reshape the size of 6272 to 7×7×128.

Next is Conv2DTranspose layer, it is a reverse of Conv2D which was introduced in CNN section. This layer transforms the input of 7×7×128 to the output of 14×14×128. After that normalization and leaky ReLU layers are followed.

Then again, another Conv2DTranspose layer transforms data to output of 28×28×64, and again another normalization and leaky ReLU followed.

Finally, a Conv2D layer transforms it to 28×28×1.

In summary, the generator takes random noises of size 100 as input and produces the images of 28×28×1.

The code snippets are shown as below,

```
1    def generator(noise_shape):
2      generator = Sequential(name="Generator")
3      generator.add(Dense(7 * 7 * 128,
4                      input_dim=noise_shape))
5      generator.add(BatchNormalization())
6      generator.add(LeakyReLU(alpha=0.2))
7      generator.add(Reshape((7, 7, 128)))
8
9      generator.add(Conv2DTranspose(128, (5, 5),
10                     strides=(2, 2), padding="same"))
11     generator.add(BatchNormalization())
12     generator.add(LeakyReLU(alpha=0.2))
13
14     generator.add(Conv2DTranspose(64, (5, 5),
15                     strides=(2, 2), padding="same"))
16     generator.add(BatchNormalization())
17     generator.add(LeakyReLU(alpha=0.2))
18     generator.add(Conv2D(1, (7, 7),
19                     activation="sigmoid",padding="same"))
20     generator.compile(
21         loss="binary_crossentropy",
22         optimizer=Adam(learning_rate=0.0002,
23                        beta_1=0.5),
24         metrics=["accuracy"] )
25     return generator
```

Line 1 to 19 implements the architecture of Figure **4.81**, and line 20 to 24 compile the model. As suggested by the DCGAN paper, the Adam optimizer is used to compile the model with learning rate=0.0002 and beta_1=0.5.

Discriminator Model

The architecture of discriminator is shown in Figure 4.82. It takes input data in the size of 28×28×1, the output of generator and the original dataset are all in the same size.

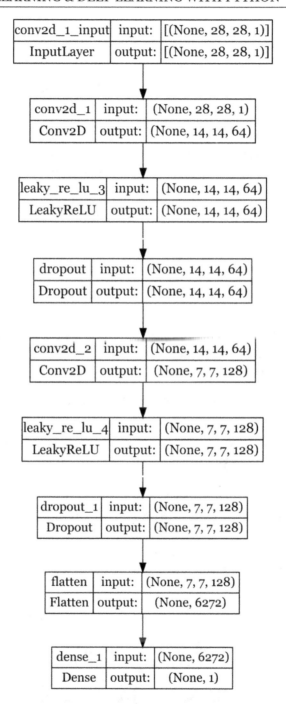

Figure 4.82 Discriminator Architecture

The discriminator is basically same as a CNN, there are a number of convolution layers, and the outputs are fed to the fully connected layers, see section 4.10.5 for details.

Now back to Figure 4.82, after the Input layer, there is a Conv2D layer to convert data to 14×14 with 64 kernels, see section 4.10.2 for details of Conv2D.

There is a LeakyReLU layer followed, it applies the leaky ReLU activation function on the data. And a Dropout layer is followed, the purpose is to reduce overfitting, see section 4.9.6 for details.

Then another set of Conv2D, LeakyReLU and Dropout layers are followed, they convert the data again to 7×7 with 128 kernels.

A flatten layer transforms the data of 7×7×128 to a 1-D array of size 6272, and then feed the data to the fully connected layer.

The fully connected layer has only one dense layer here in this example, which could have more layers though. It transforms the input of 6272 to one output, which is a probability of true or false, if the probability is near 1 then true, otherwise false.

In summary, the discriminator is exactly in opposite to generator, it takes the input image of 28×28×1 and performs the convolutional operations as a normal CNN model does, finally output a probability value to indicate the image is true or false. Typically, the images from the original dataset are considered true, and the synthetic image from generator are false, however the generator is trying its best to produce synthetic images so that the discriminator identifies them as true.

```
26    def discriminator(in_shape=(28, 28, 1)):
27        discriminator = Sequential(name='Discriminator')
28        discriminator.add(
29            Conv2D(64, (5, 5), strides=(2, 2),
30                    padding="same", input_shape=in_shape))
31        discriminator.add(LeakyReLU(alpha=0.2))
32        discriminator.add(Dropout(0.3))
33        discriminator.add(Conv2D(128, (5, 5),
34            strides=(2, 2), padding="same"))
35        discriminator.add(LeakyReLU(alpha=0.2))
```

```
36      discriminator.add(Dropout(0.3))
37      discriminator.add(Flatten())
38      discriminator.add(Dense(1, activation="sigmoid"))
39      discriminator.compile(
40          loss="binary_crossentropy",
41          optimizer=Adam(learning_rate=0.0002,
42                          beta_1=0.5),
43          metrics=["accuracy"])
44      return discriminator
```

Line 26 to 38 implements the architecture in Figure 4.82, and line 39 to 43 compile the model. And based on the DCGAN paper, the Adam optimizer with learning rate=0.0002 and beta_1=0.5 is used for the discriminator.

Generative Adversarial Network (GAN) Model

The architecture of GAN is shown in Figure 4.83. It connects the generator and discriminator models.

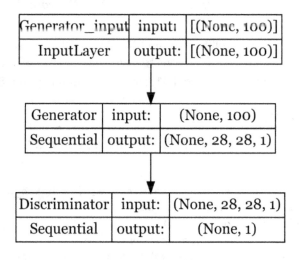

Figure 4.83 GAN Architecture

The input layer takes random noise vectors of size 100, and feed to the generator model, whose output is 28×28×1, and then the discriminator model is connected.

In this case the layers are not the *keras* build-in layers, instead they are models previous built, this demonstrates the flexibilities of *keras* for building models.

In summary, the GAN model takes random noises as input, the generator produces synthetic images of 28×28×1, and the discriminator identify the images as true or false.

```
45   def gan(g_model, d_model):
46     d_model.trainable = False
47     model = Sequential(name='GAN')
48     model.add(g_model)
49     model.add(d_model)
50     opt = Adam(learning_rate=0.0002, beta_1=0.5)
51     model.compile(loss="binary_crossentropy",
52                       optimizer=opt)
53     return model
```

Line 45 to 49 implement the architecture of Figure 4.83, then compile the model. Line 46 sets the discriminator not trainable, when training the GAN model only the generator is trained, not the discriminator.

The full source code is at *Generative_Adversarial_Networks.ipynb* in *Github* repository. There are some other functions defined like generating random noises, creating fake data and real data, displaying sample images, etc. There are also functions to save and load models, as well as generate the diagrams of Figure **4.81**, Figure 4.82 and Figure 4.83.

Train the GAN Model

In the training process, the discriminator and generator will be trained in alternation.

```
54   bat_per_epo = int(X_train.shape[0] / batch_size)
55   half_batch = int(batch_size / 2)
56   for i in range(epochs):
57     for j in range(bat_per_epo):
58       X_real, y_real = make_real_data(X_train,
59                             half_batch)
60       X_fake, y_fake = make_fake_data(g_model,
61                             noise_shape, half_batch)
62       X, y = np.vstack((X_real, X_fake)),
63                             np.vstack((y_real, y_fake))
64       d_loss, d_acc = d_model.train_on_batch(X, y)
65       X_gan = make_noices(noise_shape, batch_size)
66       y_gan = np.ones((batch_size, 1))
```

```
67        g_loss, g_acc = gan_model.train_on_batch(
68                      X_gan, y_gan)
```

Line 58 and 59 create real data from dataset, line 60 and 61 create fake data from generator model, line 62 and 63 combine them together. And line 64 train the discriminator model with the real and fake data.

Line 65 create random noises, and line 66 label them as 1, this is the trick when training the GAN model, the idea is trying to make the model think these are real data (label of 1).

Line 67 and 68 train the GAN model, as explained earlier the discriminator is set not trainable in GAN model, therefore this step will train the generator only.

Because of the amount of dataset and the complexities of the model, training could take hours, it's suggested using GPU to perform the calculation. Even with GPU, depends on the hardware specs, it could take overnight to complete 200 epochs of training. Google Colab environment might not support long time running with GPU, there could be some cooling down time. To perform this level of calculation or training, you might want to setup a local environment running Python Jupyter with tensorflow and GPU, or purchase a paid plan with Google Colab or other cloud GPU service providers such as Saturn Cloud (https://saturncloud.io/)

Produce Synthetic Images

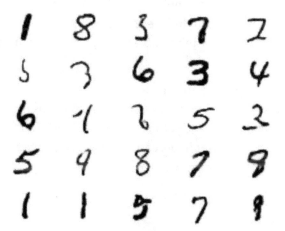

Figure 4.84 Synthetic Images

After the GAN model is trained, the generator can be used to produce synthetic images, as shown in Figure 4.84.

These images are not from the original dataset but produced by the trained generator model.

4.12.3 The Variations of GAN

There are many types of variations or extensions on the top of basic GAN, the previous section 4.12.2 was Deep Convolutional Generative Adversarial Network (DCGAN), which is a variation or extension of GAN. It utilizes the deep convolutional neural network on both the generator and discriminator models to produce the high-quality synthetic images. The basic GAN will also do the jobs however the final results of the synthetic images include some noises and not as good as that of DCGAN.

In addition to DCGAN there are several other popular variations of GAN. This book will not include the implementations of them, if interested you might want to practice them with the help of TF-GAN, which is a Google provided lightweight library for building and training GANs in 2017, at https://ai.googleblog.com/2017/12/tfgan-lightweight-library-for.html, there are many tutorials by internet search as well.

Vanilla GAN

Vanilla GAN is the basic and simplest type of GAN, both the generator and discriminator are made of multi-layer perceptron (MLP), which are artificial neural networks with multiple layers, which was introduced in Figure 4.53.

The concepts and structures of vanilla GAN are same as DCGAN in previous section 4.12.2, the differences are DCGAN is using CNN for both the generator and the discriminator while Vanilla GAN is using MLP for both. Because CNN is better in processing images, as the results DCGAN can produce synthetic images with better qualities.

Conditional GAN (cGAN)

The conditional GAN or cGAN will add some more information on top of the basic GAN, for example the class label. In the example of above section 4.12.2, the label of digital handwritten will be fed into both the generator and discriminator models, so that the GAN model will be trained not only with the random noise vectors but also the labels.

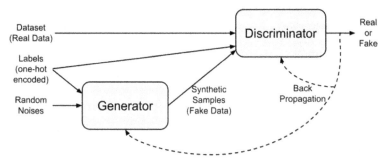

Figure 4.85 Conditional GAN

Finally, the generator is able to produce the synthetic samples based on random noises and labels, when provide label as 2 for example, it can produce the hand-written images for 2, and so on.

See the paper at material #31 in References section.

CycleGAN

CycleGANs learn to transform images from one set of images to another set. For example, a CycleGAN can take the images of horse and turn them into the images of zebra, or vise versa. It does not require the paired data with the images, meaning not need information like labels for the images, and not need a horse image paired with a zebra.

There are two datasets, one is horse, another is zebra. The CycleGAN model includes two GANs, meaning two generators and two discriminators. The first GAN transforms the horses to zebras, and the second transforms the zebras to horses.

The first GAN:

- Generator: takes horses as input and produce zebras as output.
- Discriminator: compare the produced zebras with those from the zebra dataset and decide the likelihood of similarity.

The second GAN:

- Generator: takes zebras as input and produce horses as output.
- Discriminator: compare the produced horses with those from the horse dataset and decide the likelihood of similarity.

So far with two GANs in place, it's possible to produce the synthetic images of both zebras and horses, but not the translations between them.

Now combine the two GANs together, train and update them with cycle consistency loss, this include forward and backward cycle consistency loss:

Forward cycle consistency loss:

- Input horses to the first GAN, and zebras are produced.
- Input the produced zebras to the second GAN and horses are produced.
- Compare the produced horses with those in horse dataset.

Backward cycle consistency loss:

- Input zebras to the second GAN, and horses are produced.
- Input the horses to the first GAN and zebras are produced.
- Compare the zebras with those in zebra dataset.

The CycleGAN can be applied to not only the horse to zebra, but also the apple to orange, summer to winter and so on. See the paper at material #32 in References section.

Text to Image with GAN

Sometimes we want to generate images as described by texts, this involves the natural language processing (NLP) and image processing. GAN can be used to produce images based on text descriptions, for example, produce the image of human face based on the described facial traits.

Similar to the cGAN as Figure 4.85, instead of labels, the textual descriptions will be fed into both generator and discriminator as inputs. The labels in cGAN for number 0 to 9 are categorical variable and can be one-hot encoded as 10-dimensional vectors, but this technique is not applicable to the texts, because the texts are not categorical variables and they have far more unique values.

Text embedding is a widely used technique in natural language processing (NLP), it's the vector representation of textual data. Text embedding can be considered as a translation from human-readable text to computer-readable vectors. We have used the embedding in section 4.11.4 – Model-based Recommendation System, where the userId and movieId are embedded into 64-dimensional vectors, although they are not textual data.

The textual descriptions are embedded into, for example, 256-dimensional vectors, then feed into both the generator and discriminator, as shown in Figure 4.86:

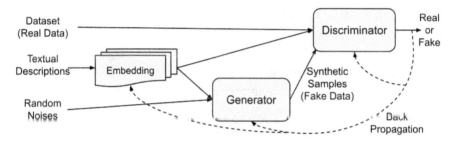

Figure 4.86 Text to Image with GAN

The random noises plus embedded textual descriptions are fed into the generator to produce synthetic images; the real images from dataset, the embedded textual descriptions and synthetic images are fed into the discriminator to determine the probabilities of real or fake. The loss will be backpropagated to the discriminator, generator and embedding to update them.

After the GAN model is trained, the generator can produce the synthetic images from textual descriptions and random noises.

See the paper at material #33 in References section.

Super Resolution GAN (SRGAN)

Super resolution GAN (SRGAN) is to transform the low-resolution pictures into the high-resolution ones by increasing the resolution and add details to fill the blurry areas of the picture. Both the generator and discriminator are using convolutional neural networks (CNNs).

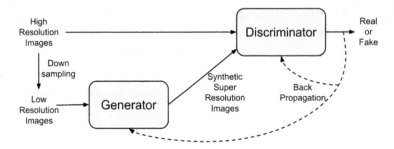

Figure 4.87 Super Resolution GAN (SRGAN)

As shown in Figure 4.87, during the training process, the high-resolution (HR) images are down-sampled to the low-resolution (LR) images, then feed into the generator, which produce the synthetic super-resolution (SR) images. The synthetic SR images and the original HR Images are fed into discriminator to determine the probabilities of real or fake. And the losses are backpropagated to both generator and discriminator.

As the results, the trained SRGAN takes the blurry images as input and produces the sharper images.

The paper of SRGAN is at material #34 in References section, Figure 4 in page 5 of the paper shows the architectures of the generator and the discriminator, the diagram is not included in this book, but feel free to reference the original paper. The notation of "k3n64s1" stands for the convolution layer with 3×3 kernel and 64 filters with stride of 1; similarly, "k3n512s2" stands for 3×3 kernel and 512 filters with stride of 2, and so on. The loss functions are also described in the paper.

The authors of the paper performed experiments on the widely used benchmark datasets and the SRGAN achieved 4× up-sampling of the resolution.

Index

References

1. https://web.mit.edu/15.053/www/AMP-Appendix-A.pdf
2. https://web.stanford.edu/~boyd/vmls/vmls.pdf
3. https://www.tntech.edu/cas/pdf/math/techreports/TR-2018-2.pdf
4. http://www.cs.toronto.edu/~jepson/csc420/notes/introSVD.pdf
5. https://www.cs.cmu.edu/~venkatg/teaching/CStheory-infoage/book-chapter-4.pdf
6. https://online.stat.psu.edu/stat505/book/export/html/636
7. https://ocw.mit.edu/courses/res-18-001-calculus-online-textbook-spring-2005/resources/mitres_18_001_strang_2/
8. http://www.math.toronto.edu/ivrii/PDE-textbook/PDE-textbook.pdf
9. http://www.cs.utsa.edu/~bylander/cs3343/notes/learning-by-gradient-descent.pdf
10. https://optimization.cbe.cornell.edu/index.php?title=Stochastic_gradient_descent
11. https://mgcub.ac.in/pdf/material/202004290203577d596f1ec8.pdf
12. https://www.cs.toronto.edu/~rgrosse/courses/csc311_f20/readings/notes_on_linear_regression.pdf
13. https://ftp.idu.ac.id/wp-content/uploads/ebook/ip/REGRESI%20LOGISTIK/Practical%20Guide%20to%20Logistic%20Regression%20(%20PDFDrive%20).pdf
14. https://web.stanford.edu/~jurafsky/slp3/5.pdf
15. https://medium.com/analytics-vidhya/logistic-regression-with-gradient-descent-explained-machine-learning-a9a12b38d710
16. http://deeplearning.stanford.edu/tutorial/supervised/SoftmaxRegression/
17. https://stanford.edu/~cpiech/cs221/handouts/kmeans.html
18. https://www.stat.cmu.edu/~cshalizi/uADA/12/lectures/ch18.pdf
19. http://cda.psych.uiuc.edu/statistical_learning_course/Jolliffe%20I.%20Principal%20Component%20Analysis%20(2ed.,%20Springer,%202002)(518s)_MVsa_.pdf
20. https://nlp.stanford.edu/IR-book/pdf/15svm.pdf
21. https://www.ams.org/journals/bull/1954-60-05/S0002-9904-1954-09828-2/S0002-9904-1954-09828-2.pdf

22. https://insightsimaging.springeropen.com/articles/10.1007/s13244-018-0639-9
23. https://jmlr.org/papers/volume15/srivastava14a/srivastava14a.pdf
24. http://yann.lecun.com/exdb/publis/pdf/lecun-01a.pdf
25. https://www.cs.toronto.edu/~rgrosse/courses/csc321_2018/tutorials/tut6_slides.pdf
26. https://www.researchgate.net/publication/337105858_Transfer_learning_using_VGG-16_with_Deep_Convolutional_Neural_Network_for_Classifying_Images
27. https://www.cs.colostate.edu/~dwhite54/InceptionNetworkOverview.pdf
28. http://ursula.chem.yale.edu/~batista/classes/CHEM584/Resnet.pdf
29. https://arxiv.org/abs/1406.2661
30. https://arxiv.org/abs/1511.06434
31. https://arxiv.org/abs/1411.1784
32. https://arxiv.org/abs/1703.10593
33. https://arxiv.org/abs/1605.05396
34. https://arxiv.org/abs/1609.04802

About the Author

James Chen, a highly accomplished IT professional with a solid academic background, holds a degree from Tsinghua University, one of China's most prestigious universities, and has developed a deep understanding of computer science theory and practices. With his extensive technical background, James has played key roles in designing and developing cutting-edge software solutions for a variety of industries including technology, financial, healthcare, e-commerce, etc. He has been working with all aspects of system design and development and actively contributed as the lead implementer of complex multi-clients and multi-tiered systems such as web systems, traditional n-tiered systems, mobile applications, and mixed software/hardware systems. He has a talent for identifying key business problems and designing customized solutions that are both efficient and effective.

His wide-ranging technical interests led him to the emerging fields of computer vision and machine learning since 2016, James has a passion for artificial intelligence and has honed his skills in this area through a combination of academic study and practical experiences. He has developed an in-depth understanding of the latest tools and techniques in computer vision and machine learning and is always looking for new ways to apply this knowledge to real-world problems.

MACHINE LEARNING & DEEP LEARNING WITH PYTHON

by James Chen, 2023